Get Seen

Get Seen

Online Video Secrets to Building Your Business

STEVE GARFIELD

WILEY

John Wiley & Sons, Inc.

Published by John Wiley & Sons, Inc., Hoboken, New Jersey.
Published simultaneously in Canada.

For general information on our other products and services or for technical support, please contact our Customer Care Department within the United States at (800) 762-2974, outside the United States at (317) 572-3993 or fax (317) 572-4002.

Wiley also publishes its books in a variety of electronic formats. Some content that appears in print may not be available in electronic books. For more information about Wiley products, visit our web site at www.wiley.com.

ISBN 978-0470-52546-3

Printed in the United States of America.

10 9 8 7 6 5 4 3 2 1

This book is for Carol, my co-host in life and of
The Carol and Steve Show.

Contents

Foreword

For marketers like me, the frustration of relying exclusively on expensive advertising and of trying to convince the media to pay attention is long gone. Yes, mainstream media are still important, but today the better way to get seen is to create something compelling and publish it on the Web for free.

All people and organizations—political candidates, nonprofits, rock bands, independent consultants, educational institutions, companies large and small—possess, via the Web, the power to elevate themselves to a position of importance. In the new marketplace of ideas, organizations deliver the right information to buyers, just at the time when they are most receptive to the information.

The tools at our disposal as marketers include all kinds of web-based media that can deliver our own thoughtful and informative content. These media include web sites, blogs, e-books, white papers, images, photos, audio content, games, and even virtual reality. Organizations gain credibility and loyalty with buyers through content, and smart marketers now think and act like publishers in order to create and deliver content targeted directly at their audience.

One of the most powerful and effective forms of online content is video. But you must already know that, because you've picked up this book!

For the past year, I've been obsessed with creating videos. I use a Flip video camera, a small and inexpensive digital video recorder that I take with me everywhere. I never know where or when a great video interview opportunity might present itself. I was certainly glad I had my Flip camera when I interviewed Amanda Palmer, lead singer for the punk band The Dresden Dolls. And when I met Fritz Henderson, CEO of General Motors. There are also many occasions when I realize an idea will be best expressed on video, as in my short clip "Do you sell camels?," which I filmed outside Riyadh, Saudi Arabia.

"This is Steve Garfield from SteveGarfield.com."

Each time I hear Steve's signature opening, a smile crosses my face, because I know the video he is introducing will be both interesting and entertaining. Steve is a pioneer. He started combining his blog with video clips way back in early 2004 (before YouTube). At the time his hybrid was a bit strange. But it was something new and revolutionary, and he was among the first to do it.

Some four years later, Steve's citizen journalism during the U.S. presidential election was seen by thousands of people. Then CNN found him. They put his content on television and on the popular CNN.com web site, and then it was seen by millions. You see, self-publishing your video on the Web is to *Get Seen*. As Steve shows in this book, quality web video can earn you a huge audience. Video can tell a story, and it has great potential for applications in citizen journalism, marketing, or simply sharing moments of your life with the circle of people who are important to you.

Steve showed me just how damn easy it is to get going. I freely admit that I'm a technical dummy. I wouldn't know a line of HTML if it bit me on the butt. But Steve shares how even a technophobe like me can shoot a great video and post it online for the world to see. I now do videos nearly every week. Some have been seen thousands of times. Steve created a monster (a good one) in me, and he'll do the same for you!

But this book is packed with much more than just basics for beginners. Steve digs into details that will benefit even veteran video experts who want to hone their online video efforts. I'm thinking in particular of his treatment of camera choice, lighting, sound, and distribution platforms, but this list just scratches the surface.

I love that Steve has written the book like a really big blog post. It's accessible and practical and it reads like something you'd study for fun rather than for work. Steve delivers it all in a blogger style that says: "I gotta keep your interest or I know that you'll click away to somewhere else."

The new publishing model on the Web is not about hype or spin or messages. It is about delivering valuable content when and where it is needed and, in the process, branding you or your organization as a leader. Perhaps more than any other medium, video can help you do all this (and much more).

So grab your camera, start recording, and remember to have fun!

David Meerman Scott
Businessweek bestselling author of
The New Rules of Marketing & PR
www.WebInkNow.com
twitter.com/dmscott

Introduction

... this land we've all been harvesting for the past decade (not forgetting the early days of dial-up and streaming videos) is full of intensely passionate people. Whether it's the actor/director/writer who can't get a job in traditional Hollywood, the entrepreneur who is using video to promote their work, the artist experimenting with the form itself, the activist using video to bring a cause to light, or the new mom sending video of her newborn to family and friends—we all have the ability to tell our story.

—Zadi Diaz, new media producer and co-founder of Smashface Productions, 1st Annual Streamy Awards: Once in a Lifetime[1]

Hi everyone, this is Steve Garfield from SteveGarfield.com.[2] I'm here in my book. Thanks for reading.

Video is everywhere. It permeates many aspects of our lives every day. The ability to record video is as easy as pushing a button on any number of devices. Because of this ease and availability, video can be a powerful tool for you and your business.

I am one of the first bloggers to figure out how to put video on a blog. I had been producing videos and blogging for years, but never had put video on my blog and had never seen anyone else do it either.

On January 1, 2004, I created Steve Garfield's Video Blog.[3]

I visited Apple.com and learned how to utilize the language of the Web, HTML, to enable me to embed a video and link to it from within a blog post. I became part of a community of video bloggers, and have been sharing my knowledge online and in classes and workshops ever since.

---

[1] http://www.zadidiaz.com/home/2009/3/31/1st-annual-streamy-awards-once-in-a-lifetime.html

[2] http://SteveGarfield.com

[3] http://stevegarfield.blogs.com

This book will demystify that process of recording and sharing video. It's a lot easier now than it was back in 2004. There are so many ways to do it. I'll share some of the tools you can use to capture video, and once you've got the video, show you where you should put it.

This book also encompasses the knowledge of other online video pioneers who are figuring out how to be successful telling stories and establishing a following. I've interviewed these successful people who are using video in many different ways. Read their stories, then follow my step-by-step guides that show you how you can follow their lead.

Since starting my video blog on January 1, 2004, I've watched on-line video grow into something I could never have imagined. It's time for a new handbook to review how people have become successful, and share with you the tools you'll need to use today.

What Is Videoblogging?

The technical definition of video blogging is video on a blog. Blogging allows anyone with access to a computer the ability to have their thoughts seen and shared. Video blogging just adds a video component.

People want to share their stories.

You can share your stories on the Web by using text, audio, photos, and video. Compelling videos can enhance engagement and prompt people to participate. This participation can range from leaving a comment on someone else's video to becoming part of a campaign to elect the president of the United States by shooting and sharing a video with a Flip camera.

Secret: Your video does not have to be professionally produced to be successful and tell a story.

Video blogging opened up the ability to share videos with others, just like blogging allowed people to easily share stories.

Cable TV has a finite audience and once your video is shown, it's gone. How do viewers give you feedback? Write to the station? Doesn't happen.

With new media a new two-way engagement is possible.

When you take a look at the video landscape there are many genres that make up video on the Web.

> **GET SEEN: The Secret to Online Video is to create good content.**

Good content gets viewed, commented on, and passed around. In this book I show you many different ways to create great content.

Even if you don't want to be seen on camera, you can create impressive web video.

Why Put Video on the Web?

Video allows you to *tell a much richer story* than you ever could with just words or pictures alone. Video enables you to *engage* the viewer emotionally. It's the same reason why TV became popular—video stimulates more of your senses.

One of the most important powers of video is the ability to *make a connection* with a viewer. As a longtime video blogger, I've seen viewers feel like they actually get to know you on a much more personal level than text or photos offer. You'll see in my story how I became friends with *Late Night* star Jimmy Fallon.

Video enables you to tell a story and connect with people on a more personal level. Those people could end up being important to you and to your business. Let's say that you post a video online and someone with 500,000 followers on Twitter reposts it; maybe someone on your local news station sees the video and broadcasts it; maybe Oprah or Ellen find it amusing and broadcast it to millions more. You can't guarantee that will happen, but if you don't put video out there, you can guarantee that it won't.

Before putting video on the Web, you might want to set some goals to gauge your success. These could be as simple as counting the number of views, comments, or time spent viewing a video.

Video is just one part of a marketing plan. It fits certain messages and people better than others.

It doesn't cost much to get started. You can start with an inexpensive video solution and spend more money as you progress if you like.

In my case, as time has gone on, my equipment has actually become less expensive and of greater quality.

Who Are the Right People to Start Video Blogging?

The right people to start video blogging are those with a passion to tell a story. One of the most passionate people out there right now telling stories with video is Gary Vaynerchuk. If you look up Gary Vaynerchuk on Google, the first entry to come up is Gary's site with the description, "Gary Vaynerchuk's place to talk about his passions, hustle, wine, and business."[4,5]

Okay, so Gary wrote that description, but isn't that what *you* want? To have the first result on Google be written by you?

Video blogging can help make that happen. Video blogging means putting video in a blog. When you do that you gain all the power of blogging.

> **GET SEEN: Add text to your video blog entries so that they are indexed by Google and show up in Google searches.**

Let's look at some examples of people who should be putting video online:

- A company that wants to tell a story.
- A journalist who wants to show the world an unfiltered video on something.
- An artist who wants to show her fans the creative process.

Hearing from Successful People

This book includes interviews with many people who are successful in online video. Read about their stories and the tools they use. Many times when you hear someone speaking at a conference, they generally talk about their video production. Then, invariably what happens is

---

[4]Gary Vaynerchuk on Google: http://tinyurl.com/garyvee-passion
[5]Gary's site: http://garyvaynerchuk.com/

that someone comes up to the mic during the Q&A sessions and asks what kind of camera they use and what type of mic. I asked and they answered, so you see technical sections of some of the interviews in the book where you can hear exactly what these video producers use to make their videos. You can even think of it as a shopping list.

If you are inspired by one of the interviews, I include step-by-step guides to show you how to produce your own video that mirror the successful producers. So, if you're interested in producing a live show, I show you how. Want to find out the fastest way to get started, I cover that, too.

Who Should Be Using This Book and Why?

If you or your company is considering putting video on the Web, you have many confusing options. It's like trying to choose a color and type of stain for your deck. There are myriad color samples and transparencies to choose from.

I appreciate what the paint company wants to do by giving us all these choices, but it would be much easier if they offered a gallon of Mahogany Semi-Transparent stain on the shelf with the label that read, "This is our most popular and people like it!"

That's what I'm going to review in the book. I show you a variety of video blogging styles, and then provide step-by-step instructions on how to use the best platforms.

You have many options for how to share your story. These options include recording video, broadcasting live video, recording screen casts, and displaying photo slides shows, to name a few.

> **GET SEEN: Your videos don't have to have people in them. You can have successful videos that tell a story with words and pictures.**

There's also a mountain of video equipment choices that changes every day. I spend a lot of time on Twitter and e-mail helping people decide which camera they should buy. You have options that include using an existing point and shoot digital camera, cell phone, Flip camera, miniDV tape camera, hard drive camera, memory card camera, standard definition, HD, and the list goes on and on.

GET SEEN: Take a look to see if your digital still camera has a video option. If it does, you can start shooting web video with it right away.

There's a wide variety of cameras, microphones, and other equipment available, however, depending on your plans, you can find the right equipment for you. I help you decide among the many camera choices out there by running through some popular models and telling you the pros and cons of different models. I also take a look at some microphone and lighting solutions.

The Early Days of Video

My experience in video production began with many years of volunteering at public access TV stations in the suburbs of Boston. During that time I was also very active in college radio. I pursued these interests "on the side" because my parents always wanted me to pursue a career in accounting.

My professional career has included jobs in programming, sales, marketing, and web development. While in those jobs, I continued to be involved in media. At one point I was producer of a morning radio show in Boston at the same time as being national marketing manager for a major computer distributor. I worked at the radio station from 3:30 A.M. to 9:30 A.M., then went in to work at the computer distributor from 10 A.M. to 7 P.M. I loved working at the radio station and took pride in my audio edits.

I finally combined my knowledge of computers and video editing in a job at a local HD video production company where I was an online editor, working with video producers to prepare HD footage for air on cable TV. No accounting experience was needed.

Around that same time I was also regularly producing online videos for my blog. *Time* magazine ran a story about video blogging that featured me, called "See Me, Blog Me."[6] The author, Jeffrey Ressner wrote, "someday anyone could conceivably mount original programming, bypassing the usual broadcast networks and cable outlets." That day is here. I showed the article around the office. I then taught some of the

---

[6]http://bit.ly/SeeMeTime

producers I worked with how to set up a video blog. Ryan Hodson and Amy Carpenter were two of the people I trained. They went on to produce popular video blogs and continue to work in online video.

One of the most exciting aspects of the early days of online video was the difference between the reach of online video compared to video shown on cable TV. Online video had an unlimited audience with the added benefit of on-demand viewing and the ability to connect with the producer, be it via e-mail or comments on the video blog.

Strategy

This book contains many examples of successful implementations of a video strategy. Much like blogging, there are certain steps you can take to become successful.

Five steps to be successful:

1. **Publish on a regular basis.** This lets people know that they can expect new videos at a certain interval.

2. **Set your videos free.** Publish to more than one location. This lets your videos organically find their audience. You might get a loyal following on some smaller niche video sites, but those viewers could turn out to be your most ardent supporters who end up spreading the word about you. Also make sure your videos are easy to share by providing sharing features like embed codes, "tweet this" buttons, and "e-mail this" links.

3. **Be real.** Make videos about something that you are passionate about. Gary Vaynerchuk has become extremely popular by producing a daily show about wine. He's an expert on that. He produces his show with one camera, one light, in one take. Web video can be produced at little cost. You can hire production crews or learn production to make your videos look like TV or Hollywood productions, and that's fine, but you can also try to do something different. Give viewers a behind-the-scenes look at what it's like to work with you or your company. You can be real. Viewers will appreciate it.

4. **Have a conversation.** The immediacy of web video allows you to connect with your viewers. They'll be able to comment back in many different ways including text, audio, photo, and video.

Encourage that communication. Incorporate viewer content in your videos. The wisdom of the audience is great and you'll be richer for sharing with them. Tools like Twitter, Facebook, and Seesmic allow you to engage in rich communication.

5. **Listen.** Even more important than focusing on your message, listen to the market. Listen to your customers. Listen to your audience to see what they are saying. See what they want and provide that. See what they want to share and help them get seen.

Learning from Others

This book is set up to teach what the best are doing in video blogging. I have interviewed the best video producers and included those interviews here. Many of the interviews were recorded on video and are available on the book web site.[7]

You can read about their stories and the tools they use. While many people were putting video on the Web prior to embedding it in blogs, this book covers how to effectively use video in the video blogging space. I asked how they did it, and they answered, so you learn about the technical aspects of exactly what these video producers use to make their videos. You can think of them as potential shopping lists.

One thing to keep in mind: Posting video to the Web is more than just putting video on a web page. Your video can be a conversation starter. Take part. Have fun.

Let me know how you are doing.

Visit SteveGarfield.com[8] and join the online conversation about topics covered in this book. Ask questions and share your own videos and experiences.

I have links to online sites, examples, and equipment you can use to get started in online video.

See you online.

Enjoy!

Steve Garfield
SteveGarfield.com
twitter.com/stevegarfield

---

[7]http://stevegarfield.com/getseen
[8]http://SteveGarfield.com

Hey, I Feel Like I Already Know You

One of the most compelling reasons to use video to communicate ideas is the sense of familiarity it creates.

That's me and Jimmy Fallon! (See Figure FM.1.)

Interview: Jimmy Fallon—Late Night with Jimmy Fallon

Figure FM.1   Steve and Jimmy at CES Las Vegas

WHAT DOES JIMMY FALLON KNOW ABOUT BLOGGING?

Jimmy Fallon started a video blog as he prepared to start hosting Late Night with Jimmy Fallon on NBC. Late Night with Jimmy Fallon was a 2009 Emmy® Award winner for Outstanding Creative Achievement in Interactive Media and Fallon was recognized with a Webby award in 2009 as Person of the Year[9] for actively engaging with his audience online.

With the help of co-producer Gavin Purcell, Fallon began using social media tools like Twitter,[10] Twitpic, and video blogging,

(continued)

---

[9]http://www.webbyawards.com/webbys/specialachievement13.php/#fallon
[10]http://twitter.com/jimmyfallon

and has been using them to communicate with his fans in much the same way as Barack Obama[11] and Ashton Kutcher.[12]

From the start, Fallon's Late Night with Jimmy Fallon video blog was authentic and personal—a perfect example of how to start a conversation on the Web. Fallon produced one video a day from the beginning of the video blog up until his premiere show.

Since the video blog was interactive, I posted a text comment about how he was using the word video blog incorrectly. Fallon was saying that he was going to make a new video blog every day. What he was actually doing was making a new post, which included a video to his video blog every day. Fallon called me out in his first video that answered some of the text comments he received.[13] He thanked me for writing in and said that he would now use the word video blog correctly.

The next week, Fallon asked for videos. I sent in a video and asked: *"It's great to see you video blogging, I love the behind-the-scenes stuff and I'm excited about the possibility of you including content from the people formally known as the audience. What are you going to do with that, how are you going to include us?"*

In his first video, answering video comments, Fallon responded to my video, referring to me as *"Steve Garfield, our old pal."*[14]

He said: *"Thanks, that's a good question, Steve Garfield. We want to include the audience as much as we can. . . . This will carry over to our show . . . I think it's awesome. Whatever's coming out, however we can incorporate technology with the audience, and our show, you will be on the show. Good question."*

It was exciting.

Fallon also embraced Twitter, and actually used it, even using twitpic to send in photos from his iPhone. Really groundbreaking

---

[11] http://twitter.com/barackobama
[12] http://twitter.com/aplusk
[13] http://offonatangent.blogspot.com/2008/12/i-was-on-late-night-with-jimmy-fallon.html
[14] http://offonatangent.blogspot.com/2008/12/ask-jimmy-fallon-how-are-you-going-to.html

stuff from someone whose career was in traditional media and was about to have a nightly TV talk show.

Social media is more than just a way to get followers, though, it's a way to establish or expand interaction.

When Fallon and I finally met at CES in Las Vegas,[15] he felt like he knew me, and I felt like I knew him (see Figure FM.1). That's what can happen when you become active in social media, particularly with video on the Web.

When we met and I interviewed him on video, I captured the moment of recognition—the moment he said that he felt like he already knew me. That's one of the most powerful features of online video—it connects people in the most personal of ways.

Steve Garfield: You've embraced the Internet and not too many people who have TV shows actually talk to their viewers. What do you feel about that?

Jimmy Fallon: It's been really fun. I have to be honest, it's like really fun. I've always like done little things here and there, you know, I jumped on people's Facebooks here and there or did these quick little things, but I never really jumped right in until we hired Gavin Purcell who was this mastermind, came from a television show you might know called "Attack of the Show" and he was like, "Dude, I got to set you up with Facebook and Twitter." He mentioned like four other different things. We're doing Digg—just seeing what the Internet is capable of. Right now technology is so good. I think right now it's almost peaking. I think it's still good right now and then you come to the show like this and you realize, "We've got a long way to go," but I mean right now, it's so much fun. You get to hear comments from people who tell you that, "You say the word um too many times," and you go, "Oh, yeah, I guess I do."

(continued)

[15]http://stevegarfield.blogs.com/videoblog/2009/01/jimmy-fallon-talks-with-steve-garfield-about-his-new-show-late-night-with-jimmy-fallon.html

Steve Garfield: How do you think that your show is going to change things?

Jimmy Fallon: What's cool about it now is that we're coming in at like the ground floor so no one else is doing this right now. We're trying all different things. We're doing Twitter, we're doing Facebook, we're doing Digg, we're just going around and we have latenightwithjimmyfallon.com where we're just answering questions to your comments and we're doing not only video comments but also your typed out comments, but we want to see how we can play and what we could do with it. I think there are a lot of things we can do. Please, check out www.latenightwithjimmy fallon.com[16] and just check out our videos, check out the archives, comment, tell me what you think, good or bad. I want to hear anything you want to say and I'm open to ideas you have and I'm just so excited to get back to you.

Watch a video of the full interview.[17]

The story gets even better. I went to New York City for a business trip and let Jimmy know I was coming. He reserved me a VIP seat for the taping of his show. At the end of the show he invited me backstage. While we were chatting he asked if I wanted to shoot a video.

I used my Nokia N95-3 with Qik software to live stream an interview with Jimmy from his dressing room and the set.[18]

It all started with my comment on his video blog.

GET SEEN: When you watch a video on the Web, leave a comment. You never know where it might lead.

---

[16]http://www.latenightwithjimmyfallon.com

[17]http://blip.tv/file/1654903/

[18]http://offonatangent.blogspot.com/2009/05/exclusive-behind-scenes-interview-and.html

Creating

Choosing a Camera

Today, many still digital cameras have excellent video capabilities.

What camera should you use to shoot video? An easy way to start out is to answer this question: *What camera do you have?*

> **GET SEEN: Many people don't know or have never tried out the video feature of their cell phones or digital still cameras. That's a good place to start.**

Many times I get into conversations with people who are interested in putting video on the Web, but are intimidated by all the camera choices (see Figure 1.1).

At a recent conference in Boston I started to review the differences between these choices with an attendee. We'll call her Ellen, because that was her name.

Some cameras are easy to use and get started with, while others are expandable and provide more features. As we went down the list of cameras I asked Ellen if she had a camera. She did, and pulled an older model Kodak camera out of her bag. We looked at it and *yes*, it had a *video* setting. Ellen was thrilled and is going to use that camera to get started and learn about shooting video. Her existing camera might just be all she needs. Your camera might be all you need, too.

After you shoot some video with your camera, copy the video from your camera to your computer according to the manufacturers' directions, and then you can post it to sites like YouTube and Facebook.

Figure 1.1   iPhone 3GS, point-and-shoot, and pocket video cameras

Choosing the Best Camera for Your Needs

When I first started shooting video, it was with a Canon PowerShot S400 Digital Elph. It took movies at 320 × 240 and had a three-minute time limit. I used the camera for more than a year and never hit the limit because all my videos were short. I'd shoot little clips and then edit them together and post them online.

Now you have many more choices in both quality and shooting length.

SEVEN THINGS TO CONSIDER WHEN CHOOSING A CAMERA

    1. **Camera Size:** How does the camera feel in your hands? Will you be comfortable shooting with it? Do you like a small or large camera? Do you want to carry a camera with you all the time, in your pocket? How large is the view screen? A larger screen makes it easier to shoot and review your footage.

2. **Video Format:** Do you want to shoot HD video? Consumer grade HD, AVCHD, or standard HD? Are you satisfied with standard resolution? Where is your final destination for the video? Online, Computer? DVD? TV? Do you want to be able to copy the files off the camera to edit them directly?

3. **Sound:** Is the on-camera microphone good enough for your needs? Do you want the ability to plug in an external microphone? Do you want a headphone jack to monitor sound as you shoot?

4. **Tripod Mount:** Do you want an option to be able to attach a tripod to keep the camera steady?

5. **Expandability:** Do you want to be able to replace the batteries and storage on the camera? Some cameras can only be recharged via USB while others support replaceable batteries. Where is the video stored? Internal memory, SD card, memory stick, hard disk, DVD, or tape?

6. **Streaming:** If you are interested in streaming live video, does the camera have video-out ports that allow you to stream? You need Firewire if you want to stream to a computer.

7. **Price:** What's your price point? An inexpensive camera is a great way to get started. You can always decide to spend more for additional features later.

There are many choices out there in the market for video cameras. I review some of them here and touch on many different elements to consider.

I've also set up a community for the book at www.stevegarfield. com/getseen. There you can join the discussions and share your experiences with cameras. As I say when speaking, the intelligence is in the room, and in this case, it's with the readers. I'd love to hear your thoughts and experiences. The camera market is always changing and we'll be able to keep up with it in the Get Seen online community.

To help you narrow down your choices, you can also visit and check out David Pogue's Pogue-O-Matic.[1] It's a fun web application.

---

[1] http://bit.ly/7I8Q

Pocket Video Cameras

Let's take a look at some selected pocket video cameras. The dollar signs following each camera indicate its relative cost.

THE FLIP—JUST PRESS A RED BUTTON TO RECORD—$

The Flip video camera revolutionized the way people shoot video. To record a video with the Flip video camera, you just press a red button. Very easy. That's the key feature of the Flip, making it easy to record video. The Flip also comes with software, FlipShare, which also makes it easy to post a video to YouTube and MySpace. Facebook uploading was added in version 5.0.

The Flip Ultra and UltraHD models have replaceable batteries, the Mino and MinoHD do not. They are rechargeable.

It's amazing how small the Flip MinoHD camera is. In day-to-day use, I've never run out of battery power.

Charging

Although the documentation says that charging takes about three hours, it took mine six hours for its first charge. At least that's when the flashing light stopped blinking indicating a full charge. All Flips can be charged via USB or Power Adapter.

Versions of the Flip: Flip Ultra, Flip UltraHD, Flip Mino, Flip MinoHD 60 min, Flip MinoHD 120 min

Each Flip version starts to focus at a certain distance. It won't be a problem when you are shooting video of someone else. It does become important when you want to shoot a video of yourself. Here are the different versions of the camera and starting focus distance.

Flip MinoHD 60 min—4' 11.05" (1.5m)

Flip MinoHD 120 min— 2' 7.49" (.8m)

Flip Mino—3' 3.37" (1m)

Flip UltraHD—4' 11.05" (1.5m)

Flip Ultra—2' 7.49" (0.8m)

In practice, with the Flip MinoHD, I've found that you can get closer than the 1.5m minimum distance, although you will notice that things in the background are more in focus than your interview subject if they are standing about three feet away from you.

With the Flip MinoHD it takes just three steps to put an HD-quality video on the Web.

Step 1: Record

Step 2: Save

Step 3: Send

The Flip is so small that you would think nothing of dropping it in your pocket, or purse, when running out for the day. One word of caution, some of the Flips have small video displays. The revised **Flip minoHD, 120 min** has a larger 2-inch display which makes it easier to see when you are filming and reviewing footage. If you have poor eyesight, make sure to consider a pocket video camera with a larger display.

Video Formats .AVI and .MP4

The Flip Mino saves videos in .AVI format while the Flip MinoHD saves files in .MP4. This becomes important depending on the editing software you will be using to edit your movies. If you use the included FlipShare software, you don't need to be concerned about it.

The Flip could have become the fourth item in our morning mantra: keys, wallet, phone, flip—but then the iPhone added video and changed everything.

IPHONE 3GS—THE NEW MORNING MANTRA: KEYS, WALLET, IPHONE—$–$$

The iPhone 3GS will allow you to record and share moments online, right away. It's convenient to have a video camera feature on your cell phone. You always have the ability to record a video, along with the added benefit of an onboard cell network or Wi-Fi connectivity that allows you to share your video online.

The quality of the video, although not HD, is very good.

The iPhone 3GS does not have image stabilization in-built, so you have to do that yourself. I find that leaning the camera up against something like a pole or a wall works well.

Recording Video with an iPhone 3GS

Step 1: Open the Camera Application and switch to Movie mode.

Step 2: Press the red button to start recording your movie.

Step 3: Press the red button to stop recording.

Note: You can rotate the iPhone 3GS sideways and shoot a widescreen video.

When you go into the Camera app on the iPhone 3GS you can select Photo or Movie. Capture video at 30 frames per second, then you can optionally trim the video, and send it via E-mail, MMS, Send to Mobile Me, or Send to YouTube.

GET SEEN: Video on the iPhone 3GS is the new home movie.

GET SEEN: Let's make this easy. If you want to share video online, get an iPhone 3GS, record a video and click, "Send to YouTube."

GET SEEN: The quality of the iPhone 3GS audio and video, combined with direct upload to YouTube, changes everything.

GET SEEN: iPhone microphones improve audio quality. Brando Workshop makes a flexible mini capsule microphone that can be pointed at the person who is speaking. This works really well.

GET SEEN: The iPod nano shoots video but the lens is inconveniently placed at the bottom.

KODAK ZI8—REMOVABLE BATTERY, SD STORAGE, AND AUDIO-IN—$

The Kodak Zi8 has a number of features that make it stand out from other pocket cameras. It has built-in image stabilization, takes full HD 1080p video, and can record up to 10 hours of video when you add a 32GB memory card.

The Zi8 also has face detection that places emphasis on people so that when you are shooting someone, the camera adjusts the exposure and white balance to make sure that you get the best image of the subject.

The most impressive addition to the pocket camera market is an external stereo microphone jack. This feature allows you to attach an external microphone for better sound capture. There are many microphone options available and the one that Kodak has tested successfully is the Sony ECM-DS70P Electret Condenser Stereo Microphone.[2] I've tested the Audio Technica ATR-3350 Lavalier Omnidirectional Condenser Microphone.[3] It's a very inexpensive high-quality mono microphone.

The Zi8 also comes with a Kodak Li-Ion Rechargeable battery and supports removable storage on SD cards. You can charge up the phone via its USB jack. It also shoots still images at 5.3 MP.

In hands-on testing with the Kodak Zi8, I found that it was a fun and easy camera to use. I shot a number of outdoor test videos including cars at 720p 60 fps,[4] cars at 1080p,[5] and sunflowers[6] to get a feel for the different recording modes. All the footage looks very good.

The 60 frames per second mode (fps) lets you capture fast moving action.

Here's a list of formats that the Zi8 shoots in:

1080p (1920 × 1080, 30 fps)

720p/60 fps (1280 × 720, 60 fps)

720p (1280 × 720, 30 fps)

WVGA (848 × 480, 30 fps)

---

[2] http://bit.ly/ECM-DS70P

[3] http://bit.ly/ATR3350

[4] http://stevegarfield.blogs.com/videoblog/2009/08/cars-720p-60fps-kodak-zi8-test-2.html

[5] http://stevegarfield.blogs.com/videoblog/2009/08/cars-1080p-kodak-zi8-test.html

[6] http://stevegarfield.blogs.com/videoblog/2009/08/kodak-zi8-camera-test-watering-sunflowers-1080x720p.html

One thing to be aware of is the distance at which the camera is in focus, a little over 3 feet. So don't get too close to your subject or they'll be out of focus.

Macro mode focuses at 15 cm or about 6 inches.

Undocumented Manual Focus

Tobias Lind found an undocumented feature on the previous model, the Zi6.[7] You can slide the focus control, which is normally used to go from Standard to Macro mode, to focus on points in between. To do this you just carefully slide the focus control up and down.

The Kodak Zi8 has a nice large 2-inch display that makes it easy to monitor what you are shooting and gives you a good look at videos that you want to play back and review on the device.

> **GET SEEN: Best portable pocket video camera set up with dual mics: Kodak Zi8, (2) Audio Technica ATR 3350, Headphone Splitter, Gorillapod (tripod). These mics record in mono, so when you export your video, choose mono instead of stereo output. Adding a mixer like the Azden Cam3 would allow you to control the volume of each mic.**
>
> **GET SEEN: Mic Options: Handheld—Audio Technica ATM 10A, Shotgun—Rode VideoMic, Sennheiser MKE 400.**

SD780 IS—Canon Point-and-Shoot Cameras—$

Canon's line of consumer point-and-shoot cameras also shoot video. Their product line is always changing. It's another good brand to consider for a camera that's easy to carry around that can shoot both still photos and video.

Looking at the current line up, one popular model is the SD780 IS. The SD780 IS has some great features, including image stabilization, 12.1 megapixel CCD for photo capture, and video recording to H.264

---

[7] http://www.vimeo.com/2791881

.MOV files, which can be directly edited unlike other formats like AVCHD, which need to be converted prior to editing.

PANASONIC DMC-FX37—WIDE ANGLE AND A BIG DISPLAY—$-$$

The Panasonic DMC-FX37 is both a still camera and a video camera. The FX37 has a Leica 25mm wide-angle lens. This allows you to get a larger picture than cameras like the Flip and Kodak Zi6. The wide-angle lens also lets you get closer to your subject, when doing an interview, so you can get better sound by having them closer to the in-built microphone. The FX37 also has a much larger display, so you can more easily see what you are shooting, and play back what you've shot.

Although the microphone is situated at the top of the camera, I haven't had a problem recording good audio.

Small enough to carry around in your pocket, or purse, with a big display screen, the FX37 also has the added feature of supporting both replaceable batteries and SD storage card.

Disclosure: I received this Panasonic FX37 as part of the Panasonic Living in HD program.[8]

GET SEEN: The Panasonic FX37 can be thought of as a hybrid combination of some of the best features of the Flip MinoHD and Kodak Zi8. In addition, it takes some really great photos.

SONY WEBBIE HD CAMERA—$

The Sony Webbie HD camera has a sticker on it that says "Self Recording," so you know it was designed with video bloggers in mind; video bloggers who like to shoot video of themselves from an extended arm.

The Sony Webbie HD has a swivel lens that allows you to shoot what's in front of you, and then with a swivel motion, film yourself.

---

[8] http://livinginhd.com

Out of the box, I took the Webbie out for a walk. In bright sunlight I found the display screen hard to view. It was a sunny day.

I started recording video of my walk and swiveled the camera around to shoot both myself, and in the direction that I was walking.

While narrating the scene, I noticed that the microphone is in the front of the camera. So it would make sense to speak into the front instead of the back.

I also tried placing the Webbie on a tabletop to let it stand alone while shooting so that the table acted as a tripod.

The Webbie almost toppled over but I finally got it to stand on its own.

Note: The Webbie supports shooting in either High Definition (1440 × 1080/30p, 1280 × 720/30p) or Standard Definition (640 × 480/30p) format.

You change formats via a button on the side of the camera located just under the Menu button. It has the image of a trash can on it, but it's actually a two-function button. Press that button, choose your movie size, then press the button again.

One thing that's nice about the Webbie is that it's also a still camera with scene selection mode. You can choose a mode to help the camera understand the lighting situation. Modes are Sports, Landscape, Low Light, Backlight, and Auto.

Pocket Camera Summary

On a recent trip to Nantucket I took the Hy-Line high-speed ferry from Hyannis, Massachusetts. When arriving at Nantucket, you sail by the famous Brant Point Lighthouse. I had three cameras with me, a Panasonic Lumix DMC-TS1, Panasonic Lumix DMC-FX37 (see Figure 1.2), and my iPhone 3GS. This was a good test to see which camera would perform best.

The TS1 took a standard shot zoomed in. The FX37 took a wideangle shot, also zoomed in, and the iPhone took a regular shot that wasn't zoomed in because the camera has no zoom.

In this case, the FX37 produced the best video because of wide angle combined with zoom.

Figure 1.2   Panasonic Lumix DMC FX37 versus Flip minoHD

Here's a summary comparison of the Flip UltraHD and Flip MinoHD, iPhone 3GS, Panasonic FX37, Sony Webbie HD, and Kodak Zi8.

The Sony Webbie has a neat swivel lens *and* records 1080p.

The Kodak Zi8 is set apart from all other pocket HD cameras by its audio-in jack. Removable rechargeable battery and storage are also nice features. The view screen is large, allowing easy viewing while recording and playback.

The Flip UltraHD supports replaceable batteries and comes with an AA rechargeable battery pack.

The original Flip MinoHD, 60 min is the smallest and easiest to carry around. The revised Flip MinoHD, 120 min, is slightly larger with a 2-inch display. The FlipShare editing software is great for newbies. It depends on your level of expertise.

I like the Panasonic FX37 best for point-and-shoot HD video and I love the wide-angle lens. The camera also takes great photos. The sound is good if you are close to your subject.

I like the iPhone 3GS for everyday non-HD video because of its ease of sharing online and the benefit of not having to carry around a second device.

Note: None of the pocket HD flip-type cameras can live-stream. The USB ports on them are for file transfer, not webcam use.

Other Options: Pocket Video Cameras

THE SAMSON ZOOM Q3[9] —BETTER SOUND—$$

The Q3 shoots 640 × 480 video with built-in stereo condenser microphone. It's from the same manufacturer of the very popular Zoom H2 audio recorder. The Q3 accepts up to a 32GB SDHC card for 16 hours of recording time. This video recorder includes a headphone jack and has the best audio recording features in the pocket video camera range. Too bad it doesn't record HD video. The Q3 also includes HandyShare editing software.

RCA SMALL WONDER—NOT MAC COMPATIBLE—$

The RCA Small Wonder has some of the great features of all the previous cameras, but the AVI files produced by this camera are not Mac compatible. Once transferred to a Mac you can use a program like iSquint to convert the AVI files into Mac compatible MP4s.

This camera has 2GB internal memory and an expansion slot for SD memory cards up to 16GB in size. It has a lithium-ion battery pack that provides up to two hours of use.

It shoots HD-quality video at 1280 × 720 resolution and also shoots 5 megapixel still photos. Other video options on the camera are Light Quality (640 × 480) and Web Quality (448 × 336).

The RCA Small Wonder also has a flip-out lens so you can see yourself in the 2.43″ LCD display. The microphone is in the front of the camera.

---

[9] http://www.samsontech.com/products/productpage.cfm?prodID=2020&brandID=4

CREATIVE VADO HD—$

This camera is also 1280 × 720. It has 8GB of internal memory. The Creative Vado HD also has a removable lithium-ion battery. The Creative Vado HD includes Windows software that lets you post videos online to sites like YouTube and Photobucket.

SANYO XACTI VPC-HD2000—$$

Moving up in features, the Sanyo Xacti VPC-HD2000 shoots full high-definition 1080p video and has in-built image stabilization. The camera has a 10× optical zoom lens. For audio it has a built-in stereo microphone and also features a microphone input and headphone output.

This camera sits right between the pocket HD cameras and higher end HD cameras. The combination of both microphone in and headphone jack make it a camera to seriously consider.

SANYO XACTI VPC-CG10—$

The Sanyo Xacti VPC-CG10 is similar in form factor to the VPC-HD2000 but shoots 1280 × 720p video and has in-built image stabilization. For audio, the VPC-CG10 has a built-in stereo microphone, but no headphone output.

Moving up from pocket cameras, here are some higher end cameras to consider for shooting video.

Higher End Video Cameras

TAPE-BASED VERSUS FLASH MEMORY CAMERAS

Tape-based cameras, miniDV included, most likely will have a Firewire interface. The reason for this is that in order to move video off a tape, streaming in real time, you need a fast interface. Firewire provides this interface.

With memory card–based video cameras, when you want to transfer your videos to a computer, you can copy them directly from the memory card to the computer by using a memory card reader, or via the camera's USB interface. USB on a video camera is made for file transfer and not for streaming.

That's why tape-based cameras have Firewire ports. The Firewire port is also important for those of you who want to live-stream, with a video camera, to the Web by using platforms like Ustream and Livestream. These platforms require video cameras with Firewire interfaces. They will, however, also support USB webcams for live streaming.

CANON HV20—$$

The Canon HV20 HD video camera records to miniDV tape. The HV20 also had a Firewire interface on it. This allows the camera to support live streaming.

PANASONIC SD100—$$

The Panasonic SD100 camera has many features that entry-level cameras do not have. Most important is both an audio-in and audio-out jack to both record and monitor sound. The SD100 also supports manual controls for white balance, shutter speed from 1/50th to 1/8000th, and iris from F16 to F1.8. These settings allow you to control the quality of video to a much greater extent than standard pocket video cameras. These settings are good in low light situations. With a standard pocket video camera, you need to add more light. With a camera like this, you can let more light in by slowing down the shutter speed or opening up the iris.

This would be a good camera to consider if you want to upgrade your video and audio quality. The SD100 also has a 12× optical zoom, which allows you to zoom in without losing video quality like you would on cameras that only support digital zoom.

This camera records video by using the AVCHD format at 1920 × 1080. AVCHD video needs to be imported into video-editing software and converted before you can edit it. In a program like iMovie 09, this happens automatically when the program imports the video.

Note: Two hours of AVCHD footage take two hours to import. Two hours of Quicktime video can be edited right away. So if you want fast, use a camera that captures Quicktime.

In video production, it's always a good idea to buy the highest quality camera so your end result looks as good as possible. If there's a chance that your video might end up on TV, it's good to have a 1920 × 1080 option.

Most video-sharing sites only support up to 1080 × 720 at this time, so depending on the site, you would export your video as 1080 × 720 prior to uploading. Some sites allow 1080 × 720 uploads, but convert to 1280 × 720 for display.

In comparison, the Panasonic FX37 records videos as MP4. You can copy those files from the SD card and edit them directly with programs like QuickTime Pro or iMovie.

Editing programs like iMovie automatically convert the files for you.

To enable headphone use on the Panasonic HDC-SD100 to monitor audio while recording, you have to make sure that the AV jack is set to Headphones and not AV-out. This tip works for Sony cameras, too. You'll know the jack is set incorrectly if you hear horrible static.

To set the AV jack to headphones, flip open the camera display and press Menu, then navigate to Setup, AV Jack, and select Headphone.

Note: This camera does not have a Firewire port to support live streaming.

Disclosure: I received the Panasonic SD100 as a gift from Panasonic for attending the Consumer Electronics Show as their guest.

JVC GY-HM100—SAVES FILES AS MP4 OR QUICKTIME—$$$

JVC recently introduced the GY-HM100. This camera can record high-quality native QuickTime files for immediate editing within Final Cut Pro.[10] Direct editing of QuickTime files is a huge benefit. This camera also can record in MP4 format for editing in Avid, Adobe Premiere Pro, Sony Vegas, and other programs.

---

[10] http://www.macvideo.tv/camera-technology/features/index.cfm?articleId=109356

Other Options: Cell Phone Cameras

NOKIA N95-3

I've been a member of the Nokia blogger program for a number of years. Having the ability to get hands-on experience with their products allowed me to see how far I could push the limit in video production.

I currently use the Nokia N95 to broadcast live video using a service called Qik.[11] I'll cover how to do that in the Live section of this book.

I've also used the N95 to record over one years' worth of videos for the video blog Spices of Life.[12]

For the weekly Spices of Life show, I recorded video at 640 × 480, 30 frames per second. The quality looks very good for web video. At one point I was able to get three Nokia phones and did a three-camera shoot for Spices of Life.

Connecting a Microphone to the Nokia N95-3

You can use the Nokia N95-3's A/V cable to attach a powered microphone to get audio-in.

These are the parts you'll need:

RadioShack Gold Series Phono-to-Phono Audio Coupler[13]

Gold Series Adapter, 1/8″ Phone Plug to Phono Jack[14]

Sure Matching Transformer Model No: A96F

Powered microphone

These connectors attach to what is normally used at the Yellow video-out cable. The parts allow you to attach a microphone as audio in.

---

[11] http://qik.com
[12] http://spicesoflife.com
[13] http://www.radioshack.com/product/index.jsp?productId=2103236
[14] http://www.radioshack.com/product/index.jsp?productId=2103708

Samsung i8910 (OmniaHD)

Although I haven't had the chance to try this camera yet, I'd like to mention it here because it's an HD camera *and* a phone.

The OmniaHD has an 8.1-megapixel camera that can record 720p HD video.

> **GET SEEN: Take a look at the features of your cell phone and shoot a video with it. You might be surprised at the quality. Or not. It's a good way to start.**

Other Options: 35mm and Micro Four Thirds Cameras

Many high end 35mm cameras, including models from Canon and Nikon, now have the additional feature of being able to shoot HD video. These cameras give the photographer aperture control, which controls how much of the image is in focus. Photographers have been able to get amazing quality from these cameras because of the advanced optics in the cameras. These cameras are limited in length of shooting time and audio features.

Watch this J!NX Commercial[15] featuring Zadi Diaz of Epic Fu. It was shot by the Bui Brothers on a Canon 5D Mark II camera. In this blog post,[16] the Bui brothers explain the shoot.

Panasonic Lumix GH1

The Panasonic Lumix GH1[17] is a very small Micro Four Thirds camera which also shoots high-resolution full HD (1920 × 1080) video at 24 fps or smooth HD video (1280 × 720) movie at 60 fps using an AVCHD format (MPEG-4/H.264).

This camera supports auto-focus, depth of field, ISO settings, plus it supports multiple lenses. You can also manually set the shutter speed and aperture.

---

[15] http://vimeo.com/6245064

[16] http://bit.ly/jinx_bui

[17] http://www.panasonic.com/lumix

Interview: Tim Street

Tools: Flip, mDialog, iMovie

Tim Street[18] is Creator/Executive Producer of the Popular Viral Video French Maid TV with more than 30 million downloads of his online videos. Tim has produced short- and long-form TV for Paramount, Universal, Warner Bros., ABC, CBS, NBC, FOX, The WB, UPN, Fine Living, Food Network, Game Show Network, Nickelodeon, Spike TV, and many others. Tim regularly appears on the podcast This Week in Media and in 2009 Tim was inducted into the International Academy of Web Television.

We met at the SXSW conference and talked about the flip camera and how to get your videos noticed.

Tim Street: I don't remember how I got turned on to the Flip, but it's always in my pocket and I just pull it out, record video just like that, and then I can turn around on myself if I need to and you can see the video right there. The other thing that's really cool about it is like when you get done shooting, you just flip open the USB and this plugs in right to your computer. So, I just plug that in and I can pull all the videos over and upload them immediately, tag them, get them up on my blog pretty quick.

The Flip saves videos as .AVI files, so I just drag and drop the AVIs over onto my desktop and then I upload them to video hosting site mDialog[19] because mDialog is a sponsor of mine and I love mDialog. So, I upload them to mDialog and then I take and embed for mDialog and drop that into my WordPress blog at 1timstreet.com.

I'll bring the videos into iMovie and the only reason I edit is if there's some kind of mess up. I'll cut that out or if I need to edit something, but usually I just add a text overlay with the name of the person who's talking and then I output that as a .mov and

---

[18] http://1timstreet.com
[19] http://www.mdialog.com/

upload it to mDialog, grab the embed, and then put that into WordPress.

Whenever there is a technological advance in entertainment, spectacle comes first, then story. YouTube has been that spectacle. Take a look at the early days of filming. There were these brothers, the Lumiere Brothers, they shot footage of a train pulling into a station. People paid money to go into a movie theater and watch a train pull into a station and they ran out of the movie theaters scared to death. They were screaming and jumping over each other because they thought they were going to get hit by the train. They didn't understand the technology.

YouTube is kind of the same way. We're watching all these cats swinging on ceiling fan videos and we're getting involved in these news stories like the phenomenon of Lonelygirl15[20] where we don't know if it's real or if it's not real and then eventually we find out it's not real. [Author's note: Lonelygirl15 was a scripted video blog series that led the audience to believe that it was real.] That's kind of where we're at. We've seen this spectacle. We're slowly moving into story right now, but any good media—whether it's a good book, whether it's a good film, whether it's a good TV show—it needs to move emotion. It needs to engage the audience. If you can give yourself chills, you can give other people chills. There you go. That's the secret.

Watch the video of our full interview.[21]

GET SEEN: Here's the secret to online video. If you want to get an audience, if you want to make money, if you want to be noticed in online video, you need to move two or more emotions, have a spectacle, and a little bit of story.

---

[20] http://www.lg15.com/
[21] http://blip.tv/file/1944543/

Interview: Jacob Soboroff

Tools: Flip

Jacob Soboroff works on the Web and on TV. Soboroff is the executive director of "Why Tuesday?"[22] and a correspondent for AMC news and the AMC network. He contributes to NPR Weekend Soapbox, which is the blog from Weekend Edition on NPR.

> *Steve Garfield: What is your advice for people who want to put video online.*
>
> *Jacob Soboroff: Just do it. Grab a camera like a Flip camera, and just start shooting. Hit Record. Something that is as simple as this, you take the Flip cam, you plug the thing into your computer, you drag it, you drop it, and at this point it's so easy. In about three steps, you can have a piece of video online. Bring a camera with you everywhere.*

GET SEEN: Take a Flip cam and just start walking around with it and put video online. Online video is easier than ever.

Watch a video of the full interview.[23]

Interview: Dunkley Gyimah

Tools: Flip

David Dunkley Gyimah has 20 years' broadcast experience and 14 years online. We talked about how the small size of the Flip camera makes interviews more personal.

> *Steve Garfield: What's happening in citizen journalism right now? What are people doing and what should they be doing?*

---

[22] http://Whytuesday.org
[23] http://blip.tv/file/1943810/

Dunkley Gyimah: That's a big question. People are doing amazing things. There are different variations of video journalism. People are mashing up cultures. People are shooting this and they are shooting that. The industry is back to front and it's front to back. People are trying to sort out a new aesthetic as to what's going to be big online when we get out of this mess of an economic crisis and, you know, jobs become more available.

SG: If someone wanted to get started telling stories and putting them up on the Web, what do you advise?

DG: The Flip is a great camera for the intimacy because you don't actually realize you've been intimate. In the end, this is not about the technology per se even though we need breakthroughs. We need to have that camera to tell the story. We have to tell our story.

GET SEEN: Ultimately it's you as a storyteller what really matters.

It's what you do behind it. It's the kind of gray matter of your visualization that makes everything work.

SG: Okay. Great. Now, if people want to find you on the Web, where do they go?

DG: They go to viewmagazine.tv or they go to my blog, which is viewmag.blogspot.com,[24] *or if they get really lost, here's my party kick. You just google David Apple. I think of about 96 million, I think I'm number one.*

SG: Excellent. I actually also have a Blogspot blog because I'm kind of loyal to it, you know? I was one of the first, you probably were, too, and there's nothing wrong with it. It works, right?

DG: Yeah, yeah, yeah. My friends say you can go to WordPress and I'm like, "Oh, look. If it's good, if your

(continued)

---

[24] http://viewmag.blogspot.com

blog is doing something, making content, people will find you whether you're at Blogspot, marstock, whatever the case is." So, you know, it's content that matters.

SG: And if you use WordPress, then you're going to have to start being a database administrator and administrating everything and you don't want to do that. You just want it up there and you want to go tell stories, right?

DG: Absolutely, absolutely, and that's why you're a genius. That is why you, Mr. Garfield, are a genius. He's laughing. You can't hold it back. He's laughing. You have to turn the camera around.

Watch the video of our interview.[25] Note: Marstock is a joke.

---

[25]http://blip.tv/file/1943737/

2

Lighting and Sound

For a number of years I worked at WGBH in Boston on their yearly auction. One year I was a producer for all the video segments that ran throughout the live show. This included videos about trips, cars, and local restaurants.

Many times I'd write a script and a shot list for a video segment, then I'd go out with a camera crew and we'd film the spot. An example script might have been for a new car, where the voiceover was going to talk about certain features of the car such as the leather interior, the navigation system, or enhanced tires. So the shot list would include:

- Interior Seating
- Navigation System
- Wheels

The camera people at WGBH are some of the most talented out there. I learned a lot from them on these shoots. One of the most important things I learned was that you don't always need to use additional light (see Figure 2.1). Available light is sometimes your best source of light.

Lighting

It's easy to grab a video camera and start shooting without thinking about lighting. You might think everything looks fine and just push your red button and start recording, but if you experiment, you'll

Figure 2.1   Tota Light Kit

realize that your resulting video will look better when it's lit well, whether naturally or by adding artificial light.

AVAILABLE LIGHT

When I'm out shooting video for the Web, I'll take a look at my surroundings and look for the light. After I find it, I'll place my subject so that the light is shining on them.

Also, just turn on all the lights in the location. Sometimes that's the easiest way to get more light.

ON CAMERA LIGHT

I have a small on-camera light that has come in handy many times. Once I was shooting in a dimly lit bar, and the on-camera light brightened up my subject's face just enough to make the shot work.

There are many new LED on camera light kits to choose from that don't get hot. Consider a Sima SL-20LX Ultra Bright Video Light with bracket.[1] Configurations of this light include different numbers of LEDs. Try them out to see which one is best for you.

---

[1] http://www.amazon.com/Sima-SL-20LX-Ultra-Bright-Silver/dp/B000WKW69Q

Your options for using a light like this range from being on camera, off to the side using a metal bracket that supports both the camera and the light, or on a support stand of its own.

I used this Sima light attached to my Panasonic FX37 camera to record introductions with people at a meeting.[2]

It's really bright. It doesn't make sense to attach it to a camera that is going to be close to the subject. The specs say the light is effective between 15 and 25 feet, so you might want to consider that when purchasing.

The light is powered by a rechargeable, nonreplaceable lithium-ion battery. It takes two to three hours to charge, and provides 45 to 60 minutes of light. The light does not work with the AC adapter plugged in.

Light Kits

There are many light kits available for online video producers. I have a Tota light kit, which includes two lights. Many times I just use one of these lights off to the side of the camera.

Beware though, these light kits get hot and the bulbs need to be replaced over time. The newer LED kits do not throw off heat and don't need to be replaced.

Lamps

Regular household lamps can also be used for lighting. Many home improvement stores sell lighting kits that will do a fine job of lighting. Consider a round Japanese LED paper lantern to add overall lighting.

Advanced Lighting

Here are some lighting terms and techniques you might use.

Key Light: The key light is the main light for your subject; this light is usually placed on the left or right side of the camera.

Fill: The fill light is placed on the other side of the camera. It fills in shadows created by the key light.

---

[2] http://bostonmediamakers.wordpress.com/2009/05/05/next-meeting-sunday-june-7-2009/

Figure 2.2   AT2020 USB Microphone

Back Light: The back light is placed behind the subject.

Background Light: The background light is used to light up the background. You see this used many times on TV interviews.

> **GET SEEN: Many times it's easy to move your subject near a window or outdoors to make use of available light.**

Sound

Before I tell you how to get good sound (see Figure 2.2), I want to share a quote with you from Gary Vaynerchuk.[3] Vaynerchuk produces a daily video show about wine[4] and has thousands of passionate fans. The quote is from Vaynerchuk's book, *Crush It!*:[5]

> *One of the silliest questions I get is, "What kind of mic do you use?" To that I reply, why are you even worrying about that? Your content has nothing to do with the mic, the camera,*

---

[3] http://garyvaynerchuk.com/
[4] http://tv.winelibrary.com/
[5] http://crushitbook.com

the lighting, or the set. The day I filmed my first video I sent the stock boy out to buy a $400 video camera from Best Buy (now I use a fancy Sony that cost a few thousand bucks, but most of my recent shows I taped on a $150 Flip Cam and they look fine). Watch the show, what do you see? It's me, sometimes an awesome guest ranging from my dad to Wayne Gretzky to Jim Cramer, some bottles of wine, and a Jets spit bucket. I only invest effort and thought into what I care about and what I need to create: great content.

Gary goes on to say:

your authenticity will be at the root of your appeal and is what will keep people coming to your site and spread the word about your personal brand, service, or whatever you are offering. If you want to dominate the social media game, all of your effort has to come from the heart; and it can't come from the heart in the passionate, irrational, wholehearted way it needs to if you're trying to be anyone but yourself. Authenticity is what will make it possible for you to put in the kind of hustle necessary to crush it.

I like Gary. You can't help but be inspired by his passion. I agree with him that you should jump in and start producing videos with what you have, just keep it real. As you make videos, you'll decide what you want to improve. Do you want better lighting, could the sound be better?

I was recently at the Inbound Marketing Summit 09 in Foxboro, MA, at Gillette Stadium, home of the New England Patriots. Gary has a goal of filming his Wine Library Show in every NFL stadium. Here's a great photo of Gary filming his show (see Figure 2.3).[6]

At the same time that everything is wrong with this, everything is right.

Gary has one of the most popular video shows on the Internet, and for this one, **he's done everything wrong**.

He's filming it with a handheld flip cam, he's backlit with the sun pointing towards the camera, he has no additional lighting, there's

---

[6] http://bit.ly/gary_gillette

Figure 2.3   Gary Vaynerchuk filming Wine Library TV at
Gillette Stadium with a Flip camera
Source: © Derek Wilmot. www.derekwilmot.com.

some kind of air conditioner noise in the background, and the audio
isn't the best quality. He isn't caught up in all the technical requirements of light kits, lav mics, extra batteries, power cords, tripods,
steady shots, multiple shots, or anything remotely requiring knowledge of video production.

He's also done everything right.

He's accomplishing his goal of filming his show at Gillette Stadium,
home of the New England Patriots, he's passionate about what he is
doing, and he's sharing his love and knowledge of wine.

It works.

Make Gary's example work for you by getting involved in
online video and starting a show about something you are passionate
about.

Now that you're inspired, let's move on and talk about producing
videos with good audio, because although it seems counterintuitive,
what's most important in a video shoot is sound. When you think about
it, even a well-shot video can become unwatchable when there's bad
sound.

Maybe there's a constant hiss running through the video. When
I hear something like that, it makes it hard for me to continue
watching.

With point-and-shoot cameras, they almost never have a headphone output. So with those cameras, you just need to be aware of your surroundings and any sounds that might affect your filming. Think about sounds that might become a distraction—birds, dogs barking, airplanes flying overhead. If you are inside, make sure the windows are closed and everyone's cell phones are turned off.

TIP: In a kitchen shooting video? Unplug the refrigerator and put your car keys inside.
That way when you are ready to leave and go to get your car keys, you'll be reminded to plug the refrigerator back in.

Here are some tips on sound that I've learned over the years:

- Wear headphones to monitor the sound. You might think that you can put on headphones, check out the sound, and then take the headphones off. Wrong. You can't.
  You've got to monitor the sound through headphones. Sometimes you may encounter a mechanical problem that introduces hiss or clicks. You need to be able to hear that coming off the camera to know that you have to fix it.

- Use an external microphone with your webcam. For webcam videos, you can use a microphone to enhance the sound quality of our videos. Sometimes your webcam also contains a microphone. For computers with built-in webcams, use an external microphone

Here's a test video I made using the audio-technica AT2020 USB mic.[7]

The sound quality is significantly improved.

The audio-technica AT2020 USB mic comes with a desktop stand. If your computer is on the same desk as the mic, the vibration of the hard drive might be picked up by the microphone. You can get a mic stand for your microphone and attach the audio-technica AT2020 USB mic to it. That removes all desktop vibration.

---

[7] http://www.youtube.com/watch?v=xnTVVxdz7zg

Here's a quick video I made with the microphone attached to a floor stand.[8]

One more thing you should consider is a windscreen/pop filter. This screen reduces the "P sound" when you speak. The P sound is the letter P.

Here's a video I made to show the difference, AT2020 Mic Test with Windscreen/Pop Filter.[9]

USE AN EXTERNAL MICROPHONE WITH YOUR CAMERA

If your camera supports it, use an external microphone. Especially in a noisy situation, an external microphone gives you much better sound.

A handheld mic is good to use for a single stand-up report for an interview between two people. If you are the only one on the shoot, put your camera on a tripod, flip the viewfinder so you can see yourself, press record, and record your report.

A lavaliere mic is also good. I've used a Sennheiser lav mic kit for years. It comes with one wireless live mic and a wireless adapter for a handheld mic. A less expensive option is the Audio Technica ATR-3350 Lavalier Omnidirectional Condenser Microphone.

In order to get these mics attached to the mic in port on my camera I needed a breakout box that converted XLR mic connections to the audio in port on the camera.

TIP: When purchasing microphones for your camera make sure you know if it requires a powered mic or not. Some video cameras will not accept audio from a microphone unless they supply power.

A couple of good choices for shotgun microphones for video cameras are the Sennheiser MKE400 and the Rode VideoMic.

One of my shooting setups is made up of these items:

Panasonic HDC-SD100 and Sennheiser ME66 powered shotgun mic with a Shure line matching transformer A96.

---

[8] http://www.youtube.com/watch?v=YB81Jb8xgtw
[9] http://www.youtube.com/watch?v=mlu57_0-Z0U

The Panasonic HDC-SD100 has a standard consumer mic in port.

The Sennheiser ME66 shotgun mic has an XLR connector.

The Sennheiser ME66 won't connect into the camera so I had to add a Shure line matching transformer, the A96F.

If your camera does not have a microphone input, you can record your audio with a separate audio recorder.

RECORDING SOUND ON A SEPARATE DEVICE

One method of making sure that you get good sound is to use a dedicated audio device and sync it up to the video later. One device to consider is the Zoom H4n Handy Portable Digital Recorder. The H4n has two built-in stereo mics and two XLR inputs, so you can record from four mics at once. The H2 is an earlier model and costs less. These recorders can also be used as microphones if your camera has a mic-in jack.

My friend and video producer David Tamés[10] calls this a Double System. It's easy to record, but you have to make sure that you'll be able to combine the video and audio later in your video editing system. It's a good idea to make a clap at the start, so that when you are editing, you'll know where to sync up the sound. In practice, this method works for short videos. On longer videos, the audio and video might drift out of sync and you'll have to adjust for it in the editing process.

There are many methods to help find the right sync point, including a Hollywood-style clapboard, actual clapping, and flashing a light.

If you use Final Cut Pro, there's a third-party package called PluralEyes[11] that automatically syncs your audio and video. It takes one or more video tracks and matches them to the audio. PluralEyes acts something like a plug-in; it is a stand-alone application that gets installed into the Applications folder.

---

[10] http://kino-eye.com
[11] http://www.singularsoftware.com/pluraleyes/

Four Steps

Step 1: Save the project

Step 2: Create a sequence called "PluralEyes"

Step 3: Add clips to the sequence

Step 4: Start PluralEyes and choose Sync

Interview: Israel Hyman aka Izzy Video

Tools: Sony PMW-EX1

Tools: Chimera Triolet lights, Arri fresnel lights

Tools: Westcott Scrim Jims

Tools: Sennheiser ME66 shotgun microphone, Sennheiser Evolution G2 Series

Tools: Heil PR40 studio microphone, Aphex 230 Master Voice Channel, Sennheiser HD202 headphones

WHY YOU SHOULD KNOW ISRAEL HYMAN

Israel Hyman aka Izzy Video[12] has devoted the last several years to showing others how easy it is to shoot video. Hyman says it's not the "black art" that people sometimes pretend it is. Developing skills with video is as easy as learning the principles and then practicing them.

> *Steve Garfield: What makes a successful video?*
>
> *Israel Hyman: Clean, understandable audio really helps a video. It's important to get the microphone next to the talent. This means that it's usually a bad idea to use the microphone on the camera. When you use the built-in microphone, you end up recording the camera operator's voice louder than the talent's. Also, the microphone on the camera usually picks up the "whine" of the camera as well as all kinds of unnecessary room noise.*

---

[12]http://www.izzyvideo.com/

Use a separate microphone, and get it close to the talent. This produces much better results.

SG: What audio advice would you give to a business getting started in online video.

IH: When you've decided on your budget for your video, don't forget about audio. In my opinion, three priorities go like this:

1. *Lighting*
2. *Audio*
3. *Camera*

Spending on lighting and audio are higher priorities than spending on the camera.

Many people do just the opposite. They spend most of their budget on a high-quality camera and leave little for lighting and audio gear. They end up with video that looks and sounds bad. Get good lights and good audio gear, and as nice of a camera as you can afford with the money that remains.

SG: What selection of video equipment do you use and why?

IH: My camera is a Sony PMW-EX1, which records a full 1920 x 1080p signal at a very high image quality. It doesn't use tape. It records to little Express Card solid state media called SxS cards, which allows me to use a tapeless workflow. This means I can shoot video, transfer the video files to my computer, and start editing within minutes. This allows a much faster workflow than using tape.

The camera is important, but I've spent more on lighting equipment than I have on my camera. Good lighting is the real secret to getting good video, and few people give lighting the attention it deserves.

If I'm shooting indoors, I use Chimera Triolet lights inside of soft boxes (Chimera Video Pro series) as the key and fill lights. These soft boxes produce a nice, soft

(continued)

fill light that is flattering on many women and some men. I'll usually use the medium and large soft boxes when I'm shooting women, and the small soft box when I'm shooting men. These soft boxes are a critical part of my setup because of the way they affect the quality of the light, and how that in turn affects the way the talent looks on camera.

Arri fresnel lights (usually 150 watt and 300 watt lights) as the separation lights and background lights. The separation light is the final part of "three-point lighting" along with the key light and the fill light. The separation light creates a rim of light around the talent that separates them from the background and adds to the 3-D look of the video. The background lights illuminate the background behind the talent.

By the way, I'm a big fan of having a completely black background. This works best when you want the viewer to focus 100 percent on your talent. Black backgrounds are fast to set up, and they eliminate all distractions. Also, they look great on the Web and keep your file sizes down.

If I'm shooting outdoors, I use a complete set of Westcott Scrim Jims to control the sunlight and build a three-point lighting setup outdoors. I'll usually position the sun behind the talent at an angle, and then reflect sunlight into the talent's face with a Scrim Jim reflector. I'll reduce the intensity of the sunlight with a Scrim Jim diffusion panel or a black net (if I don't want to soften the sunlight).

SG: What makes a successful video? What selection of audio equipment do you use and why?

IH: I have a few different microphones I use in my videos. My favorite is the Sennheiser ME66 shotgun microphone, because of the quality of audio it produces. Whenever I can, I position this microphone just above the talent's mouth, outside the top of the frame. Sometimes this isn't practical because the talent is moving around a lot. Whenever this happens, I rely on a little lavalier microphone. The system I use is called the Sennheiser Evolution G2 Series. It's a wireless system that comes with a couple of ME2 lavelier (lapel) mics, and the transmitters and receivers you need to get the audio into your camera. Although they don't sound as good as the shotgun mic, when the talent needs to be free to move, I use them.

My camera has XLR ports on it, so I use standard XLR cables to get the audio from the microphones into my camera.

During postproduction, one of the final steps I take in editing footage is to send the audio tracks to Soundtrack Pro to "sweet" it. Usually this means I compress the audio levels a bit to help make the talent sound more "present." Sometimes I might need to use noise-reduction tools to eliminate unwanted ambient noise, but usually I do a pretty good job of getting good audio when I'm shooting, so I rarely end up doing noise-reduction.

What I've described so far is the audio portion of shooting video, but I have a different setup for the voiceovers I do. Whether I'm adding narration or doing instructional screencasts, I use more of a studio setup. I have a Heil PR40 studio microphone. I send the audio from this microphone into an Aphex 230 Master Voice Channel to compress and enhance the audio, and then I send it into my computer through an optical cable. I monitor this all the while with Sennheiser HD202 headphones.

SG: What video advice would you give to a business getting started in online video.

IH: I believe that anyone can learn to shoot and edit video (note that I'm biased because I train people on video). It's a basic skill set. You learn the skills, and then you can do it. However, this takes time and commitment. If you decide that you'd rather devote

(continued)

your time to other things, then consider hiring someone else to do the video production.

If you decide to learn video yourself, congratulations. I believe that video is an amazing art form. It's technical and visual. It combines photography with motion and audio. It's simple to learn and can bring you joy for the rest of your life. Whether you're shooting an advertisement for your latest product or video blogging about your thoughts on politics, it's always a wonderful experience. It's magical, and it's within your reach.

GET SEEN: Spending on lighting and audio are higher priorities than spending on the camera.

GET SEEN: Anyone can learn to shoot and edit video.

3

Making Videos Without a Video Camera

Make a Screencast

Hey wait a minute, you don't even *need* a camera to make video for the Internet. You can record what's on your screen.

Let's say you want to make a video of some activity on your computer. The easy way to do that is to make a screencast (see Figure 3.1), a recording of your computer screen.

A screencast lets you record what happens on your computer screen, computer audio, and microphone at the same time. Optionally you could also record from a video camera, but that would defeat the purpose of the title of this section. Hmm, maybe I need to retitle this section?

Let's take a look at making a video using a free online screencast tool as well as a few other methods for including photo slideshows. Learn how to have animated characters do your talking for you!

JING

A nice tool you can use to create a screencast is a web application called Jing.[1] You don't even have to download or purchase Jing to get started. All you have to do is visit www.jingproject.com.

With Jing, you start it up, press record, and then anything that you display on your computer screen is recorded, all audio, too, for

---

[1] http://www.jingproject.com/

Figure 3.1   Screenr Screencast
Source: http://screenr.com/BUs.

up to five minutes. There's also a Pro version of Jing[2] that supports MPEG-4/H.264 and YouTube uploads. The free version records SWF video files which can be played by Adobe Flash player.

Four Steps

Step 1: Start up Jing. Click the crosshairs to select what you want to record. You can place your cursor in the window you want to record and click to select it.

Step 2: In the menu at the bottom of the screen, Click Capture a Video. A countdown starts and then you start recording.

Step 3: When you are done, Click the STOP button.

Step 4: You can click Play to check your recording. Then Click Screencast.com to upload the video.

When you are done recording your screencast, you have the option to save it, or to upload it for free to screencast.com. Hosting on screencast.com is also free for 2GB of storage space, and 2GB of

[2] http://www.jingproject.com/pro/

monthly bandwidth. You can upgrade screencast.com hosting to a Pro version.[3] The Pro version allows 25GB of storage space and 200GB of monthly bandwidth. The Pro version also lets you customize what appears to viewers.

I recorded an example screencast[4] of all the web sites I posted to my Twitter stream one day.

So if you don't want to be on camera, but still want to make web video, a screencast is a great way to be creative and stay behind the scenes.

OTHER WEB-BASED SCREENCAST OPTIONS

Screenjelly[5] is a web site that allows you to record what's on your screen and add voice. The Screenjelly site allows you to make up to a three-minute recording. A drop-down menu allows you to choose which microphone to use, or to not record video at all.

Another web-based screencast application is Screenr.[6] I guess I could call it a ScreencastTwitter but that might be somewhat ridiculous, although you sign into this web-based screen casting application via Twitter. Record your screencast, then you can optionally send out a link to your screencast to Twitter. You can also publish to YouTube or embed the screencast on your own site.

SCREENCAST SOFTWARE OPTIONS

QuickTime X, included with Mac OS X Leopard, now includes a screen capture feature.

Other Mac screen recording applications include SnapZ Pro X,[7] ScreenFlow,[8] and iShowU HD and HD Pro.[9]

PC screen recording applications include Camtasia Studio,[10] which also works on the Mac, and Adobe Captivate.[11]

---

[3] http://www.jingproject.com/pro
[4] http://screencast.com/t/mV7ywaPFj
[5] http://www.screenjelly.com/
[6] http://screenr.com/
[7] http://www.ambrosiasw.com/utilities/snapzprox/
[8] http://www.telestream.net/screen-flow/overview.htm
[9] http://store.shinywhitebox.com/ishowuhd/main.html
[10] http://www.techsmith.com/camtasia.asp
[11] http://tryit.adobe.com/us/captivate/

Make a Video Slideshow with iPhoto

This is for Mac users. iPhoto has a feature that lets you create a movie out of your photos. You click the Slideshow button and choose how you want your slide show to look. You can modify how the slide show looks by clicking the Gear icon on the running slide show's pop-up menu. The options you can control are Theme, Music, and Settings. Then export the slide show to disk.

Five Steps

Step 1: Put the photos you want to use in a Photo Album. To do this, select the photos and choose File, Make New Folder from the selection.

Step 2: Select that Photo Album and choose File, Export.

Step 3: Click Slideshow. Choose the size in the Export Photos Dialog Box. Uncheck Automatically send slideshow to iTunes if you don't want the exported video in iTunes. Click Export.

Step 4: Choose where you want to save it. The default location is the iPhoto Slideshows folder. Click OK.

Step 5: Upload the slide show to the Web. See the How to Upload a Video to YouTube and How to Upload a Video to Facebook sections in Chapter 6.

Here's a sample video slide show I made of my neighborhood's First Thursday Kickoff 2009 using photos, music, and iPhoto.[12]

Make a Photo Slideshow with Animoto

Animoto rocks! It's so easy to make a slide show with it. You can make 30-seconds-long slide shows set to music with Animoto,[13] and there is no cost. Full-length video costs $3 and can be downloaded. An All-Access pass costs $30 to make and download unlimited videos.

---

[12] http://www.youtube.com/watch?v=uHrw-D-r9I
[13] http://animoto.com/

Seven Steps

Step 1: Click Create Video.

Step 2: Choose your video type: Animoto Short or Full-Length.

Step 3: Get your images. Upload from your computer, retrieve from another site, or select from their collection.

Step 4: Add text, rotate and/or spotlight images. Click Continue.

Step 5: Get your music. Select from their collection or Upload from your computer. Save and Continue.

Step 6: Customize the video length, image pacing, and video cover screen. Click Continue.

Step 7: Click Create Video.

Once created, your options are to Remix, E-mail, Post online, Download, Send to YouTube, or upgrade to DVD quality.

Here's a sample video I made with three photos and three pieces of text.[14]

Interview: Photography—Wm Marc Salsberry
WHY YOU SHOULD KNOW WM MARC SALSBERRY

Wm Marc Salsberry figured out how to make videos from his photographs without knowing how to edit video. He uses Animoto.

Salsberry is a producer, director, and event photographer as well as media correspondent and consultant. Salsberry writes articles on events and helps to set up interviews and stories for TechZulu.[15] Salsberry is on the Web on Tumblr, wm-marc.tumblr.com, Facebook, and Flickr, and his Twitter name is the same thing, wmmarc.

(continued)

---

[14] http://animoto.com/play/nclL3Wm1S4N39M11IWf61g
[15] http://techzulu.com/

Steve Garfield: How do you use video in your photography business?

Wm Marc Salsberry: There's a company called Animoto.[16] It takes your photographs and puts them all together and basically creates a music video with all sorts of animation and it just looks amazing. It takes my photographs that I think, quite frankly I've been told, they look really good, and make them look spectacular, but as a medium, video has a much better ability to share with people. So, whenever I have my iPhone, I go and I whip it out. I just take it out and I show them a video[17] of what it is that I do. So, instead of being able to have them flip through one or two pictures at a time, I will click the video on and then they can see it and this is what Animoto does. It takes these pictures and puts something into a platform and a medium that is just so much easier to digest. So, as far as video goes, I think that any photographer really has that in mind.

Make Robots Do Your Bidding and Talk for You

Another cool way to make videos without a camera is with the web site xtranormal.[18] Xtranormal (see Figure 3.2) is a web site that makes talking animations based on your text.

All you do is type in text and drag in camera directions, and xtranormal makes a video for you using animation.

Here's one I made to promote my friend John Herman's video blog, Strange Deaths.[19]

The free account is lots of fun. Upgrade to a premium account and you can make longer movies with no post-roll advertisements. You also get high-quality downloads.

---

[16]http://Animoto.com
[17]http://animoto.com/play/9dajCuOr7Ndv8MkgMWyqog
[18] http://www.xtranormal.com/
[19] http://bit.ly/B11jH

Figure 3.2   Talking Robots: Turn Text into Movie

Remix, Reuse, Recycle

WGBH has a wealth of videos that they've made public for you to use in your own projects.[20]

You can download these clips and use them in your own projects as long as you attribute the work to The WGBH Educational Foundation and provide a link to the Creative Commons license.

The Internet Archive[21] is also a good site to find videos that you can use in your own projects. Share your own videos there for others to use, too.

---

[20] http://lab.wgbh.org/sandbox
[21] http://www.archive.org/

4

Recording and Shooting

Be Like the Web Video Stars and Use a Webcam

Shooting video of yourself talking to a webcam is great practice. It's even more than just practice, it might be the only camera that you have available to shoot video.

I've used the iSight webcam on my MacBook Pro to record a video that ended up on CNN (see Figure 4.1).[1]

I was up in Maine for my niece's wedding and hurricane Kyle was approaching the coast. I grabbed my MacBook Pro with its built-in iSight camera and went to the coast of York, Maine. My wife Carol held up an umbrella, and I recorded a report from the shoreline. All I used was my MacBook Pro, its in-built webcam, and QuickTime Pro to record. After recording the video we drove over to the York Public Library and I used their free Wi-Fi to send the video into CNN iReport.

We then met the family for breakfast across the street. Shortly thereafter I got a call on my cell phone. It was CNN. I had to excuse myself from the table. I said, "Sorry, I've got to take this call, it's CNN." Ha! That was fun. The producer at CNN was calling to confirm the details of my video. Soon after, they showed it on CNN.

So don't be intimidated by people who suggest that you need to buy thousands and thousands of dollars worth of audio, video, lighting, and computer equipment to produce good video. If you want to get started recording video, all you need is a webcam.

In my example I recorded the video to the computer using Quick-Time Pro.

---

[1] http://www.ireport.com/docs/DOC-97376

Figure 4.1   Reporting with a MacBook Pro for CNN iReport

Here's how to record a video with QuickTime Pro and upload it to CNN iReport.

Recording with QuickTime Pro

Step 1: Open QuickTime Pro.

Step 2: Select New Movie Recording from the Edit menu.

Step 3: Click the Red button to record.

Step 4: Click the Black Square button to stop recording.

Step 5: Save the video.

Uploading to CNN iReport

Step 1: Go to iReport.com.[2]

Step 2: Sign in and Click *Upload Now*!

---

[2] http://ireport.com

Step 3: Click Choose File to select and upload a video file.

Step 4: Select your video and Click Choose.

Step 5: Enter a Title, Description, Assignment, and Tags. Choose if you want your video to be able to be downloaded. Enter the story location and date. Agree to the terms of use. Click Submit.

GET SEEN: CNN also has an iPhone application that allows you to file video reports directly to iReport.

Quick Capture

If you have a computer with a webcam, you can record and publish a quick video.

That's the quickest and easiest way to get a video online. For those of you who've never done it, it gives you a sense of how easy it can be.

You can record directly from a webcam to online sites like YouTube, Facebook, and Seesmic, among others. It's easy because when you stop recording, your video is already online.

When using a webcam, consider the height of the camera. If you are using a laptop, the camera will be on your desk and pointed up at you. That's not the most flattering angle. Put your laptop on top of a stack of books to make the height of the camera at eye level.

Recording by using a webcam saves you the step of recording to a camera first. The quality depends on the webcam you are using. Keep in mind that using a webcam and recording directly to your computer, instead of directly to an online site, ensures that you get the best quality because you are recording direct to your local disk instead of recording remotely to a web site.

On Mac OS X you can use QuickTime X to record a video and then send the video to YouTube, Mobile Me, or e-mail.

TIP: On a Mac when recording from an iSight webcam using iMovie, at its larger file size of 1024 × 576, you can post to YouTube as HD video at 1280 × 720, and it looks good.[3]

---

[3] http://www.youtube.com/watch?v=xnTVVxdz7zg

TIP: You can also record with QuickTime Pro at 640 × 480 in H.264 quality and post to YouTube at 1280 × 720 and it looks good, too.[4]

Note: One issue with recording video to a web site is that sometimes your audio goes out of sync with your video. For quick video recording from a webcam I like to use Seesmic.[5]

Let's look at some step-by-step examples of how to record a video directly to a web site and how to record a video and upload it to a web site.

QUICK START: HOW TO RECORD A VIDEO WITH YOUTUBE

In this example we are going to record a video directly to the YouTube site.

Four Steps

Go to the main YouTube page.

Step 1: Click Upload. Click Record From Webcam. Click Allow, to allow Adobe Flash Player access to your camera and microphone. YouTube then searches for your camera. Use the drop down menus to select your camera if needed.

Step 2: Click Ready to Record.

Step 3: Click the red square button to stop recording.

Step 4: Click Publish to post your video to YouTube.

You can also Preview it or Re-record.

GET SEEN: Once you have a video on YouTube you can copy the Embed code on the right-hand side of the page and paste that to your web site or blog.

---

[4] http://www.youtube.com/watch?v=YB81Jb8xgt
[5] http://seesmic.com

GET SEEN: Add your blog to the YouTube share options on the Blog Setup page.[6]

GET SEEN: Set up YouTube to AutoShare[7] each of your new videos to Facebook.

GET SEEN: Engage the camera lens, not the screen. You can take a quick look at your screen or viewfinder to see how the shot is framed, but when recording your video, look into the camera lens.

QUICK START: HOW TO RECORD A VIDEO WITH FACEBOOK

In this example we are going to record a video directly to the Facebook site.

Five Steps

Go to the Facebook home page.

Step 1: Click in the white space writing area of the "What's on your mind?" box. Optionally, you can enter descriptive text.

Step 2: Click Video.

Step 3: Click Record a Video with a Webcam. Click Allow, then click Close. This allows Adobe Flash Player access to your webcam.

Step 4: Click the red Record button. Record your video. Click the black Stop Record button to stop. At this point you can play your recorded video and choose to re-record it if you want by pressing Reset and then recording again.

Step 5: Click Share.

GET SEEN: From the video's Facebook page you can click the Embed in the Video button and copy the Embed code

---

[6]http://www.youtube.com/account#blog/blogs
[7]http://www.youtube.com/my_videos_upload

and display this video on any site on the Web. When you record directly to an online site like this, you shoot your video in one take and have to re-record if you want to do it over. Some people like this procedure because it makes you practice until you get your video how you like it.

Liz Gannes reports for New TeeVee that according to Chris Putnam, software engineer and the lead video developer for Facebook, "40 percent of Facebook video uploads come from webcams. Facebook receives some 415,000 video uploads per day, with 155,000 of them from webcams."[8]

SHARE QUICK VIDEOS WITH TWITTER

One thing people want to do is easily share videos. Twitter (twitter.com) lets you easily share text. Combine video with Twitter and you can easily share videos.

It reminds me of the early video blogging days, video + blogging = video blogging. Video + Twitter = videotwitter. What you are basically doing is recording a video and sharing a link to it on Twitter.

QUICK START: YOUTUBE TO TWITTER

A simple way to do this is to record a video on YouTube and then post a link to it on Twitter.

YouTube has made it easy by including a Twitter option under the Share options under each video.

Four Steps

Step 1: Navigate to the YouTube page of the video you want to share on Twitter.

Step 2: Click Share.

Step 3: Click Twitter.

---

[8] http://newteevee.com/2009/03/29/facebook-40-of-videos-are-webcam-uploads/

Step 4: YouTube will open a new browser window and prefill the text entry area with your video title and a link. Modify that text, if you like, and click update.

You can also set up YouTube to AutoShare[9] each of your new videos to Twitter.

Other Options for Quick Recording and Sharing Video via Twitter

Twitvid

Twitvid[10] allows you to upload a video file or record from a webcam, enter a text message, and tweet the message with a link to your video.

Three Steps

Step 1: Sign in to Twitvid with your Twitter username and password and click Record from Webcam. If the Adobe Flash Player Settings box appears, click Allow, then click Close.

Step 2: Click red Record button.

Step 3: Click the black Stop Recording button. Then you can Playback and re-record if you like.

Step 4: Add or change twitter message text (optional).

Step 5: Click Tweet Video!.

Note: You can alternately upload a video file or send in a video via e-mail. You can also send your video to YouTube.

When you watch the video, there's an embedded chat room that lets you chat with other people who are watching the video at the same time.

Example: http://www.twitvid.com/5E39B

---

[9] http://www.youtube.com/my_videos_upload
[10] http://www.twitvid.com/

12 Seconds

Is 12 Seconds[11] of video the equivalent of 140 characters on Twitter? The people at 12 Seconds seem to think so.

This video-sharing site lets you record 12 seconds of video and post it to the Web.

Two Steps

Step 1: Sign in to 12 Seconds with your Twitter username and password or connect your 12 Seconds account to Twitter and click the Record tab (allow Flash access to your camera and mic).

Step 2: Click Record It

After recording your video, a link to it is posted to Twitter. The resulting video gets its own page, embed code, tiny12.tv URL link and the ability to download either an MP4 or FLV version.

@replies and DMs show up on 12 Seconds in a feed. Included in each message is the ability to reply with Twitter or 12 Seconds. Very cool.[12]

yfrog.us

With yfrog, yfrog.com, you can upload a prerecorded video from your computer, record with a webcam, or upload from a URL.

Three Steps

Step 1: Sign in to yfrog.us with your Twitter Username/Password.

Step 2: Upload a video, record with a webcam, or enter a URL. (You have to have already recorded a video.)

Step 3: Click Post It.

I use the Tweetie Mac desktop application. That lets you record a video directly from Tweetie and post a link to Twitter. Tweetie does not allow you to choose a camera or review the video prior to saving and posting.

---

[11] http://12seconds.tv

[12] http://12seconds.tv/channel/stevegarfield/182552

Note: You can also send in videos via e-mail, web upload, iPhone application (Tweetero), or 3rd Party Application. http://yfrog.com/partners.php

vidly

Vidly[13] lets you upload video and tweet it using your existing Twitter username and password. It also lets you post a video directly from your webcam.

Three Steps

Step 1: Sign in to vidly.com and click Record from webcam.

Step 2: Click Stop Recording. Then you can Playback and re-record if you like.

Step 3: Enter your Twitter username/password and click Upload Video.

Here's a video I recorded about David Pogue's book, *The World According to Twitter.*[14] I'm a co-author ;-). Once the video is saved, you can also post it to Facebook or e-mail it.

For this video I used an iSight webcam and a USB AT2020 mic.

Need More Time? Say It in 25 Seconds with Tweetube

Tweetube[15] uses a desktop application to allow you to record 25 seconds of video. Tweetube then uploads the video and posts a link to the video on Twitter.

All you have to do to get started is press a little red button to record. So easy.

Here's my test post on Twitter:[16]

---

[13] http://vidly.com
[14] http://vidly.com/acil
[15] http://www.tweetube.com/share
[16] http://twitter.com/stevegarfield/status/1576324107

"http://tweetube.com/1G7[17] - twee tube, tweet ube, tweet tube! Record 25 seconds and post to Twitter.

```
1 minute ago  from  TweeTube"
```

I like this method because it records locally and gives you a high-quality recording, then it handles the uploading and posting, including posting to Twitter.

Note: Your videos also end up on the public tweetube time-line.[18] That feature is optional though, and you can turn it off in your account settings.

One issue I came across: after recording a video, if the upload failed, you have to re-record your video.

Tech Specs for Tweetube

For those interested in the recording specs, here they are:

Y'CbCr 4:2:2 = yuvy, 320 × 240, Millions

32-bit Float (Little Endian), Stereo, 44.100 kHz

QUICK START: HOW TO RECORD A VIDEO WITH SEESMIC

To start a video conversation with Seesmic, you go to Seesmic.com[19] and sign up.

Two Steps

Step 1: Click Start a new Conversation. Record a video using your webcam. Press Stop.

Step 2: After recording, you give your video a title and click Post Video.

---

[17] http://tweetube.com/1G7

[18] http://www.tweetube.com/timeline

[19] http://video.seesmic.com/

Optionally, you can enter a description, language, privacy level, and creative commons license. You can also click a checkbox to share a link to your video on Twitter.

Note: Seesmic uses Adobe Flash Player. To change your recording settings, you right click on our video. From there you can change your camera and/or microphone.

Note: After you record your video, you can watch it and re-record it if you like. It's good practice if you are uncomfortable in front of the camera. The process of re-recording will help you make a better video. Record it until you are happy with it.

Once you've recorded your video, it shows up on the Public Timeline where anyone else can watch it and comment on it.

If you click Go to Video, you then have a few more options available to you. You can grab the embed code and paste the video somewhere else, like on your blog. When you do that, the video can be played from your blog, and people can respond with video on your blog, too. It's video blogging made easy.

There's also download links for the flv and MP4 version of your recording.

Conversations with Seesmic

What sets Seesmic apart is the ability for someone watching your video to join the conversation by recording a response video. The steps are the same as above.

These conversations can take place on the Seesmic site, your blog, or in desktop application.

When embedded on a blog, the conversation is embedded, too.

Right at the bottom of the video, any video responses are displayed. Want to respond to a Seesmic video while watching an embedded video on a blog? You can reply using Seesmic, right from that blog post without having to go back to Seesmic.

Interview: Loic Le Meur

WHY YOU SHOULD KNOW LOIC LE MEUR

Loic Le Meur is the founder and CEO of video conversation site Seesmic.com. Seesmic also makes a Twitter and social software client, Seesmic Desktop.

Loic also founded and hosts the number one tech event in Europe, LeWeb.net, with his wife Geraldine. Prior to Seesmic and LeWeb, Loic started several other businesses such as Six Apart Europe, RapidSite, a web-hosting service (acquired by France Telecom in 1999) as well as B2L, an interactive agency in 1999 (acquired by BBDO).

> **GET SEEN: Seesmic lets you share in a second and you don't have to manipulate any file, you don't have to upload anything, you just press a button.**

Loic Le Meur: Yes, Seesmic lets you share in a second and you don't have to manipulate any file, you don't have to upload anything, you just press a button. You record yourself, you press stop and it's up. You have no delay. YouTube takes 20 minutes to put your video up whether you record or you upload. We are also building a conversation. It's all in video threading. That is our difference: people can reply and it's doing pretty well.

Steve Garfield: Can you offer some examples of how a business might use Seesmic?

LM: A business like JetBlue, for example, would use Seesmic to help give a face to the company. People want to see the faces behind brands. They want to know who they are talking to if they have a question, complaint, or suggestion. I think it would be a fantastic experiment for brands to create a live focus group, listening to . . . they pay fortunes, those brands, basically to have

(continued)

feedback from customers and here, it's like Twitter but all in video. You can get instant customer suggestions and feedback from around the country or around the world actually.

SG: And how about newspapers? I think some newspapers have experimented with having like conversations with their readers?

LM: Yes, The Washington Post *has asked their readers to publish video comments from around the world around politics, the BBC is asking questions to their audience, and also a Seesmic community.*[20] *During the inauguration, for example, we got 50 video replies that day, and what's exciting is they took the video replies and put them on TV. They mashed them up, put them on TV. So, that's like a video conversation on TV. I don't see why TV should still be this 1950s, one-way media that you talk and I can't see you, I can't answer. So, we're going to make it many-to-many both ways.*

SG: You know, I participated in some of that BBC campaign and I agree that the people formally known as the audience can now contribute to big media.

Note: I talk in greater detail about streaming live to the BBC in the Broadcast Live Chapter.

LM: Yeah. There is no reason why the social conversation should be so huge on social software and blogs but not in video. It's just not happened yet and I'm very confident that it will. It's really about having people get used to talking to a camera, not being shy, not thinking too much about it, just busting it.

SG: When I think about putting video on the Web very quickly, I think Seesmic because you can just press a red button and it's on the Web and then you can embed it and put it elsewhere. Do you find people do that as a quick way of sharing their message?

---

[20]http://seesmic.com/bbchaveyoursay

LM: Yeah, or just post it to Twitter as a link. Again, you don't think too much. You just press, ping, it's up. Otherwise, video is too complicated. The reason why we did it is also because it's just too complicated to have a conversation if you have to wait 20 minutes each time.

SG: So, following on that, what's the secret of online video?

LM: There is no secret, but I think everybody will realize that for their brand whether it's their personal brand or like a company, putting a face. It's like meeting you in real life. It's you and that's very, very important. With the people in my community, we connect in a very deep way because I watch them, they watch me, and we talk. In video, we're just not used to it. We're used to being passive in front of a TV. It's going to change. Its power is really huge.

Watch the video of our interview.[21]

Disclosure: I liked the idea of Seesmic so much, I invested in the company.

Talking Heads: Recording a Skype Video Chat

One of the hardest things to do with online video is to record a remote video call between two people for later broadcast. There are a few solutions available. Call Recorder[22] is one. It allows you to record a private two-person Skype[23] video chat video call. In Chapter 7, we'll look at alternative ways of recording live public conversations.

Interviews with a split screen where two people are talking are broadcast on TV all the time. The default display for a Skype video chat is to have your video in a little box, and the person you are talking to taking up the full frame. In this example I'm talking to Social Media Evangelist Bryan Person.[24]

---

[21] http://blip.tv/file/1944030/

[22] http://www.ecamm.com/mac/callrecorder/

[23] http://www.skype.com/

[24] http://bryanperson.com/

Figure 4.2   Skype video chat recorded with Call Recorder

We weren't actually doing an interview for broadcast so we were not concerned with looking into the camera.

When recording interviews like this, match up both people in both size and orientation. Advise the person you are interviewing to look into the camera. Have them set their camera at eye level so they aren't looking down.

With Call Recorder software, you can record your Skype video call and have the resulting QuickTime video file display the call participants side by side (see Figure 4.2).

You need to make sure that your computer is fast enough to capture a clean recording without any audio or video breaks. I suggest closing all unnecessary programs before starting a recording.

If your recorded video goes out of sync between the audio and video, you'll need to edit the video in a program like Final Cut Pro to sync up the audio to the video. Basically that entails slipping the audio track a few frames to match the person talking with the audio.

The Church of the Customer blog has a great post about this process entitled "How to produce a 2-person video blog post."[25]

---

[25] http://www.churchofcustomer.com/2009/03/how-to-produce-a-2person-video-post.html

Figure 4.3   Chatting with Whit Scott Using Wetoku
Source: http://wetoku.com/video/0336jap2.

TALKING HEADS: WETOKU

Wetoku[26] (see Figure 4.3) is a web-based application that lets you record a two-person talking head interview and save it for embedding on the Web.

Seven Steps

Step 1: Click Start New Interview.

Step 2: Enter the Title, Interviewer, Interviewee, Location, and Description. Click Next.

Step 3: Copy and send the supplied invitation link to your interviewee and allow wetoku access to your camera and microphone.

Step 4: After your interviewee enters the chat, click the Record button.

Step 5: When finished, click the Stop button.

Step 6: Click Done.

Step 7: Your video is now on a page of its own and you can grab the embed code to post it on the Web.

---

[26] http://robo.to/

Figure 4.4   Video Shoot with Ann Handley,
MarketingProfs

Enhanced features include higher quality video without pixelation, video editing, custom logo, custom embeddable player, and the ability to import pre-roll/post-roll video.

Video Avatars

Robo.to[27] hosts really short silent movies of people looking into their webcams.

Visit robo.to. Once there, you can sign in and record a short silent video of yourself. Then copy the embed code and paste that anywhere you want your video avatar to show up.

If you want to have some fun, visit robo.to TV[28] and watch everyone else's videos.

Here's mine.[29]

Great Video, Simple Techniques

Your video will end up being successful depending on your content. How you shoot that content is important (see Figure 4.4). You can

---

[27] http://robo.to/tv
[28] http://robo.to/stevegarfield
[29] http://wetoku.com/

start out with the simplest camera and move on to more elaborate setups. What's most important is the content.

Great content can be produced with the simplest tools. As mentioned earlier, you can create a video starting with a regular point and shoot camera that also shoots video.

There are lots of places to learn how to shoot video. Film school is one place. Looking at other videos is another good way to get ideas. If you see something you like, try to emulate some of the elements.

Rule of Thirds

I learned how to shoot good video by doing a lot of photography. In photography classes you learn techniques like the Rule of Thirds. This is one of the most helpful rules for framing shots. Although it's called a rule, feel free to break it.

You can think of the Rule of Thirds as a tic-tac-toe layout superimposed on top of your viewfinder. Some cameras even have a feature that puts these lines right on the viewfinder.

What you end up with are four intersecting lines. Place your point of interest at one of the intersections.

Keep the End Result in Mind

When you are shooting video, keep the end result in mind. If I'm shooting a quick video, I think about what my first image is. Many times, if I shoot a video and don't edit it at all, the hosting provider takes the first frame and makes it the thumbnail for the video. The thumbnail is the still image that is used on video-hosting sites to promote your video.

Make your first image interesting.

Next, I think about what my introduction is going to be. Many times I introduce who I am and where we are. Most of the time in my first-person videos, I start off with, "This is Steve Garfield from SteveGarfield.com." I do that in case my video is reposted and separated from the associated text and description. That way the viewer always knows where to visit on the Web to find more information.

I like to have most of my videos have a beginning, middle, and end. So after I've made my introduction, I might interview someone or give a video tour of a location.

Then to wrap up, I share a web site where viewers can find more information about whatever was covered in the video. I'll talk about the techniques I use when shooting interviews; I shoot a lot of them. You can use these techniques in any type of video shoot.

The Interview

When conducting an interview, think of it as having a conversation, but not a regular conversation. In an interview, you want to let the interviewee have a chance to speak. In normal conversation you might want to acknowledge what the other person is saying by saying "yes, ah ha," and other verbal confirmations—in a video interview you don't want to do that.

Let the other person talk and complete a sentence. When the person is finished, pause a moment. This gives the interviewee time to add an additional thought. If you talk over the interviewee, it'll be hard to edit the interview later.

It's good to research the person you are interviewing, but don't come to the interview with a list of 10 questions. That will inhibit the interview. If you've got points you want to cover, list them out as bullet points to refer to, but don't go down your interview questions in order from 1 to 10.

Listen to what the interviewee is saying and follow up with questions based on what you hear. Ask what is interesting to you. Be present in the moment.

THE INTERVIEW—BASIC

Here's an example of an interview done in one shot. The interviewee knows what they are going to talk about, and starts off the interview by saying who they are.

I shot this video with my mom, Millie Garfield; she's 84 years old and is a great storyteller. She's been featured on *ABC World News*[30] and in the book *15 Minutes of Fame, Becoming a Star in the YouTube Revolution.*[31]

The video is "My Mom's Cookies."[32] We've done a lot of videos like this. Before I turn the camera on we review that she is going to introduce herself, give her blog name, and then tell her story. What you

---

[30] ABC World News
[31] http://www.amazon.com/15-Minutes-Fame-Becoming-Revolution/dp/1592577652/
[32] http://mymomsblog.blogspot.com/2009/07/my-moms-cookies.html

can see from the video is that she's real, authentic, and comfortable. A good example for anyone. Yay mom!

When I shoot videos with my mom, I use a small camera like the Panasonic FX37. It's small enough that it doesn't get in the way. It's a great size because the interview subject forgets that a camera is even there and ends up talking to you, the videographer.

We shoot these videos in her dining room to take advantage of the natural light coming in from large sliding glass doors. I have her sit to the side so the light from the outside shines on her. I also turn on the dining room overhead light.

The sound is great because we are in a quiet environment and the camera is relatively close to the subject.

GET SEEN: If the interviewee has a number of topics they want to talk about, have them talk about the first point, then pause. Think about what they want to say for the second point, and continue. They don't have to memorize everything. You can edit together the points later and make the interviewee look good.

GET SEEN: If the interviewee gives a really long answer, you can ask them to restate their answer using fewer words. Say something like, "That was great, can you repeat that answer again but with a lot fewer words?" Since the person could have been formulating their answer the first time they answered, they will be able to be clearer and shorter the second time.

GET SEEN: "The moment you figure out that you don't have to be 'that guy' and you should be yourself is when video becomes comfortable."

The Interview—Advanced

An advanced version of the interview is done with additional equipment.

I was happy to work with Ann Handley of MarketingProfs[33] on this video[34] to open the Digital Marketing World online conference.

---

[33] http://www.marketingprofs.com/
[34] http://www.youtube.com/watch?v=3Mvvl6cGamA

The interview setup consisted of a Canon GL/2, Tota Light, and Sennheiser Lav Mic. In this setup I place the camera on the opposite side of the table, I light Ann from the side, and capture the sound directly to the camera with the lav mic. I wore headphones to monitor the quality of the audio being recorded.

> **GET SEEN: Although the sound in the room and the interviewee might sound great to you, what is being captured might not be. The mic might be picking up rustling from clothing or jewelry. You wouldn't know that by listening to the interviewee in the room, but you'd hear it right away with headphones.**

B-ROLL

Another video I shot that's a good example of using B-Roll is of the Ireland Basketball National Team.[35] B-Roll is interesting footage that you display to make the video more interesting.

I shot this video for Boston City Councillor John Tobin. I've been shooting videos for him for years. In this example, he wanted me to make sure that I interviewed Joe Walsh, Commissioner of the Great Northeast Athletic Conference. I also interviewed David Baker, assistant coach of the team.

The basketball court was noisy so I asked Coach Baker if he'd step out into the hallway for an interview. There it was much quieter and I conducted the interview.

Once I finished recording the interview, I went back to the court to shoot some B-Roll.

In this case I shot video of the team in the huddle, basketballs going through the hoop (I used a monopod for that shot), and lots of different angles of the practice and the game.

When it was time for the edit, I had great sound, and lots of extra footage to use to enhance the final video.

---

[35] http://www.votejohntobin.com/blog/_archives/2009/7/3/4243911.html

GET SEEN: When shooting B-Roll, hold steady on your shot for 7 to 10 seconds. Some things you can shoot B-Roll of are interviewee hands, the computer keyboard, and the computer screen.

A Two-Person Interview

When you are conducting an interview with someone and don't have a crew with you, a tripod and external microphone makes the shoot easier.

In this example, I produced a report for web news show Rocketboom on the Chevy Volt.[36] I was producing this shoot myself, so I used a tripod to set up the camera.

The camera I used for this shoot was a Canon GL/2. I set it up on a tripod and flipped its viewfinder around so I could frame myself and the interview subject in the shot. Then I used a handheld mic to conduct the interview.

When you watch this interview, you'll notice that it makes use of a lot of B-Roll. While conducting the interview, I made note of all the things that the interview subject was discussing. Then after the interview was complete, I went around and shot all the images. In the editing process, whenever one of those things was mentioned, I showed it in the final video.

When you watch the video, make sure that you watch until the end where someone from the crowd interrupts our interview with lots of questions. I've used this video in many journalism classes where we talk about whether that footage should be included. I'd love to hear your thoughts.

GET SEEN: When using cue cards, hold the cue card next to the lens. Don't drop the cue card on the floor—it makes too much noise. Either hand it to someone, or quietly place it down.

---

[36] http://offonatangent.blogspot.com/2009/08/rocketboom-electric-volt-car.html

Tripods and Monopods

In order to get a steadier picture, I suggest using a tripod or a monopod.

TOOLS: MONOPODS—PEDCO ULTRAPOD TRIPOD, JOBY GORILLAPOD

I like the Pedco UltraPod Tripod that you can get at REI. It's a small tabletop tripod that's easy to carry around. When closed you can also use it as a camera handle. The Joby[37] Gorillapod is flexible and allows you to attach it to irregular surfaces like a fence or a chair. There's also a whole range of larger tripods to choose from.

TOOLS: MONOPODS—MANFROTTO 680B, BRUNTON, XSHOT

The monopod I use is a Manfrotto 680B. It's big enough to support a miniDV cam and can also connect to a Flip camera or any small camera with a tripod mount. An add-on for the 680B allows it to stand by itself on three legs. Other options include the Brunton Monopod, which also acts as a walking stick, and the Xshot 2.0 Camera Extender, which allows you to extend the camera far enough away from you to be able to get an in-focus shot of yourself, or a two-shot of you and someone else.

If you don't have a tripod or monopod available, improvise. The Flip has a flat base, so you can place it on something like a windowsill and it won't topple over. Other ways to keep the camera steady are leaning it up against something stable like a lamppost or a wall.

Note: My standard style is to shoot a steady shot. That doesn't mean that you have to. You might want to move the camera around, up, down, in, out. Experiment with different styles.

Shooting Tips

Here are six shooting tips that will help you get the best footage from a pocket video camera:

---

[37] http://www.joby.com/

1. Shooting yourself? Shoot a preview video to see framing. Since most pocket cameras do not have a display that allows you to see yourself when shooting, you can shoot a preview video to see how it looks first.

2. Hold the camera steady. If you hold your arms against your body, that will keep the camera steadier than holding it out at arms length. When you hold your camera out at arms length, it usually makes for unsteady footage. Once you get some experience, you can hold your camera at arms length with a steady arm. Note: All your video doesn't have to be rock steady either, sometimes you might want a shaky shot, like you see on TV.

3. Understand where the camera starts focusing to get your subject in focus. You might have to position the camera three to four feet away to focus on the subject.

4. Put the camera in record mode early, then start the interview. That puts less focus on the camera and more on the connection between the interviewer and the interviewee.

5. It's okay to interrupt the interview and reset the camera to get a different shot; you'll be editing it later. You don't have to post the whole interview in one continuous stream and can edit things out. Pause the camera and go from a wide shot to a closer head-and-shoulders shot for visual interest.

6. When the interview is over, don't stop the camera when the interviewer ends the interview. Let the camera roll. You might get your best moment after the interview when the subject relaxes.

5

Editing

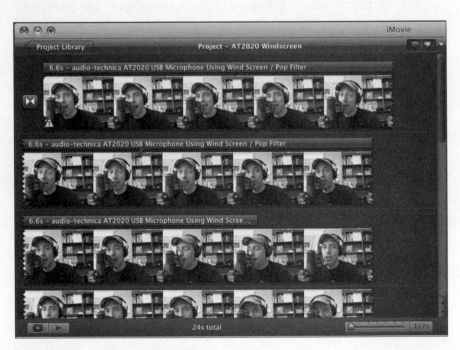

Figure 5.1   Editing with iMovie

Before you start editing you might want to consider backing up your files. If your source video is on tape, once you import your video to a computer, your original source tapes are your backup. If you recorded to a Flip camera or a SD memory card, and then moved the files to your computer, you've only got one version. If your footage is irreplaceable, you will want to consider making a backup copy. Store your footage on backup external hard drives, CDs, or DVDs.

Now let's talk about why you might or might not want to edit. For me, it depends on the situation.

Why Not Edit?

If I'm at a conference and know I'm going to be shooting lots of videos that are time sensitive, I'll want to either shoot them live to the Web without any editing, or record them to a video camera and upload them right away.

MINIMAL EDITS

For those videos that I record on a camera, I might, at a minimum, add a title and credits at the end. I'll add credits to the video so that if my video gets copied and hosted elsewhere, people will always see a URL at the end of the video so they can find their way back to me.

If I'm just working by myself and want to end the day without having any other work to do, I'll choose one of these methods.

Shoot for the Edit

Many times I shoot for the edit. This means that while I am shooting, I'm thinking ahead to what the final edit will look like.

Sometimes this means getting different angles of the action. Other times, I will have the talent re-state something that they just said. It's okay to do that. The cleaner the original video, the easier it will be to edit.

In Camera Edits

On some cameras you can do minimal editing with the video camera itself. One of the most basic ways of doing this is to plan out your shots ahead of time, and then shoot them in order, from start to finish. If your camera has a pause button, you can continue your shot right where you left off, and the final video will be the series of scenes, one after the other.

Types of Edits

There are many types of editing you can do with video. I'll give you a few simple edits that are standard, then get into specific edits you can do with different types of software.

TRIM

At the least, an edit can simply be trimming the beginning and end of a video. Maybe you set the camera up on a tripod, turn it on, and then run around to the front to start your video. At the end, you run back and shut the camera off. A trim edit would be cutting off the excess video beginning and end, so the remaining video starts and finishes with you standing in front of the camera. This type of edit can even be done on some recording devices like the iPhone.

You might even consider not editing this at all, leaving in all the running around.

TITLE AND CREDITS

The next basic edit you can do with your video is to add a title and credits. For the title you can choose to have it be the first thing people see, or you might want to have a short teaser of what's coming up, then display the title.

For ending credits, I always put in a URL. That way, if the video is embedded somewhere other than your web site, people will always be able to find their way back to you. I always use SteveGarfield.com. Although I have lots of other sites, that's the URL I use consistently on all my videos. Viewers can then navigate to my main site and find their way to my blog, video blog, or client site.

B-ROLL

In the recording and shooting chapter I suggested shooting B-Roll. B-Roll is great to layer on top of someone talking. One technique I have fun with is the L cut and J cut.

With the L cut, you overlay your B-Roll footage so that you see the new footage while still hearing audio from the current footage. With a J cut, you hear audio from the next piece of footage while still seeing the current footage.

A fun example of a J cut is seeing a reporter on location and then hearing the sound of a sheep. It tips you off that something is coming and ties the footage together. It's fun to play with.

Let's get into some specific editing software.

Quick and Easy Cut and Paste Editing with QuickTime Pro

If you want to do a quick edit using cut and paste techniques, Quick-Time Pro is a great tool to use.

It works on both a PC and Macintosh.

Sometimes if you shoot a video and all you want to do is trim the beginning and end, QuickTime Pro can help you do that very quickly. More than that, you can also cut out pieces you don't like from the middle, and move things around. It's just like using a word processor, but with video.

How To: Open Up QuickTime Pro

Select "New Movie Recording" from the edit menu.

Then click the red button to start recording. That changes the red button to a black square, and recording starts. Record your video, then press the black square, the Stop button, to stop recording.

When done you can start a quick and simple edit.

Play the video up to the point where you want the actual starting point to be.

Then press "O." This sets your out point.

When you press "O," a section of the video is selected from the very beginning of the video, up to the point where you stopped playing the video.

Cut that section out by going to the Edit menu and selecting "Cut."

Now play your video up to the point where you want to start your next cut. Press "I" for in point. Then play through the video until you get to the next part you want to keep. Press "O."

What you now have selected is video that you want to delete. It's all between your selected in and out points.

Tip: You can reset either the in or out points by placing the play-head on a new location and either pressing "I" or "O."

Once you are happy with your selection, once again, go to the Edit menu and select "Cut."

When you are happy with your video, you can save it.

Then you can also save a version for the web.

Move the playhead to an image you'd like to use for your thumbnail.

Then, to make this easy, Choose "Export for the Web ..." from the File menu.

Enter a name for your movie in the "Save As" entry area, then Select Export versions for: iPhone. Create a poster image from the current frame. Then press Export.

Note: Some video hosting sites recognize poster frame and some don't.

Your video is saved in the format of moviename.m4v.

If you double click it, it will open up in Apple iTunes. Otherwise you can right-click it open in QuickTime.

Right click on the file name, select Open With, then select Quick-Time Pro or some other video viewing application.

Next you can upload to a video sharing site of your choice.

Editing a Flip Video with FlipShare

The Flip mino HD includes a FlipShare Program that allows you to browse, play, delete, and save videos to your computer, make some movies, snap photos from your videos, and share your videos online by e-mail or upload.

The technique used by FlipShare to make movies is called an assemble edit. You assemble the pieces together one by one, adding video clips until you have a complete movie. Prior to this, you'll want to trim the beginning and end of any clips you are going to use to make the movie.

Once edited you can upload video to AOL Video, MySpace, YouTube, and other sites.

INSTALL FLIPSHARE

Open the FLIPVIDEO labeled drive that appears when you plug in your Flip camera, then launch "Setup_FlipShare" (PC) or "Start Flipshare" (Mac).

Note: Clicking on "Start FlipShare" on the FLIPVIDEO USB volume installs the FlipShare software to your Application folder on your computer.

Need support, visit the Flip support web site.[1]

After recording a **video, plug the Flip into your computer.** FlipShare opens up and displays the video you just captured. **Click "Save to Computer."**

You then get the choice if you want to "Remove videos from camcorder after saving."

Check that box. Click yes.

Now you have a new movie in your computer directory, under the current month.

When in the FlipShare movie folder, you'll see thumbnail images in video players. At the bottom right of each video is a pair of scissors. Click the scissors to bring up an edit window.

There are controls at each end of the video to help you select a new start and end point.

This feature makes it easy to trim off shaky parts of your video before sharing it.

Move the left-hand slider to the location you want the video to start, and the right-hand slider to the frame you want the video to end on.

Your video has to be three seconds or longer.

Six Steps

Step 1: Click Movie

Step 2: Drag Clips to the Arrange Window

Step 3: Add Title and Credits (Optional)

Step 4: Add Music (Optional)

Step 5: Name Your Movie

Step 6: Create Movie

Combine Clips to Make a Movie

In this step you add movies to your movie timeline.

Click Movie in the Create area at the bottom of the FlipShare screen.

---

[1] www.theflip.com/support

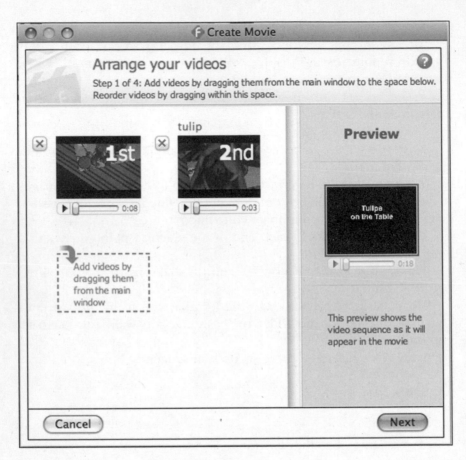

Figure 5.2   Arrange Your Videos

A Create Movie window pops up (see Figure 5.2). That's where you drag in all your clips. Combined together, they'll make up your movie.

There is a Preview movie on the right side of the Create Movie window, so you can check your results as you put your movie together.

Next, you can add a movie title, credits, and share credit with Flip, if you choose to (see Figure 5.3).

Note that you cannot change the font size, so be careful choosing your title.

For music, you can use music provided by Flip, or choose an MP3 file from your computer. Make sure you have the rights to use the music you choose.

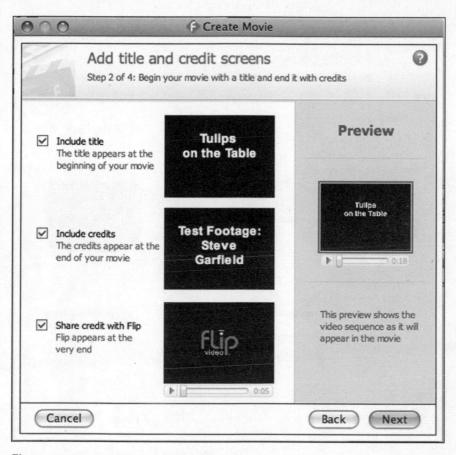

Figure 5.3   Add Title and Credit Screens

Additionally, you can choose to play the music softer or louder than the sound in your video, or only play the music and mute the sound in your video (see Figure 5.4).

The final step asks you to name your movie file that Flip will put in your My Movies folder within the FlipShare program (see Figure 5.5).

Finally, click Create Movie and your movie will be assembled and saved to disk.

At this point, you could just click Online and send the video to AOL Video, MySpace, or YouTube, but this time we'll click Share Online and select Other Web Sites.

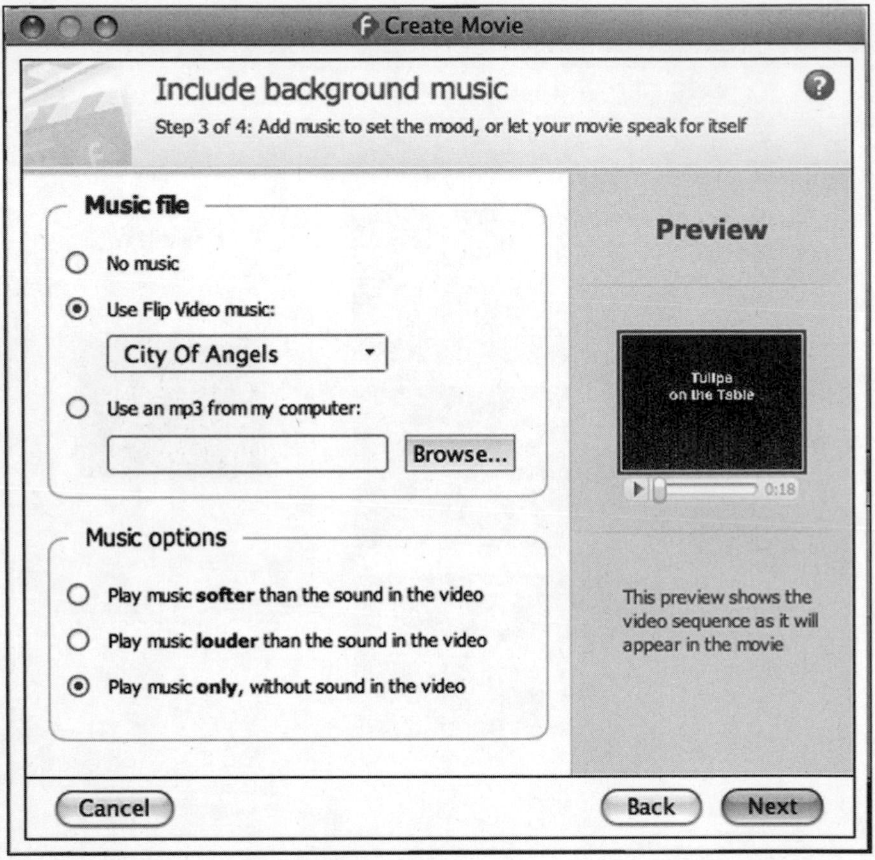

Figure 5.4   Include Background Music

You then save the video to your desktop in a folder that FlipShare creates. If you don't rename it, the folder name looks like this:

Videos for uploading 2009-03-03

The edited video is saved as 640×360. That's half the size of full 1280×720 HD resolution. If you take a look at the original MP4 file in the FlipShare Videos folder, you'll see that it's 1280×720. So by using the FlipShare editing software, although easy, it reduces the resolution.

To make this very easy, you can use an application like Flickr Uploader to send this file (since it's so small) up to Flickr for sharing.

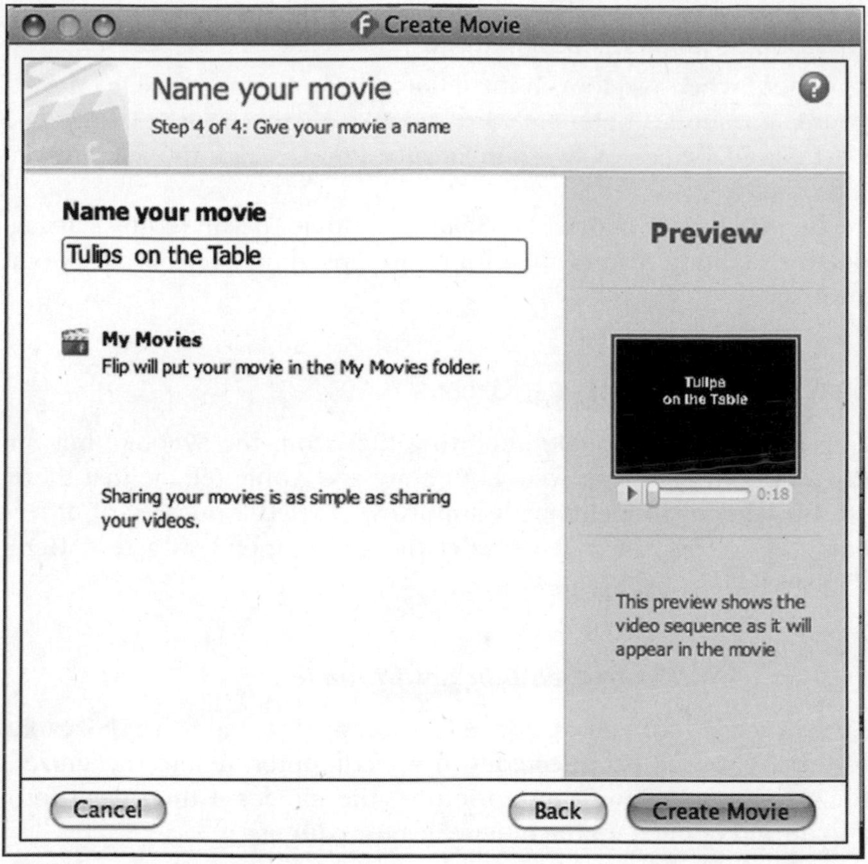

Figure 5.5   Name Your Movie

EDITING A FLIP VIDEO WITH QUICKTIME PRO

If you open the Flip mino HD video with QuickTime Pro, you can edit the full resolution 1280×720 file, then save and upload in full HD resolution.

EDITING FLIP MINO (AVI) VIDEO WITH IMOVIE

If you have a Macintosh with iPhoto configured to recognize new USB devices, iPhoto will open up and give you the option to import Flip mino .AVI files.

After import, you can look at the video from within iPhoto.

Open iMovie and generate thumbnails for the new movies that iMovie finds in iPhoto. It's automatic.

Then, when you look in the iPhoto video directory inside iMovie, your Flip mino .AVI files are there, ready for you to edit in iMovie.

I edited a video of swans in Jamaica Pond.[2] Click HQ to watch in high quality.

So you have a choice, FlipShare or iMovie. If you're just starting out with editing, you can use FlipShare and then later on check out iMovie.

Sony Webbie Movie Import Options

I had some initial trouble importing files from the Webbie, but on the second try all went well. Both Sony and Apple tell me that there are no known problems with importing. I tried a number of different ways to get the video files onto the computer as a test. Here they are:

Import with iPhoto then Edit with iMovie

To get the files onto my MacBook Pro computer I attached a USB cable to the Webbie and connected it to my computer. iPhoto recognized the device and allowed me to import the movies. I then went into iMovie and opened up the movie files for editing.

Import with iMovie

You can also import your movie files directly into iMovie by disabling the iPhoto auto import, and then just starting up iMovie after inserting the SD card into your Mac with a card reader. iMovie recognizes the files and allows you to import them.

Note: Closing iPhoto after it auto opens also works. So you don't have to disable auto import.

---

[2] http://www.youtube.com/watch?v=Dj9qjdEQrt4

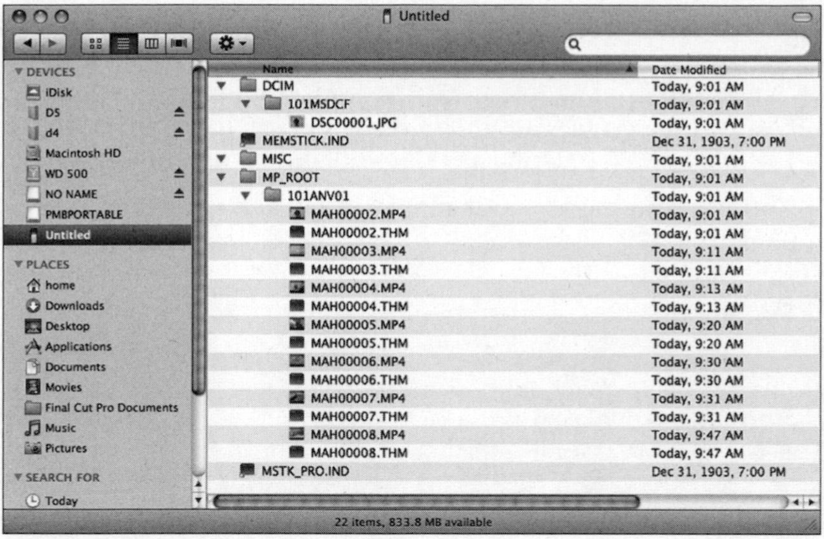

Figure 5.6   Sony Webbie Files

File Copy

You can also go to the file directory and copy the movie files, MP4 files, to your hard disk (see Figure 5.6).

iMovie File Import

The next test was to go into iMovie and import the movie files from the hard disk. To do that you choose File, Import, then select the files you want to import.

QuickTime

You can also open up the videos with QuickTime Pro to take a look and edit with basic cut and paste editing.

When I listened to the audio it turned out that it was clear both when the mic was facing me, and when it was pointing away from me.

YouTube Direct Upload of the unedited file.

I went over to YouTube[3] and directly uploaded the MP4 file[4] after copying it from the camera to the computer. Worked fine.

---

[3] http://YouTube.com
[4] http://www.youtube.com/watch?v=pVYp_PDWcNI

Windows Live Movie Maker

The easiest way to make a movie from your photos is to use Windows Live Movie Maker's AutoMovie feature. Just add photos and music and AutoMovie makes a movie for you. You can also click one button to publish your movie to YouTube.

You can also modify your movie to change transitions and add captions.

Six Steps

Step 1: Select images

Step 2: Click Make

Step 3: Rearrange your images in the storyboard (optional)

Step 4: Add a title and text effect (optional)

Step 5: Adjust the length of time it plays (optional)

Step 6: Click AutoMovie to make the movie.

Video Editing

Use the trim tool to select a beginning and end point for each of your video clips.

If you want to select another part of the same video, you can copy and paste the clip, and then trim a different part of the video.

After you have all your clips, rearrange them, just like you did for photos above.

Sharing

Upload directly to YouTube, Save as HD, Burn to DVD.

Get Movie Maker for free at http://download.live.com/movie maker.[5]

Editing Software for Mac Users—iMovie

I've used Final Cut Pro on a Macintosh for years. It's very powerful. Recently I've been using iMovie '09 instead. Apple has made it very easy

---

[5] http://download.live.com/moviemaker

to edit movies with iMovie. One nice feature allows you to add a second video track. I'll use this to add interest to an interview, and it's as easy as dragging and dropping the second track of video on top of the first video track.

GETTING VIDEO INTO IMOVIE

There are a number of ways to get iMovie to recognize your video.

1. Live—Where you record live video from a webcam or attached camera. The video you record can then be edited from within iMovie. Hooking up a camera and recording direct to disk saves a lot of time if you've got a camera that records to tape.

2. SD Card—Import pre-recorded video into iMovie from an SD card that comes from a video camera.
   1. Remove the SD card from your video camera.
   2. Insert the SD card into a card reader and plug it into your Macintosh.
   3. Open iMovie.
   4. Wait for iMovie to recognize the SD card.
   5. An import dialog box will pop up with the following options:
      Save to:
      Add to existing Event
      Create new Event
      Import 1080i video as:
      Full—1920 × 1080
      Large—960 × 540
      Cancel/OK
      Make your selections and press OK (see Figures 5.7 and 5.8).
   6. Once the import is complete, select DONE.
   7. Now that you have the video captured you need to create a new Project.
   8. Enter a Project name.

Figure 5.7   Import Dialog Box

9. Choose an aspect ratio (see Figure 5.9):

Standard (4:3)

iPhone (3:2)

Widescreen (16:9)

Once you've selected these settings, click Create.

This example is an easy edit since all I have to do is select the section of video I want and drag it up into the Project window (see Figure 5.10).

TIP: Within your video, say your web site URL, so that no matter where the video is hosted or copied to, your URL goes with it.

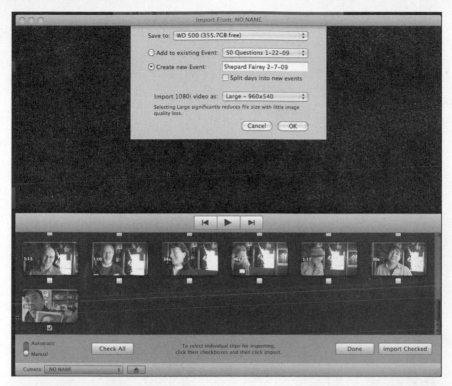

Figure 5.8   Import Dialog Box

Figure 5.9   Choose Aspect Ratio

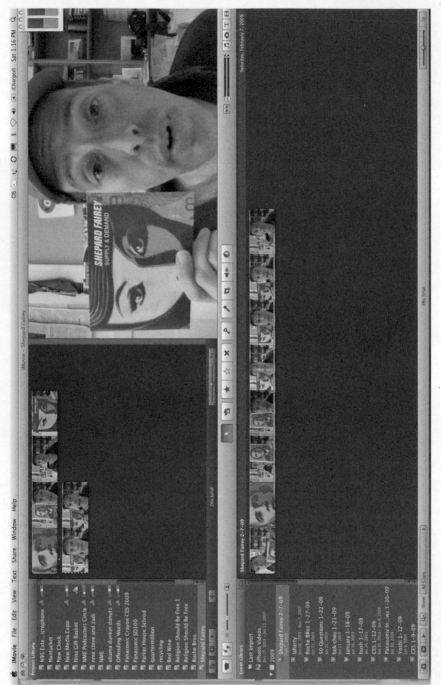

Figure 5.10 iMovie Project Window

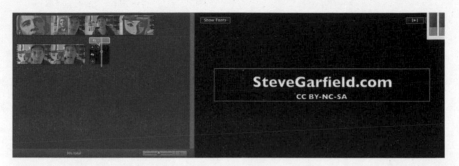

Figure 5.11   Add Credits

ADD A TITLE

To add a title, click the title icon and then select the title you want.

You can drag it in front of your movie, or you can drag it on top of the beginning of the movie.

I chose to drag it on top of the beginning of the movie so it shows up on top of the beginning video.

ADD CREDITS

For this video I clicked on the Centered credits and dragged it up into the Project window at the end of the video (see Figure 5.11).

Then you can edit the text.

I've put in my URL and Creative Commons License.

For a license I chose BY-NC-SA.

Add Natural Sound Underneath the Credits

Adding sound from an earlier part of your video underneath the credits is a good way to add interest while the credits roll. Sometimes I'll use a memorable line from the video.

To do this you select a clip from the event library, bring it up to the Project, go to the edit menu and select "detach audio."

Then move the audio that you just detached under the credits. Now select the video that the audio originally came from, and delete it.

Now you're editing just like you would be if you were using Final Cut Pro! Well, sort of.;-)

There's even more you can do with iMovie's Precision Editor. Watch Apple's excellent iMovie tutorial videos online to learn more.[6]

iMovie YouTube Direct Upload—No Waiting

To send this video directly to YouTube, select the **Share** menu, then click **YouTube**.

Note: This is one of the easiest and direct ways to post a video to YouTube. iMovie makes it very easy. It's very similar to the FlipShare software, but iMovie has a lot more video editing options.

Enter in your YouTube account information, then choose a category for your video. Add a Title, Description, and Tags to identify it.

Choose the size you want to publish. Uncheck the box "Make this movie personal" so your video will be available for anyone to see. Press Next. (See Figure 5.12.)

Exporting for Upload Elsewhere

For this video I also want to do a quick export so I can upload the video to CNN's iReport. I don't want to spend any time figuring out settings so I'll choose Share and iTunes, then I see that one of the options is for 960×540 (see Figure 5.13). That's the same quality that I imported in the first place, so I'll choose that to get the closest export quality to what was imported.

The menu option presented, Publish, is misleading, though; we aren't actually publishing the video to the online iTunes store, meaning we aren't actually saving off a copy and sending it to the iTunes site. We are exporting a version of the video locally that will be iTunes compatible.

When iMovie is done exporting the video, it automatically puts a copy in your iTunes player (see Figure 5.14).

---

[6] http://www.apple.com/ilife/tutorials/#imovie

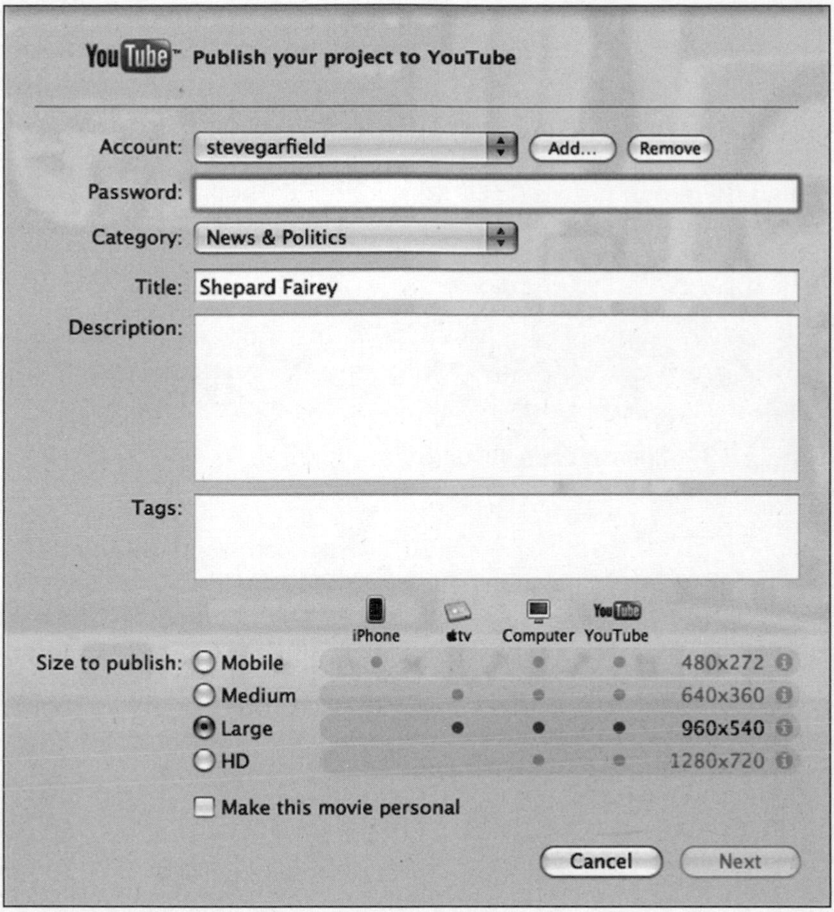

Figure 5.12   Publish Your Project to YouTube

From there, you can view it, then right-click on it to see where it is located in the Finder.

It ends up in the Movies/iMovie Sharing/iTunes folder (see Figure 5.15).

IMPORTING AVCHD VIDEO WITH IMOVIE

AVCHD[7] is Sony and Panasonic's format for HD video.

_____
[7] http://en.wikipedia.org/wiki/AVCHD

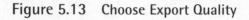

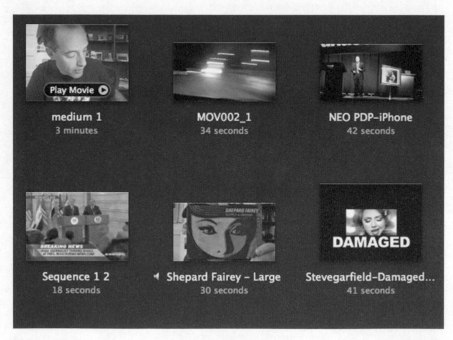

Figure 5.13   Choose Export Quality

Figure 5.14   Movie in iTunes Player

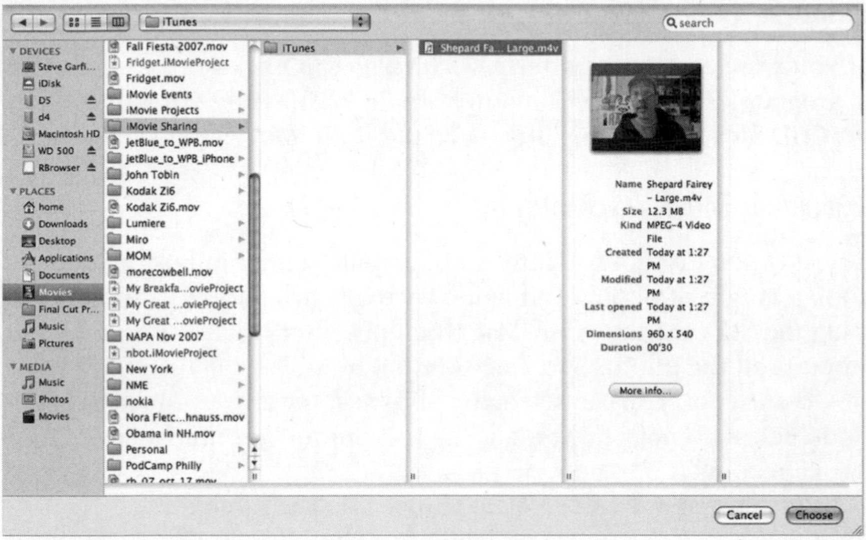

Figure 5.15   Movies/iMovie Sharing/iTunes Folder

The steps to get AVCHD video into iMovie are as follows:

Three Steps

Step 1: Insert your SD card

Step 2: In iMovie, choose Import Camera Archive. This will recognize all the movie files on the SD card and present them to you with selection boxes under each video.

Step 3: Choose the videos that you want to import into iMovie and press "Import Checked..."

A popup menu will ask if you want to import at full resolution or not. Depending on where the final output will be presented, choose full resolution of the lower resolution presented in dialog log box.

The benefit of choosing full resolution is that you can always export a lower resolution for the Web, but if you start with a lower resolution and then find that you need a higher resolution for something like TV, you won't have it.

Convert AVCHD files to Quicktime

If you want to convert your AVCHD files to Quicktime, you can use a program called MovieConverter Studio.[8] This program will convert AVCHD files that can be directly edited with iMovie and FinalCut.

IMPORTING MOVIES FROM IPHOTO

Let's say you just got back from a huge pillow fight in Boston and you took a bunch of photos and video with a Panasonic LX37. When you plug the SD card into your Mac, the computer opens up iPhoto and imports all the photos and videos into iPhoto.

That's cool. You can select the photos you want to upload to Flickr and click the Flickr button and all the photos get uploaded to your Flickr account.

But what about video? Well, you can do the same thing.

Once those videos are uploaded to iPhoto, open iMovie and wait for it to recognize the new videos. Allow iMovie to compile the thumbnails of the videos.

Then you will see a new event in the Event Library that you can edit.

In the file menu, click New Project. Then click on the Theme you want to use.

Click the check box "Automatically Add Transitions and Titles" to make it easy.

Then drag your video clips from the Event Library up to the Project Library (see Figure 5.16).

When you drag each piece of video up into the project, it will also be added into the theme you have chosen. In my example, I chose the Comic Book theme, so some of the video pieces are inserted in panes of a comic book (see Figure 5.17).

Cool, huh?

After you've completed your movie, click Share, YouTube, then put in your Password, Title, and Description. Add Tags and select the Size to Publish.

If you have HD content, choose HD, then click Next.

Then click Publish to send to YouTube. Here's the video, Boston Pillowfight 2009.[9]

It's so easy.

---

[8] http://www.apple.com/downloads/macosx/video/movieconverterstudio.html
[9] http://www.youtube.com/watch?v=xzP-dmqjVnU

Figure 5.16 Event Library and Project Library

Figure 5.17   Comic Book Theme

To recap, all you do is drag your clips into the project area, and when done, share on YouTube.

Note: To find the actual Quicktime movie file on your computer, you have to go to its project file in the iMovie Projects folder. Right-click on its name and select Show Package Contents.

In the new Finder window you'll see a movie folder. In there is your movie. In this example, mine is called 720p.mov (see Figure 5.18).

Sending a Video to CNN's iReport

Let's take this movie and upload it to CNN's iReport.
Direct your browser to http://ireport.com
Click Upload.
If you don't have an account on iReport, sign up for one.
Enter in all the information about your video, including tags, and press Submit.

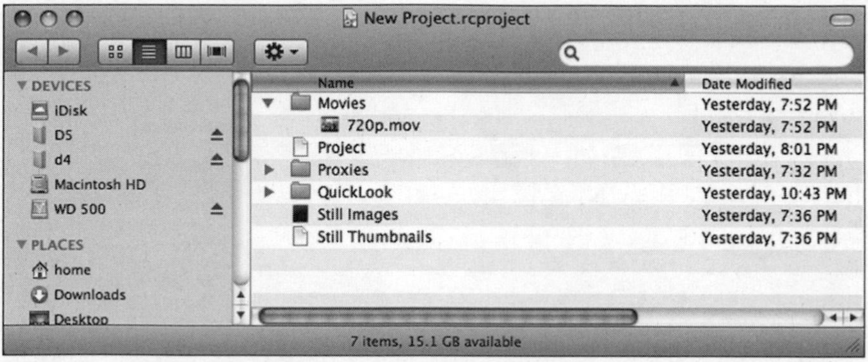

Figure 5.18   720p Movie

Required information includes:

Section 1 (see Figure 5.19):

File

Title

Description

Assignment

Tags

Allow download: Yes or No

Discretion Advised?

Section 2: Story Location and Date (see Figure 5.20):

City

State

Zip

Country

Date

Section 3: Terms of Use

☐ Yes, I have read and agree to the terms of use.

send an iReport

1 **Upload your video, image or audio files** ✳ Required fields.

✳ **Files:** (Choose File) no file selected
1. Shepard Fairey - Large.m4v - Remove

✳ **Title:** Obama HOPE poster artist Shepard Fairey arrested in Bostor

✳ **Description:**

| Plain Text |

B *I* <u>U</u> ᴬᵇᶜ✓   ⊙ Markup Help

The Boston Globe is reporting that artist Shepard Fairey was arrested last night on his way to DJ an event at the ICA art museum. No details on the arrest warrants were given.

http://bit.ly/ONc3

I'd like more information.

Requirements:
- You may upload up to 10 files at one time.
- Maximum total file size for all items: 100 MB
- We support most image, video, and audio formats, but not text or formatted documents. More on file formats »

powered by blip.tv

Assignment: iReport for CNN   ⬍
(For more details on categories, go to the Assignment Desk.)

Add your own tags: ireport_for_cnn fairey ica boston arrest warrant obama hope
(Enter one or more tags, separated by spaces.
150 chars max, up to 10 tags, 50 chars per tag.)

Download: ⊙ Yes, allow my media to be downloaded by others.
○ No, don't allow my media to be downloaded.

Discretion: ☐ Discretion Advised (ᵂᴴᴬᵀ'ˢ ᵀᴴᴵˢ?)

Figure 5.19   iReport Section 1

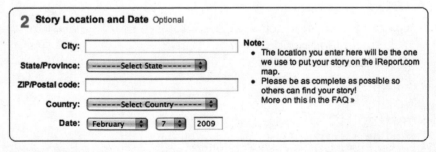

2 **Story Location and Date** Optional

City: [   ]

State/Province: [------Select State------ ⬍]

ZIP/Postal code: [   ]

Country: [------Select Country------ ⬍]

Date: [February ⬍] [7 ⬍] [2009]

Note:
- The location you enter here will be the one we use to put your story on the iReport.com map.
- Please be as complete as possible so others can find your story!
More on this in the FAQ »

Figure 5.20   iReport Section 2

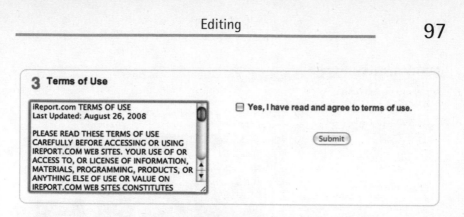

Figure 5.21   iReport Terms of Use

The terms of use are in a little square box that's hard to read (see Figure 5.21). You can't really copy and paste the terms of use by clicking and copying and pasting them, so I went into the browser and chose View Source, and copied the terms from there.

It's 5,711 words long!

I suggest taking a look at them.

Figure 5.22 shows the report up on CNN's iReport.

Compare the version up on CNN iReport with the version I exported.

See Figure 5.23 for the iTunes version.

The CNN iReport version is shown in Figure 5.24.

During the CNN conversion process from QuickTime .m4v to Flash, they changed the aspect ratio from 16:9 to 4:3. That makes it look elongated.

TIP: Prior to uploading reports to CNN iReport, change your aspect ratio to 4:3. Add letterboxing to your 16:9 videos to make them look right in the CNN player.

Exporting HD with iMovie 09

Can you export HD videos as well? Yes. iMovie 09 has an automatic setting which lets you Export HD videos to YouTube.

Figure 5.22   CNN's iReport

Figure 5.23   iTunes Version

00:02 / 00:30

Figure 5.24   CNN iReport Version

The biggest improvement in iMovie 09 is the feature to upload HD movies in 1280×720 format directly to YouTube. Now that's what we have been waiting for.

With this feature, iMovie is as easy to use as the Flip camera's FlipShare software.

Let's go through the steps to take an HD video file of a Panasonic FX37 digital camera and upload the clip to YouTube.

Here we go:

When you plug a USB card reader into a Mac, iPhoto recognizes the photos and imports the photos and videos into iMovie.

Then, when you open up iMovie, iMovie recognizes the movie files and adds them to the event library for editing.

In this example we'll use a simple video clip I recorded on a Panasonic FX37 digital camera. This still camera records HD video in 1280×720 format. Very good quality for a digital camera.

The first step is to select the section of the movie you want and drop it into the project window.

In this example we're using one clip. Now we need to add a title and credits. First the title.

You can add a title at this point. Figure 5.25 shows an example, Eating the European Way with Carol Garfield.[10]

For this video, I used the Pull Focus title effect. It's very cool. Try it.

Then for the final credits I used "Horizontal Blur." When you choose this effect, you can also choose the background image. When you drag the "Horizontal Image" title to the timeline in the project, you are presented with a number of background choices. I chose "Blobs" (see Figure 5.26).

The final credits had no sound under them, so I decided to grab some restaurant noise from the movie clip and put it under the final credits.

As of this writing, the FlipShare software does not allow uploading of HD videos. I e-mailed them, but they seem to think that sending up a smaller file is better. I don't understand why, since bandwidth is pretty fast these days.

iMovie 09 also recognizes the Flip cam and imports video from it directly, so that allows you to bypass the FlipShare software and use the more fully featured iMovie 09 (see Figure 5.27).

Advanced Video Editing for Mac Users
Final Cut Pro

There are two versions of Final Cut Pro: Final Cut Pro Express, an entry version, and Final Cut Pro 6, which is part of Final Cut Studio.

Note: You can start off editing with iMovie, then export or project to Final Cut Pro using the iMovie Export Final Cut XML menu option.

---

[10] http://www.youtube.com/watch?v=OZhZ8JmhJv4

Figure 5.25   Eating the European Way

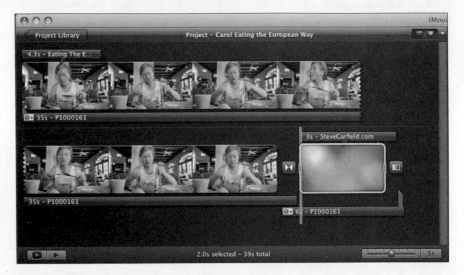

Figure 5.26   Blobs Background

FINAL CUT PRO TIPS

TIP: When you set up Final Cut Pro, store all your project files on your computer's main drive, and store all your media files on an external drive.

Final Cut Pro performs better this way.

Back up your project files. They are files that are small in size and have all the edit instructions for your videos.

When working on a Final Cut Pro Project, turn on the auto-save setting. This will save versions of your work at a specified time, like every three minutes.

Also, when you are editing, stop and think to yourself, "Have I made enough edits since my last save that if I lost everything, I'd be very upset?"

If the answer to this question is yes, then you might want to start saving alternate versions to your project file.

Let's say you have something saved as Winter Scenes. Select the project file you are working on and duplicate it. Rename the new version with an incremental number, like Winter Scenes 2.

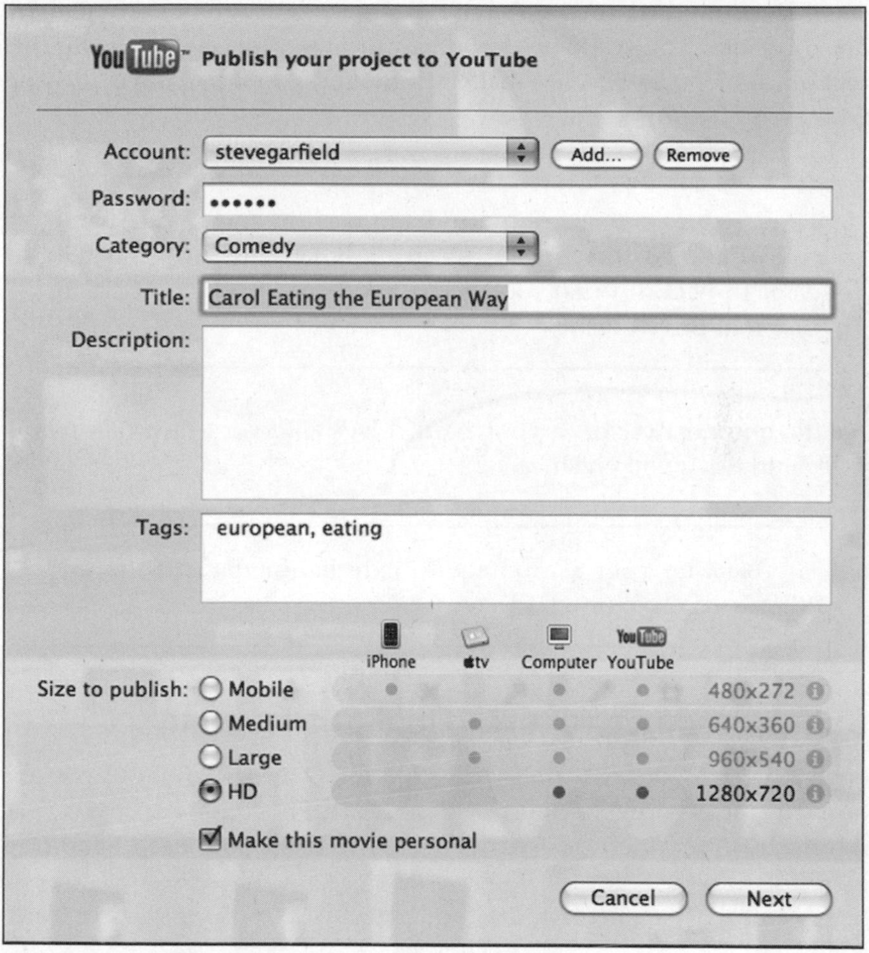

Figure 5.27   iMovie 09 Publish to YouTube

Another good time to save is when you are about to make a drastic edit to your project file. Duplicate your project file again, and name it Winter Scenes 3. Then you can make your edits and if it all comes out horribly wrong, you can just delete that version and go back to your last saved version.

With Final Cut Pro, the software does nondestructive edits. This means that your video files always remain intact. They are not changed. Final Cut Pro just saves instructions to disk on how to display the video based on our edits.

If your original media is on DV Tape, and your external hard drive crashes, you could always recapture your footage by using the recapture menu option in Final Cut Pro, and you'll still have all your edits from the project file.

TIP: If your original source footage was on an SD card, and you've copied the footage to an external hard drive, you'll want to back up that footage to one or two other media in case that drive crashes.

It's not a matter of *if* your hard drive will ever crash, it's *when* your hard drive will crash.

TIP: Back up your SD footage to external media, such as another hard drive or a DVD.

Online Resource for Free Final Cut Training

Israel Hyman,[11] known online as izzyvideo, wants to show people how easy it is to make online video. Learn Final Cut Express 4[12] is a series of free video tutorials designed to help you learn Final Cut Express.

His tutorials are great and a good place to start if you want to learn Final Cut Pro.

Roxio Creator

Roxio Creator is a Cylon—an intelligent being wrapped up inside of a computer.

If you don't want to go through the hassle of having to learn an editing program, Roxio Creator has a feature called CineMagic that will guide you through the movie making process.

You can give CineMagic some help by marking your scenes.

---

[11] http://www.izzyvideo.com/about/
[12] http://www.izzyvideo.com/learn-final-cut-express/

Unmarked—CineMagic will automatically decide whether to include the scene.

Check Marked—CineMagic will definitely include the scene.

X—CineMagic will not include the scene.

After selecting the scenes, you can add music and choose the theme for your movie.

Then you choose where the movie is going to be played: computer, TV, or Web.

Once you make those final choices, CineMagic makes your movie for you.

Once the movie is complete, you can choose to additionally edit further using VideoWave.

Editing without Editing: Animoto for Video

Earlier we saw how you could use Animoto[13] to create a video out of still photos. You can also use Animoto to make a video for you out of video clips.

Three Steps

Step 1: Upload video clips to Animoto.

Step 2: Choose highlights. Animoto suggests 3–5-second highlights.

Step 3: Create the rest of the video like we did for photos.

Video files can be up to 200mb.

Music

There have been some examples of bands embracing fans who are using their music to make videos. Some fan videos have even been wildly successful in helping to increase sales. The problem for the video producer is that history has proven that record labels don't appreciate fans making videos from their artists' music, so the fans

---

[13] http://animoto.com

don't have any guidance as to whether or not it would be okay to use a band's music.

If you put a video up on the Web using unauthorized music, one of two things could happen: It could be taken down or the band might like it.

Smaller bands have been cool with people making music videos, but major label recording groups have not. Now, with the success of the JK Wedding video[14] and its ability to sell songs for Chris Brown, things might be changing, but it's always a good idea to use podsafe music[15] and also support independent artists.

Sites for music:

Soundcloud

http://soundcloud.com/

iodapromonet

http://iodapromonet.com/

CC Mixter

http://ccmixter.org/

Jamendo

http://www.jamendo.com/

---

[14] http://www.youtube.com/watch?v=4-94JhLEiN0
[15] http://www.musicalley.com/

Sharing

6

Uploading

Sharing Your Video Online

After you shoot video with your camera, you can quickly and easily post it to sites like YouTube (see Figure 6.1)[1] and Facebook. These are two of the simplest and most popular ways to post your video to the Web. To have total control of your content, you can also put video on your own servers, a hosting provider, or content delivery network. First we look at the easiest and most popular ways to share, then we examine alternatives that provide additional features that you might want to use.

Before we jump into uploading your video onto YouTube or sharing on Facebook, you may want to consider the audience you want to view and experience your video—who may also then share it with others. Some material you may want to share with the world, and other just with a limited audience. Depending on where you host your video, there are a number of ways to protect your videos and add security and privacy protection so they can be found and viewed by only select members of your close community. Many times there's just a checkbox that allows you to make a video private. Protection is something to consider before uploading and sharing any digital content.

Let's assume you have a video that you are ready to share. Copy the video from your camera to your computer according to the manufacturer's directions.

---

[1]http://www.youtube.com/user/stevegarfield#grid/uploads

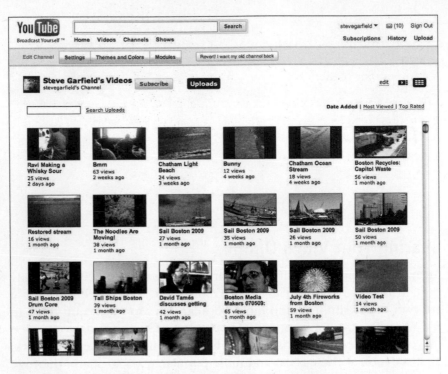

Figure 6.1   YouTube Videos—My Channel in Grid View

Uploading Video to YouTube

These steps are different than the earlier ones where we recorded a video directly to YouTube. This time we've recorded a video with a webcam or a camera, optionally edited it, and have it saved to disk. Now we upload it to YouTube.

Four Steps

Step 1: From the main YouTube page click Upload. Then, click Upload Video.

Step 2: Choose the file you want to upload.

Step 3: Add a Title, Description, and Tags.

Step 4: Click Save Changes.

GET SEEN: Once you have a video on YouTube you can copy the embed code on the right-hand side of the page and paste that to your web site or blog.

GET SEEN: YouTube can automatically update your Facebook friends, Twitter followers, and Google Reader shared items when you upload a video. From the Video File Upload page you can authorize these accounts.[2]

Notes on YouTube Video Quality:

When you upload video to YouTube there are two basic choices: (1) standard definition or (2) HD.

To optimize your videos for YouTube here are their suggested file sizes:

1920 × 1080 (1080p) or 1280 × 720

640 × 480 (4:3 SD)

YouTube provides a web page[3] that provides the settings you can use to get the best quality.

Here are YouTube's suggested settings.

Video Settings:

Resolution

Recommended: Original resolution of your video—for HD it is 1920 × 1080 (1080p) or 1280 × 720.

There is no required minimum resolution. In general the higher resolution the better and HD resolution is preferred. For older content, lower resolution is unavoidable.

Bit rate

Because bit rate is highly dependent on codec there is no recommended or minimum value. Videos should be optimized for resolution, aspect ratio, and frame rate rather than bit rate.

---

[2]http://www.youtube.com/my_videos_upload
[3]http://bit.ly/optimize_youtube

Frame rate

The frame rate of the original video should be maintained without resampling. In particular, pull-down and other frame rate resampling techniques are strongly discouraged.

Codec

H.264 or MPEG-2 preferred.

Audio Settings:

Codec

MP3 or AAC preferred

Sampling rate

44.1kHz

Channels

2 (stereo)

As you see in the section on editing in this book, some software programs, like FlipShare and iMovie, make it very easy to upload video to YouTube with just one click.

Those one-click settings are set up to produce good-looking online video. You can start with those, and then customize them if you are unhappy with the way they look. In my experience, the standard settings work great.

After you post your video to YouTube, it might take a while for your HD video (see Figure 6.2) to show up.

The YouTube Partner Program[4] page explains how you can join and receive revenue from advertising.

As a YouTube partner, you can also request to allow YouTube Downloads.[5]

When you put your video up on YouTube, you're agreeing to their terms of service.[6]

---

[4]http://www.youtube.com/partners
[5]http://bit.ly/youtube_downloads
[6]http://www.youtube.com/t/terms

Figure 6.2   HD Video as displayed on YouTube

Uploading Video to Facebook

With Facebook you can also upload your videos. Here's how.

Go to the Facebook homepage.

Five Steps

Step 1: Click in the white space writing area of the "What's in your mind?" box. You can write a description here. (This step is optional.)

Step 2: Click the image of the Video Camera.

Step 3: Click Upload a Video from your drive.

Step 4: Click Choose File. The video file size must be less than 1024 MB and 20 minutes. Choose the file.

Step 5: Click Share.

GET SEEN: If you are using Facebook Lite, lite.facebook. com, from the main page, press Post Video, then proceed from Step 4 above.

GET SEEN: From the video's page on Facebook you can click Embed the Video and copy and paste the Embed code to display this video on any site on the Web.

GET SEEN: Here's an example video that I shot in Boston, with the Kodak Zi8, Boats at Jamaica Pond in HD.[7] The standard file created by the Zi8 camera is .mov and can be directly uploaded to Facebook.

Uploading Flip Video to YouTube

The Flip camera has its own software, FlipShare, that makes it very easy to upload video to YouTube.

Run the FlipShare application.

Four Steps

Step 1: Select a video you want to send to YouTube.

You do this by selecting a folder in the computer directory, then clicking to highlight the video you want to upload to YouTube.

Step 2: Under the share section at the bottom of the screen, click Online to share it.

Your options are AOL Video, MySpace, YouTube, Other Web Sites.

Step 3: Select YouTube, click Next, enter in your username and password (see Figure 6.3), then click Login. If you don't have a YouTube account, click the "Create a YouTube account" button.

---

[7]http://www.facebook.com/video/video.php?v=127521127019

Figure 6.3   YouTube Username and Password page

Step 4: Who Should See These. Choose if the video should be public or not by clicking either "Share your items with the world" or "Private" (see Figure 6.4). Click Share.

After you do that, strangely there's no acknowledgment or progress bar. Go to your YouTube account and click to see your videos, and you see that your upload is processing (see Figure 6.5).

I made a Flip minoHD video of my refrigerator.[8] Fun times!

---

[8]http://bit.ly/flip_fridge

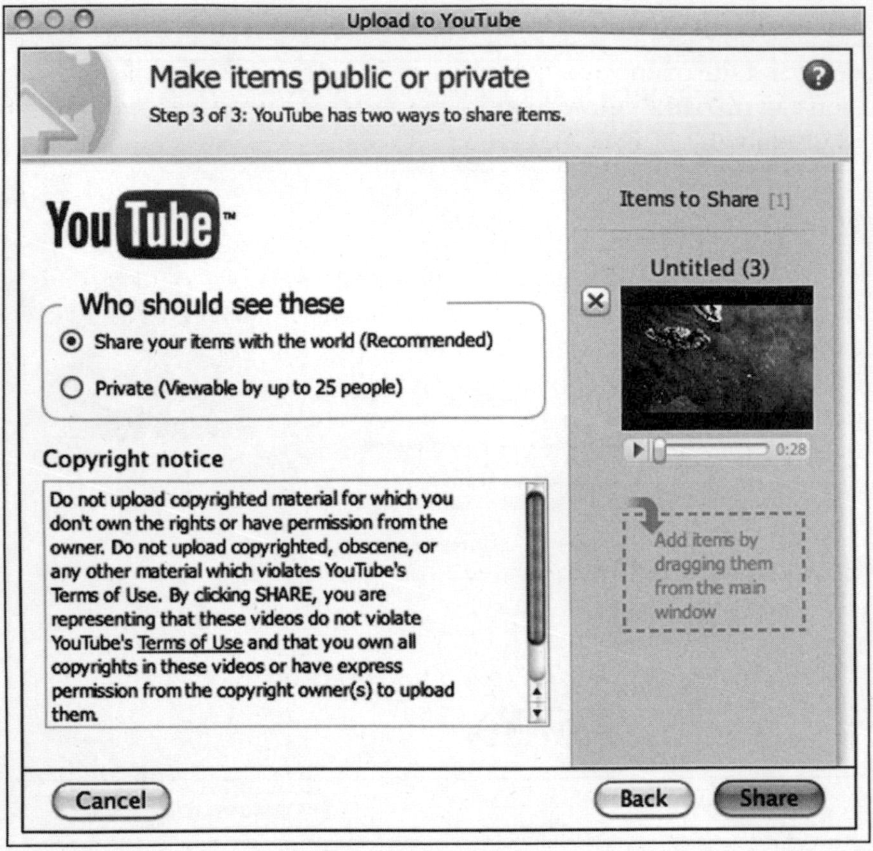

Figure 6.4   Make Items Public or Private

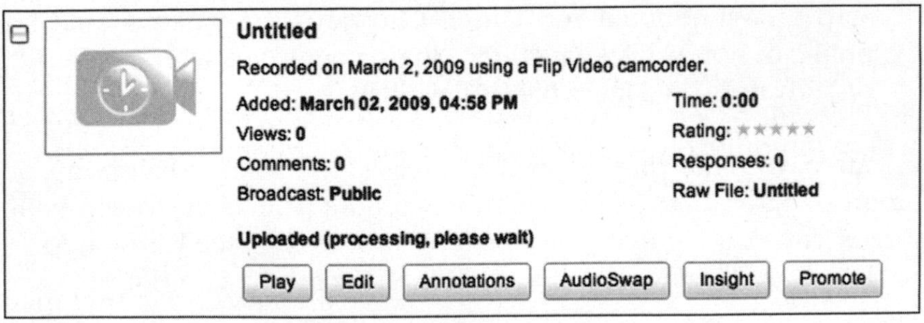

Figure 6.5   Processing Page

Uploading Video to Flickr

Flickr is a site mainly used for photo sharing, but it also supports video. You can upload a video to Flickr and then send people there to watch it, or embed it in your blog.

Flickr Video HD

Pro account users can upload unlimited HD video up to 90 seconds in length and up to 500 MB in size. Free accounts can upload two videos a month with a 150MB file size limit.

I recorded a 14-second video of Cable Beach in the Bahamas[9] with my Panasonic Lumix FX37. It records the files as QuickTime movie files. An easy way to post a short video to the Web is to send it up to Flickr.

How to Upload Video to Flickr via the Web

Four Steps

Step 1: From the Flickr.com home page just click Upload Photos & Video.

Step 2: Click Choose Photos and Videos. Choose the video you want to upload and click Select.

Step 3: Set the privacy of your video and click Upload Photos and Video.

Step 4: Click Add a Description. Add title, description, and tags. Click Save.

For this Bahama Beach video, prior to uploading to Flickr, I opened it up in QuickTime Pro and made it smaller. That's because I was on a slow Internet connection and wanted it to be completed faster.

To export from QuickTime Pro, here are the steps:

Choose File, Export. Then select "Movie to QuickTime Movie" in the Export drop-down menu, then click the Option button to customize your settings.

---

[9]http://www.flickr.com/photos/stevegarfield/3390395798/

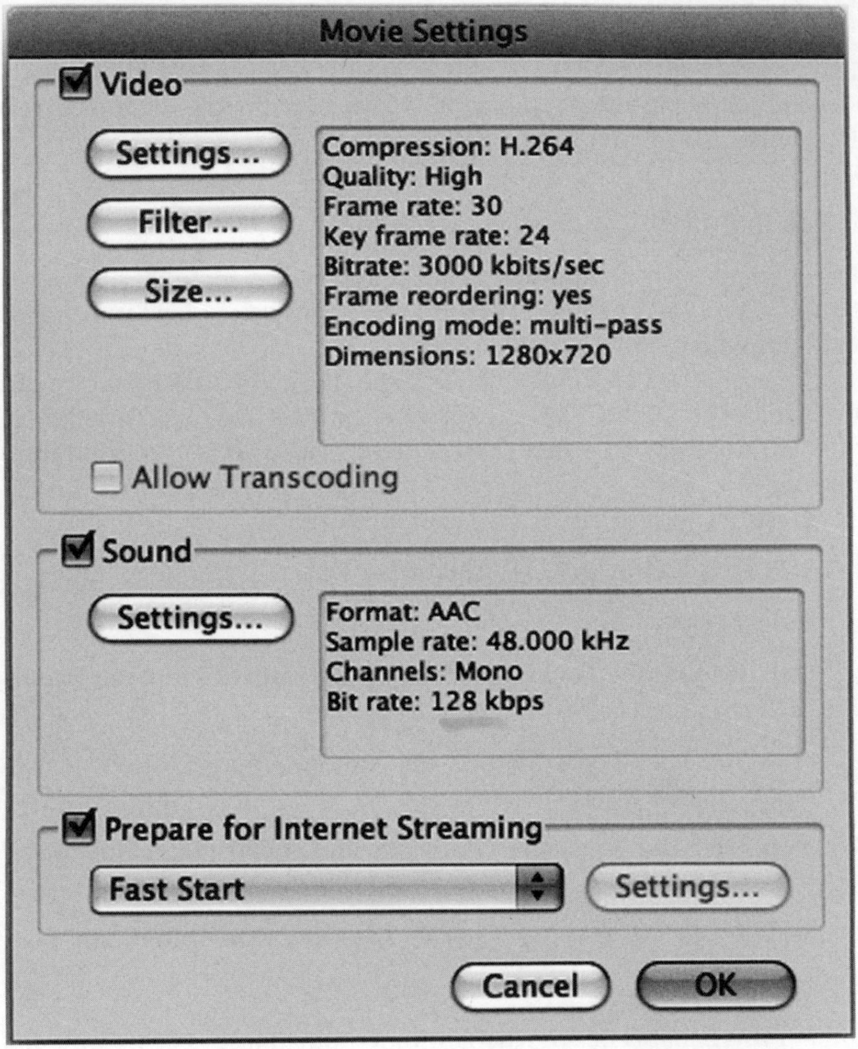

Figure 6.6   QuickTime Export Settings

Here are the settings I use for HD export (see Figure 6.6).

Video Settings:

Compression: H.264

Quality: High

Key frame rate: 24

Bitrate: 3000 kbits/sec

Frame reordering: yes

Encoding mode: multipass

Dimensions: 1280 × 720 (Current)

Audio Settings:

Format: AAC

Sample rate: 44.100 kHz

Channels: Stereo (L R)

Bit rate: 128 kbps

Here's the file information of the resulting file:

1280 × 720 AAC H.264:14 Bit rate 2, 957 4.9 MB

The original file size was 42.2 MB. It still looks good at the smaller file size. In fact, Cable Beach would look good at any file size. It's beautiful. I asked a local resident why they named it Cable Beach. She told me that it was because they put all the cables underground in this area. The same person who named the beach must have named the local grocery store. It's named City Market.

FLICKR FILE UPLOAD TOOLS

Flickr also provides a number of desktop applications[10] to help upload your photos and videos. I use Flickr Uploadr on a Mac.

Six Steps

Step 1: Copy files to computer. If you plug your SD card into a Mac, iPhoto automatically recognizes your new photos and video and lets you import them.

Step 2: Drag your selected videos to Flickr Uploader.

---

[10] http://www.flickr.com/tools/

Step 3: Add titles, descriptions, and tags.

Step 4: Press Upload.

Step 5: Once the upload is complete, you can optionally press Go to Flickr in the confirmation dialog box. Then you can modify any titles, text, and tags.

Step 6: When done, press Save. It's so easy.

FLICKR IPHONE APPLICATION

The Flickr iPhone application allows you to post your videos directly to Flickr (see Figure 6.7).

It's free in the iPhone App Store.

Once you download the Flickr iPhone App to your iPhone, you have to authorize it to access your Flickr account.

After you do that, the photo slide show that plays on the default home page will display photos from your contacts. This is very nice.

Figure 6.7 iPhone Flickr
Upload Screen

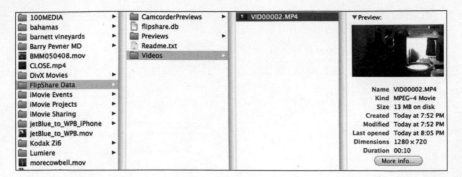

Figure 6.8   Flipshare Data and Videos

Here are the three steps to send a video up to Flickr from the Flickr iPhone App.

Three Steps

Step 1: Press the camera icon.

Step 2: Either Take a Video or Upload from your Library.

If you take a new video, after you record it you will be able to add a title, description, tags, tag your current location, and add it to a set.

Step 3: Click Upload.

UPLOADING FLIP VIDEO TO FLICKR

Let's say you want to grab a video that you recorded with a Flip camera and put it somewhere else, like on Flickr. If you've imported the video with the FlipShare software, you'll need to find it on your disk and then upload it. Here's how.

On a Mac, you'll find the video in the Flipshare Data, Video directory (see Figure 6.8). My filename is VID00002.MP4.

Three Steps

Step 1: Run Flickr Uploadr,[11] and *add* the video file (see Figure 6.9).

---

[11] http://www.flickr.com/tools/uploadr/

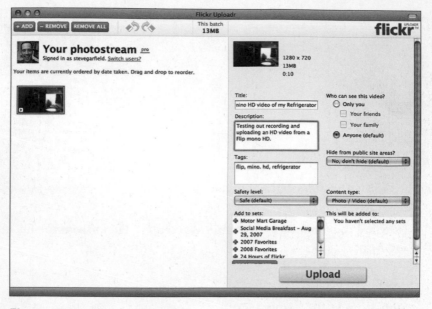

Figure 6.9   Flickr Uploadr

Step 2: Give it a title, description, and tags.

Step 3: Then press Upload.

When your upload is complete, click Go to Flickr, click Save, then wait for your video to complete processing.

And here it is in HD on Flickr.[12]

You get very good sound on the Flip minoHD, and when there is enough light, good video quality, too.

Note: Flip minoHD camera does *not* have an audio-in jack.

Uploading Video to Blip.tv

Let me start out this section by telling you that blip.tv[13] has the best support of any of my online service providers. One time, blip.tv CEO

---

[12] http://flickr.com/photos/stevegarfield/3324563400/?likes_hd=1
[13] http://blip.tv

Figure 6.10 Blip.tv CEO Mike Hudack

Mike Hudack (see Figure 6.10) responded to an urgent customer service e-mail from me while he was out at dinner in a restaurant in New York City. They care. I've worked closely with the team at blip.tv and consider them friends.

Blip.tv (see Figure 6.11) focuses on hosting shows, videos that are part of a series. Blip.tv also helps content creators make money through advertising.

I use blip.tv to host my video for a number of reasons, including the ability to share my original files, the automatic show page and player, and support for automatic cross posting. Let's take a closer look.

ORIGINAL FILES

Blip.tv allows you to access your original video files. This means that you can both embed and allow viewers to subscribe to your .mov or .mp4 files.

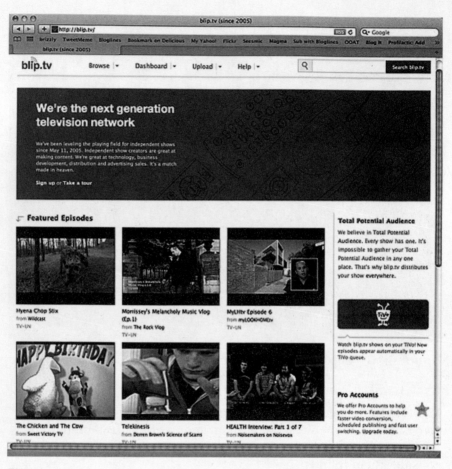

Figure 6.11   Blip.tv

This comes in very handy when you want to submit your show to the iTunes Store.

SHOW PAGE

Blip.tv has a nice show player that you can either send people to or embed on your own site.

Here's my Show Page on blip.tv[14] (see Figure 6.12).

Here's my Show Page on my own site (see Figure 6.13).

---

[14] http://stevegarfield.blip.tv/

Figure 6.12   Show Page on Blip.tv

From the show player you can get more details on a video, share it, watch in full screen, and navigate to other episodes.

It's a nice implementation that can give your show a professional look.

PUBLISHING

When you publish a video to blip.tv you have many options that let you customize your upload, including the ability to upload your own custom thumbnail image, choose a license, add descriptive tags, genre, content rating, and specify a language.

The ability to upload your own custom thumbnail is a great feature that allows the added opportunity to better market your video. Just like choosing a good image and adding text to your Show Image on the iTunes store, customizing your episode thumbnail image helps to let prospective viewers know what the episode is about.

Figure 6.13   Show Page on Steve Garfield's Site

CROSS-POSTING

When you upload your video to blip.tv, you can choose to automatically cross-post your video to a blog, del.icio.us, Flickr, YouTube, Facebook, MySpace, and other sites. You can also automatically cross-upload your video to the Internet archive. The Internet archive is a free hosting service.

TV

Users that have access to a TiVo checkbox will automatically have their videos syndicated to the TiVo box, if approved by blip.tv and TiVo.

In New York City you'll be able to watch blip.tv shows on TV. NBC has launched a digital channel focused on lifestyle. New York Nonstop is a lifestyle network.

Verizon FiOS TV will allow watching blip.tv content in Standard Definition and High Definition on demand.

Conversion

If you sign up for a Pro account, blip.tv can also automatically transcode your video to MP3 Audio (.mp3) and MPEG-4 Video (.m4v) for iPod/iPhone.

This is a great timesaver. I always have blip.tv create .mp3 and .m4v files for my videos. Otherwise, it would take extra time and work for me.

Privacy

Pro accounts can also choose to make videos private, visible with a password, and/or visible on a specified date.

Analytics

The nitty gritty. There's an engagement summary powered by Tube-Mogul (see below for more on TubeMogul). You can see how much of the video people watch. You can also see the referrers and browsers that viewers are using.

Start playback and a line will move across the graph to gauge what your audience is really interested in. Wow.

Player Appearance

The blip.tv show player can be customized with custom colors, branding, links to your own show page, and a sidebar to the right, with other recommended videos.

Fast User Switching

Fast User Switching is for an emerging class of web studios that manage a number of shows. It allows you to link your blip.tv accounts without having to log in and log out to manage accounts.

ADVERTISING

Show creators need technology, workflow automation, distribution, and ad sales. Blip.tv can take 20 to 30 shows and put them together for advertisers to advertise on a group of shows. Now the ads will show up on the Web, iTunes, and TV.

You can choose to opt-in to three types of advertising:

1. Pre-roll: Pre-roll ads run before the start of your video and are generally between 3 and 15 seconds. These advertisements often perform very well since most of your viewers will see them.

2. Post-roll: Post-roll ads start playing when your video finishes. If you're using the Show Player then post-roll ads will play in-between episodes of your show.

3. Overlay: Overlay ads are inserted in the lower third of your video. Some overlay ads will automatically shrink or hide themselves if the viewer doesn't interact with them. Viewers also have the opportunity to close the ad unit by clicking an "X" in the corner.

UPLOADING

Blip.tv provides a program called Upper Blip that lets you upload one or more videos to blip.tv at a time.

Upper Blip features a drag-and-drop interface. I use it all the time to upload videos to blip.tv.

Here's how I upload video to blip.tv:

Four Steps

Step 1: Run the Upper Blip application.

Step 2: Drag and drop one or more video files and thumbnails to Upper Blip and click Next.

Step 3: Add the descriptive information.

Step 4: Click Next to finish.

Once you enter the information, you click Next, and after the file is uploaded you can view it on blip.tv. So easy! You can also use the web interface.

GET SEEN: Use the playlist feature on blip.tv to display a selection of videos. This video playlist can then be embedded as a standalone player.

GET SEEN: To embed a blip.tv video on Facebook, paste in its blip.tv URL as a link (for example, http://blip.tv/file/2639082).

GET SEEN: Check the terms and conditions prior to hosting videos on blip.tv. Questions? Contact support@blip.tv.

Interview: Mike Hudack

WHY YOU SHOULD KNOW MIKE HUDACK

Mike Hudack is co-founder and the CEO of blip.tv. Blip.tv provides technology, distribution, marketing, and advertising sales in exchange for an advertising revenue share.

> *Mike Hudack: Our general theory is that when you're making a show, you need to have good content. That's like the price of entering. You need to have a good concept and be good at producing it but then you need a bunch of other things. So, you need hosting and workflow automation, distribution to as many different places as possible. You need a little help with marketing and your stats and all that kind of stuff and maybe, if you want, also ad sales and that's what we do.*

You can pretty much shoot with whatever you want, however you want. What's more important is the actual content. It's not how you shoot; it's what you shoot. It's if you have a good core idea, if you have an entertaining premise, if you're good at telling a story, it doesn't matter what camera you use, it doesn't matter what you do. People will enjoy it for what it is.

Blip is all about distribution. iTunes is a really important place to distribute so if you go to Blip, you can just click on distribution

(continued)

and then click on iTunes, you fill in a couple form fields and click a button. It opens up iTunes and you click another button and you have automatically submitted to iTunes. It usually takes from a day to a week to actually show up in the directory, but just by doing that you're in the directory. Our team has a relationship with the guys at iTunes as well as the people at TiVo and Sony and all these different places to help you get there and then also hopefully help you get promoted there as well.

We have a distribution relationship with Sony. So, the new Sony television ships with an Internet connection. You can just plug it into your router and you can watch Blip shows on there. If you have Verizon FiOS at home, we're on video-on-demand on FiOS. We're also on video-on-demand in some markets with Time-Warner cable, particularly in Hawaii, in Guam, and in Puerto Rico. So, those are kind of test markets we're going to try to expand nationwide with Time-Warner. We also distribute to AOL and MSN and just kind of all over the place and I should say that some of the places we distribute like TiVo, they can't take everything. We have 38,000 shows on Blip. So, our editorial team kind of picks what we're going to send there and then they also kind of have to approve it and it's because there's limited capacity on TiVo for how many things a person can browse. So, you try to send the things through that are going to do best and what we find is that with most shows, we can find the three or four or five or a dozen distribution outlets that that show is going to do best on.

There are many secrets to online video. There's no one right answer, but if I had to pick one thing, I think it would be consistency and persistence. I think that many people will go and create a show and they don't get the traction they expect in the first two weeks or the first three weeks and it kind of feels like they're doing something wrong. The reality is that it takes time to build an audience and with each successive episode, you find more people for whom this is an interesting idea, for whom this is an interesting show. There are many shows on Blip that may be in the top 10, top 20 now that took six months to find their place.

Watch the video of our interview.[15]

[15]http://blip.tv/file/1944217/

GET SEEN: We provide services to independent show creators in exchange for revenue share on the advertising.

GET SEEN: We have a distribution relationship with TiVo.

GET SEEN: The secret to online video is consistency and persistence.

Viddler

Viddler[16] lets you either record videos directly to the site or upload them. Viewers can post comments and tags at specific points of the video. This helps other viewers see points of interest in your video. It also helps you add annotations to the content.

Two Steps

Step 1: Under the Videos Menu, click Simple Upload. Other options are Batch Upload or Record from a webcam.

Step 2: Click Choose File and then enter in your video title, description, and tags. Then click Upload Video.

The video is then uploaded to Viddler and encoded into Flash. Code for you to embed your video is also presented at that time.

Another cool feature of video hosting site Viddler is its enhanced embedded player. You can add your own logo as an overlay on your videos, customize the player colors, and have the player link back to your own web site.

In addition to supporting standard HTML embed code, Viddler also provides you with the Wordpress.com custom embed code (see Figure 6.14).

The custom-embed code looks like this:

[viddler id=bb363d03&w=437&h=370]

According to the Viddler Terms of Use, "Viddler is limited to Non-Commercial use. If the primary purpose of your video is to promote

---

[16] http://www.viddler.com/

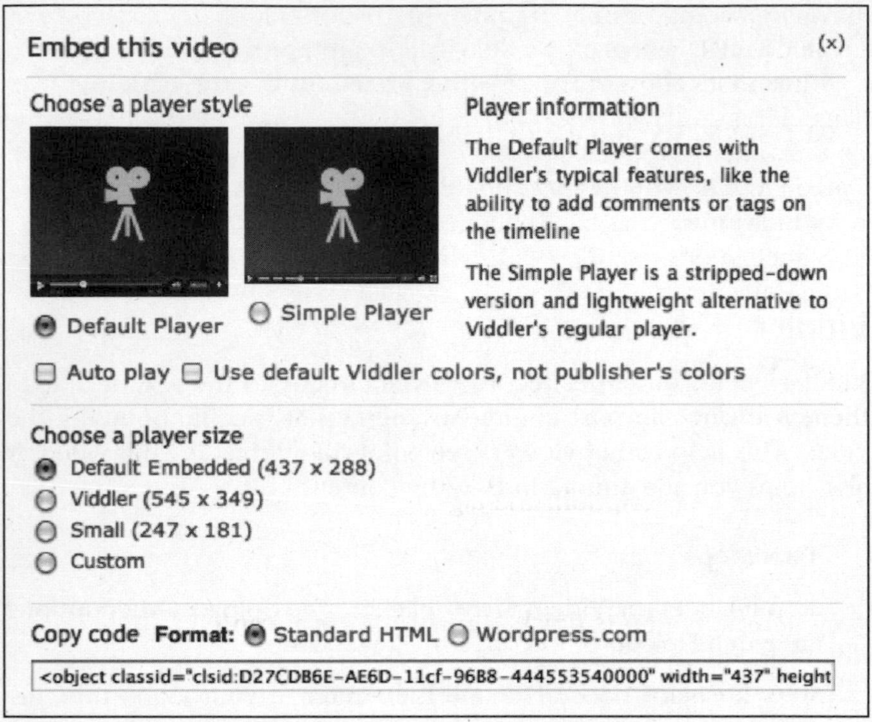

Figure 6.14   Viddler: Embed this Video Dialog Box

a product, service, event, or web site for a business, you must have a valid Viddler Business Services Contract to upload your video. You cannot present commercial videos on Viddler without a Viddler Business Contract."

Vimeo

Vimeo is one of the first video upload sites. I first saw it demonstrated by Jakob Lodwick in January 2005. That was way before YouTube. It's comprised of a community of people who are eager to interact with each other in a fun way.

There are two types of Vimeo[17] accounts, Basic and Plus. Vimeo Basic gives you 500 MB of storage a week for a basic account,

---

[17] http://vimeo.com/

allows uploading of one HD video per week, but does not allow for embedding HD video.

Vimeo Plus allows for 5GB per week, converts your video to Flash using 2-pass conversion, which makes for nicer looking videos, allows for unlimited HD video uploading, and removes banner advertising. Vimeo Plus gives you 25,000 embedded video plays and you can control which videos can be embedded as HD.

Vimeo supports 128 × 720 HD video and also allows for downloading of your original files.

Three Steps

Step 1: Click Upload.

Step 2: Choose a File to Upload. As the file uploads you can enter in its title, description, and tags.

Step 3: Click Save Changes.

When the video is finished uploading, you can click the "Go to Video" link to go to your video.

Here's a sample HD video "Girls on Dock" shot with the Kodak Zi8 at 720p 60 fps.[18]

Once the video is on Vimeo you can share it with other friends on Vimeo, or send it to other web sites like Flickr, Facebook, Twitter, Del.icio.us, Digg, StumbleUpon, or MySpace.

The Ikea Heights[19] series is a great example of a web series that uses Vimeo as its destination site.

Kaltura

Kaltura[20] is a free open-source video platform that supports uploading of video, direct recording, video players, playlists, remixing, syndication, and distribution. Look into it if you are interested in deploying your own video platform.

---

[18] http://vimeo.com/6432225
[19] http://vimeo.com/4921692
[20] http://corp.kaltura.com/

GET SEEN: Consider using Brightcove, Smugmug, or Viddler for business videos. Smugmug supports hosting of good HD quality, HQ, and iPhone versions. Visit vidcompare.com; it's a comparison service for online video platform providers. Make sure you check with the hosting provider's terms of service to make sure the content you are planning to host is approved.

Eye-Fi Explore Video Card

The Eye-Fi Explore Video Card allows you to upload photos and video via Wi-Fi from your camera. I set it up to upload photos and video to Flickr and it works!

Here's my first video sent via Wi-Fi from Panasonic DMC-FX37 using Eye-Fi.[21] I feel like Thomas Edison.

I also sent a video from the Kodak Zi6 to YouTube.[22]

Here's how you can do it, too:

Six Steps to Set Up Eye-Fi

Step 1: Plug the card and included card reader into your computer's USB port to set up the card.

Step 2: Run the Eye-Fi Manager application and create an Eye-Fi account. Optionally upgrade the firmware according to the on-screen instructions.

Step 3: Select Wireless Network. If you are setting up the card from home or work and have a wireless network, you can set it up.

Step 4: Enable Hotspots and Geotagging. In this step you can allow your Eye-Fi card to upload photos and video via Wayport locations or Open Networks that don't require you to load a browser welcome screen. You can also enable or disable Geotagging, which sends location information.

Step 5: Setup Web Sharing. Add sites you want to post your photos and videos to. I choose Flickr for photos and video.

---

[21] http://digg.com/u13kKT
[22] http://www.youtube.com/watch?v=FocxM_8pyJI

Step 6: Remove the Eye-Fi card from the card reader and insert it into your camera. Upload your first photo.

One Step to Upload a Video via Eye-Fi

Step 1: Shoot a video. It is automatically uploaded to the destination(s) you set up.

Optionally you can set up notifications. Have Eye-Fi send out an e-mail, SMS, or Twitter when your upload starts, is interrupted, resumes, or completes.

Note: The Panasonic DMC-FX37 is not officially supported by Eye-Fi. The Eye-Fi requires the movie files to be saved to the DCIM folder and in mpg, mov, flv, wmv, avi, or MP4 format. AVCHD files are not supported.

Expanding Your Viewership

If you are putting your content on the Web, you need to feel good about letting it go. Here are some ways to help your videos get seen.

FEEDBURNER

Feedburner[23] provides an RSS feed for your blog that you can take with you if you ever choose to move to another blogging platform like Wordpress or TypePad.

Choose Get Started, paste in your blog URL, check "I am a podcaster," and click Next a bunch of times. Then paste the feedburner feed URL into blogger.

E-MAIL SUBSCRIPTIONS

You can set this up for your blog at feedburner. This example will show how to add e-mail subscriptions to a Blogger blog.

Choose the Publicize menu, and select E-mail Subscriptions. Then select Use as a widget in Blogger and press [GO!].

---

[23] http://feedburner.google.com/

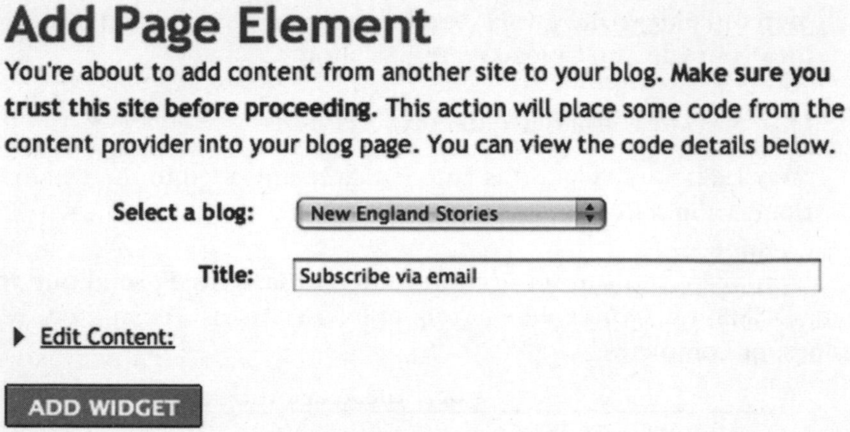

Add Page Element

You're about to add content from another site to your blog. **Make sure you trust this site before proceeding.** This action will place some code from the content provider into your blog page. You can view the code details below.

Select a blog: New England Stories

Title: Subscribe via email

▶ Edit Content:

ADD WIDGET

Figure 6.15   Add Page Element

The next page will come up with your blog and a title for the widget as it will appear on your Blogger blog. Edit the title if you like and press Add Widget (see Figure 6.15).

Your blog layout page will be displayed and you can arrange where the widget shows up. Press Save. Your blog will then have a Subscribe via E-Mail form where visitors can enter their e-mail address (see Figure 6.16).

Get the blog sent to your inbox.
Enter your email address:

Subscribe

Delivered by **FeedBurner**

Figure 6.16   Subscribe via E-Mail

Watching Videos with iTunes

Bring up the iTunes application on your computer and you can listen to music that you've either purchased online or loaded in off your CDs.

Over on the left-hand column there are selections for Movies, TV Shows, and Podcasts. That's where you'll be able to watch video on your computer.

In order to get this video content, Apple directs you to the iTunes store. Let's take a look at what you see when you click on the iTunes store link in your iTunes application.

Just under the Music category, these are the selections you can choose to find video content on the iTunes Store.

Movies: In this section you can buy and/or rent movies. Lots of Hollywood productions are featured in this section.

TV Shows: This section has current episodes of shows like *Lost*, *Gossip Girl*, and *Family Guy*. Here you can find content that is available for purchase as well as free content. You can also see the top TV episodes listed. This is a good way to catch up on TV shows you've missed if you don't have a DVR or the shows are not available on demand.

Music Videos: Music videos are available here for purchase. There are not many places to see them anymore on TV, so this is where you can find many of them.

Podcasts: The podcast section is broken into two categories once you click on it: Video Podcasts and Audio Podcasts. When the iTunes Store first started it only supported audio, and now it delivers video. Click on Video Podcasts under Categories to see what's listed in the iTunes Store.

There are a number of sections here, including New Releases, Staff Favorites, The News, How To, and Action Sports.

If you look over on the left, you'll see a number of featured providers. This is where a choice of signing up with a distributor could gain your video higher visibility on the iTunes Store. In addition to major media outlets like ABC News, CNN, and HBO, you'll also see smaller networks such as Next New Networks, Revision3, and Wizzard Media.

Finding Videos in the iTunes Store

If you know the name of a podcast or its topic, you can enter it into the search box in the iTunes Store.

A search for Yiddish, turns up my mom's Yiddish class (see Figure 6.17).

The iTunes application is also a podcasting application that allows you to subscribe to *any* podcast.

How?

First you have to record and save your video out on the Web in an iTunes-compatible format, then at the iTunes Store you can submit a Podcast (see Figure 6.18).

If you have a show and are hosting it at blip.tv, you can upgrade to a Premium Account, and have blip.tv transcode your videos to match the iTunes format. Blip.tv also lets you enter in all the custom settings to make your entries on the iTunes Store look nice.

Figure 6.19 shows the setup page on blip.tv for Millie's Yiddish Class.

Secrets to Getting Featured on the iTunes Store

If you want your videos to be featured in the iTunes Store, the first thing to do is get it listed.

Getting listed is easy if you have an RSS 2.0 feed set up that supports media enclosures.

I know. Easy for me to say. When I was doing video reports for Rocketboom, I used to ask interview subjects if their product supported RSS 2.0 with Media Enclosures. Most times the interview subject had no idea what I was talking about, even then some answered yes.

If you are posting your videos to YouTube, you don't have an RSS 2.0 with Media Enclosures because YouTube does not make the source video file available. All YouTube provides access to is the converted flash video file.

TIP: Host your videos on blip.tv with a Pro Account. blip.tv will make iTunes-compatible QuickTime videos for you.[24] Submit your iTunes podcast URL to the iTunes Store.

---

[24] http://blip.tv/prefs/itunes/

iTunes

Millie's Yiddish Class

▶ Podcasts ⟩ Video Podcasts ⟩ Language Courses ⟩ Millie's Yiddish Class

Millie Garfield
Category: Language Courses
Language: English
Free SUBSCRIBE

WEBSITE
REPORT A CONCERN
TELL A FRIEND

VIEWERS ALSO SUBSCRIBED TO
SBS Yiddish program
American Jewish Music from the Milken Archives with Leo...
This American Life
Feed Me Bubbe
Learn Hebrew Pod - Learn Conversational Hebrew by Pode...

PODCAST DESCRIPTION
Learn Yiddish online with Millie Garfield's free video blog lessons.

CUSTOMER REVIEWS

Average Rating: ★★★★★

Yiddish Rocks! ★★★★★
by Sarah99999
Hi . . . The word for matza balls is Knaidlach . . . and for chicken it's hun. I loved your site. Zul sein mit glick!

Dos is sheyn. ★★★★★
by Shlomo B.
Thank you millie, I am learning a lot, A sheyrem danke. Zai Gezunt

We Want More Millie's Yiddish! ★★★★★

See All 5 Reviews ⊕
Write a Review ⊕

▲	Name	Time	Artist	Release Dat	Description	Price	
1	Yiddish Class: Beautiful, Moon, Black Coffee, Blue, Book		Millie Garfield	9/3/07	Click To Play Also on YouTube.	Free	GET EPISODE
2	Yiddish Class: A Joke		Millie Garfield	5/14/07	Click To Play Alternate Version: ...	Free	GET EPISODE
3	Yiddish Class: Chicken Soup		Millie Garfield	4/4/07	Click To Play Alternate Version: ...	Free	GET EPISODE
4	Yiddish Class: Sweet Potatoes		Millie Garfield	2/21/07	Click To Play Alternate Version: ...	Free	GET EPISODE
5	Millie's Yiddish Class: Hot Knish		Millie Garfield	2/21/07	Click To Play Learn Yiddish onli...	Free	GET EPISODE

LIBRARY
♫ Music
Movies
TV Shows
Podcasts
Audiobooks
Applications
Radio
Ringtones

STORE
iTunes Store
Purchased

▼ PLAYLISTS
Party Shuffle
Genius
N95
90's Music
Music Videos
My Top Rated
Recently Added
Recently Played
Top 25 Most Played
Amazon Purchases
Holiday Music

Nothing
Playing

View
Search iTunes Store
apple@stevegarfield.com

Figure 6.17 Millie's Yiddish Class Podcast

Figure 6.18   Submit
a Podcast

Don't worry, you can still host your videos on YouTube, but you need to host them in another location to be able to produce an RSS 2.0 feed with Media Enclosures that the iTunes Store can read and then add to their directory.

When someone clicks on a video in the iTunes Store, often the videos are hosted elsewhere on sites like blip.tv.

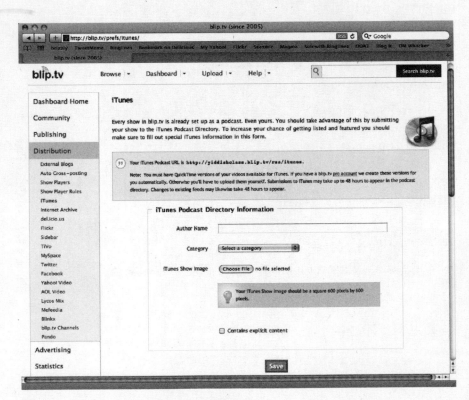

Figure 6.19   iTunes Page on blip.tv

Now, let's look at some secr
Store.

You've got to have a quality
marketing plan.

A Quality Program

Blip.tv is a good place to host yo
in shows. These shows are a lot
episodic. What's great about blip.
number one priority of the compar

A good way to be successful is
format of your show. In radio, stations use a shot clock, so that at a
certain time of day you know to tune in to get the weather report.
A good show has a consistent format that's familiar to the viewer.
Keep the show intro to less than five seconds. Introduce what's on
the show, then follow that up with your show content. EpicFu[25] does
a great job of maintaining a consistent look and feel to every show.
Finally, add end credits.

Good Metadata

When you sign up for an account on blip.tv, you initially give your
show a title. This is an important choice because that's how people
will find you on the iTunes Store.

In addition to the show title, you can add some static information
to your iTunes Store show by the listing from the blip.tv iTunes Podcast
Directory Information page (see Figure 6.20).

Author Name

Author name is important because the iTunes search ranks the show
title author name highest.

Category

Viewers will be searching for your show by category, so make sure
you put it in the right category.

---

[25] http://epicfu.com

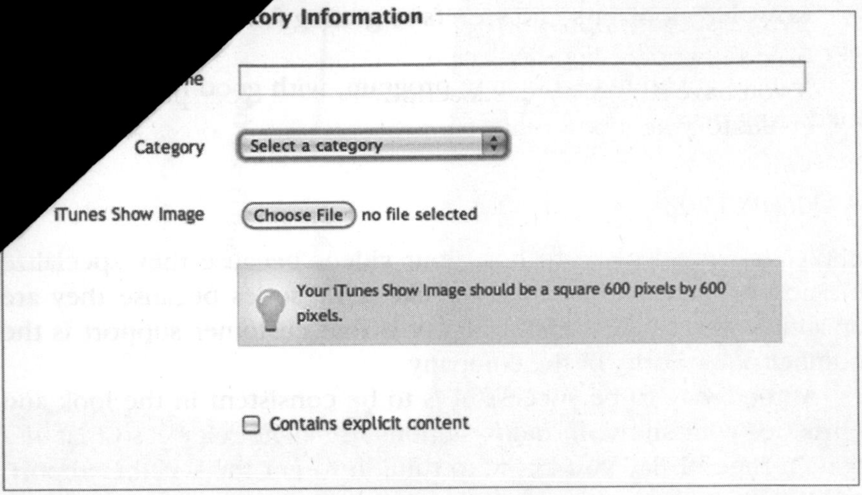

ory Information

ne	
Category	Select a category ▼
iTunes Show Image	(Choose File) no file selected

💡 Your iTunes Show Image should be a square 600 pixels by 600 pixels.

☐ Contains explicit content

Figure 6.20   Blip.tv iTunes Podcast Directory Information Entry Page

iTunes Show Image

It's good to have a clear show image. An image of a person works well with a clear text title. The graphic size you upload to blip.tv is 600 pixels by 600 pixels. The iTunes Store reduces this size for a thumbnail, to 55 pixels square. Make sure that your show image is clear at this size and that you can read any text.

ITunes Description

The iTunes description is taken from the general show description at http://blip.tv/dashboard/show_settings. Blip.tv suggests:

> Describe your subject matter, episode schedule and any other relevant info so that potential subscribers know what they'll be getting. Also make sure to include relevant search terms in your description, but be careful: iTunes will remove shows that have spammy descriptions.

A Marketing Plan

Putting your show on blip.tv and iTunes does not mean that people will find it.

Viewer subscriptions and comments on the iTunes Store will help get your show more highly rated, and a chance to get it featured.

If you have a blog, put a subscription link to your podcast there.

Promote your show with blog posts, twitter posts, and e-mail messages.

SUBMIT TO ITUNES FROM BLIP.TV

When signed on to blip.tv, under the Distribution menu choose iTunes.

Enter in all your iTunes information, including a 600 × 600 show image, and then click Add to iTunes. Blip.tv connects to iTunes and places you on a page where you can submit your blip.tv-created iTunes feed. For example: Here's the iTunes feed for Get Seen videos: feed://getseen.blip.tv/rss/itunes/.

Note: If you upgrade to a Pro version of blip.tv, blip.tv will automatically make iTunes friendly-compatible videos for you.

When you view the blip.tv iTunes RSS feed (see Figure 6.21), you'll see the iPhone/iPod friendly link in there.

You'll get a confirmation from Apple that your podcast was successfully submitted.

"Your podcast feed, [http://getseen.blip.tv/rss/itunes] was successfully added and is now under review."

TIP: To get the link of your podcast, go to the iTunes Store and right-click on your show image.

Then you can embed that link with a graphic on your blog or web page.

Your show is more than just video on a web page. That's why it's a good idea to make a blog post along with each new episode to

Figure 6.21   blip.tv iTunes RSS feed

provide show notes, and give your viewers a place to interact with you—the show creator.

TIP: Blip.tv works closely with Apple. If you've got a good show they can help you try to get it promoted on the iTunes Store.

WHY WOULD YOU PUT YOUR VIDEO ONLINE FOR FREE?

Putting your video out there for free does not mean that you are giving up ownership of your video—you still own it, but are letting others view it for free.

To let others know what they can do with your video, you can add a Creative Commons license to it. That gives others the right to use your work, without asking, as long as they follow the requirements of your license. I explain this in more detail in the next section.

Licensing: Creative Commons

Free web video is easy to find. That's because not many producers are able to charge money for web video. Hollywood producers get to charge for reruns of TV shows and movies, but independent video producers are not charging viewers.

Why is that?

One reason is that there isn't a widely distributed platform that's open to allow producers to charge for content.

iTunes charges for TV shows and movies, but only major media companies are allowed to charge. YouTube has a pay per download program for selected partners, but that's a small selection of video producers.

IN ADDITION TO COPYRIGHT–LICENSING: CREATIVE COMMONS

If you are going to be putting videos on the Web, you might try to let people know what they can and can't do with it.

You can hope that they've read *The Seven Habits of Highly Effective People*[26] by Stephen Covey and that they are values based.

I am.

That's why I put a Creative Commons[27] license on all my work. The license gives others the right to use my work without asking, as long as they follow the rules that go along with the license.

On my work I use an Attribution, Noncommercial, Share Alike Creative Commons license that can be abbreviated to BY-NC-SA.[28]

That means people can use it as long as they attribute it to me, don't use it commercially, and put the same license on it.

---

[26] https://www.stephencovey.com/7habits/7habits.php
[27] http://creativecommons.org/licenses/by/3.0/
[28] http://creativecommons.org/licenses/by-nc-sa/3.0/us/

Here are the terms of the license:

You are free:

> to Share—to copy, distribute, display, and perform the work
>
> to Remix—to make derivative works
>
> **Under the following conditions:**
>
> **Attribution.** You must attribute the work in the manner specified by the author or licensor (but not in any way that suggests that they endorse you or your use of the work).
>
> **Noncommercial.** You may not use this work for commercial purposes.
>
> **Share Alike.** If you alter, transform, or build upon this work, you may distribute the resulting work only under the same or similar license to this one.
>
> For any reuse or distribution, you must make clear to others the license terms of this work. The best way to do this is with a link to this web page.
>
> Any of the above conditions can be waived if you get permission from the copyright holder.
>
> Apart from the remix rights granted under this license, nothing in this license impairs or restricts the author's moral rights.

AL JAZEERA CREATIVE COMMONS REPOSITORY

The Al Jazeera Network has released some of its broadcast-quality footage (see Figure 6.22) under a Creative Commons 3.0 Attribution license.[29] You can use the footage in your own work with the only

---

[29] http://cc.aljazeera.net/

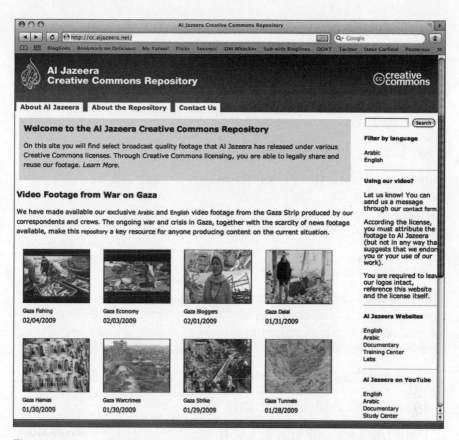

Figure 6.22   Al Jazeera Creative Commons Repository Featuring
Video Footage from War on Gaza

requirement being to acknowledge that you got the footage from Al
Jazeera.

WATCHING WHO USES YOUR CREATIVE COMMONS CONTENT

Fairshare[30] is a Creative Commons-aware self service platform that
tracks where your content is used around the Web.

You give it the RSS feed of your content, most likely a blog, and
Fairshare reports back to you via another RSS feed.

---

[30] http://beta.fairshare.cc/fairshare/

Want to Get More Views? Put Your Video on More Than One Site

If you want to get your video seen, why not place it in front of as many people as possible?

There are a few ways to automate this process.

 ## TubeMogul

TubeMogul allows you to upload your file once, and distribute it to more than one site.

TubeMogul also has statistics that allow you to track how much viewership your videos get across multiple sites.

TubeMogul Advanced Stats

TubeMogul 2.0 integrates advanced tracking technology with 15 of the top video sites' flash players, unlocking rich, standardized data on per-second audience drop-off, what sites and search terms are referring viewers, audience geography, and much more.

Interview: Mark Rotblat

Why You Should Know Mark Rotblat

Mark leads the sales and marketing efforts at TubeMogul,[31] a very cool tool that lets you distribute your videos to multiple sites and analyze statistics.

> *Mark Rotblat: If you're getting your videos out to all the distribution points where people are actually consuming content, it's a pain to upload at each of the sites. So, if you up load to us once, then you can choose the sites that you want to distribute to and we get it out to your channels. We take care of the metadata, the size requirements, transcoding issues. We get it out there then*

---

[31]http://www.tubemogul.com/

we pull back the viewership information from across those sites, so you can see in one single dashboard how your videos are performing across the Web.

More and more we're seeing higher and higher quality content, HD. They may be anywhere from 100 megabytes or 30, 40 megabytes up to 1,000 and they are distributing that content through us. So, they're really testing what platforms can provide the best return based on quality.

Number one is distribution. I mean, obviously, that plays to our product but we have found on average getting it out to more places doubles your audience. Audiences are fragmented and they want to consume the content where they want to, so get it to them.

Second is to have regular recurring content. If you don't do that, you lose audiences. If you want to build communities, you have to put it out on a regular schedule or at least regularly, and so that's a key component to being successful and then the building community aspect, that's the hard part. There are no shortcuts. You have to build your audience by that person-to-person content whether it's through friending, tweeting, or through the different profiles. That's a lot of work, but that's really critical and it's something that many people try to skirt and it hurts them.

GET SEEN: The most important things about online video are distribution and recurring content.

TubeMogul: How To

Let's take a look at the steps needed to use TubeMogul to distribute your content, starting with the TubeMogul Welcome screen (see Figure 6.23).

Five Steps

Step 1: Sign in.

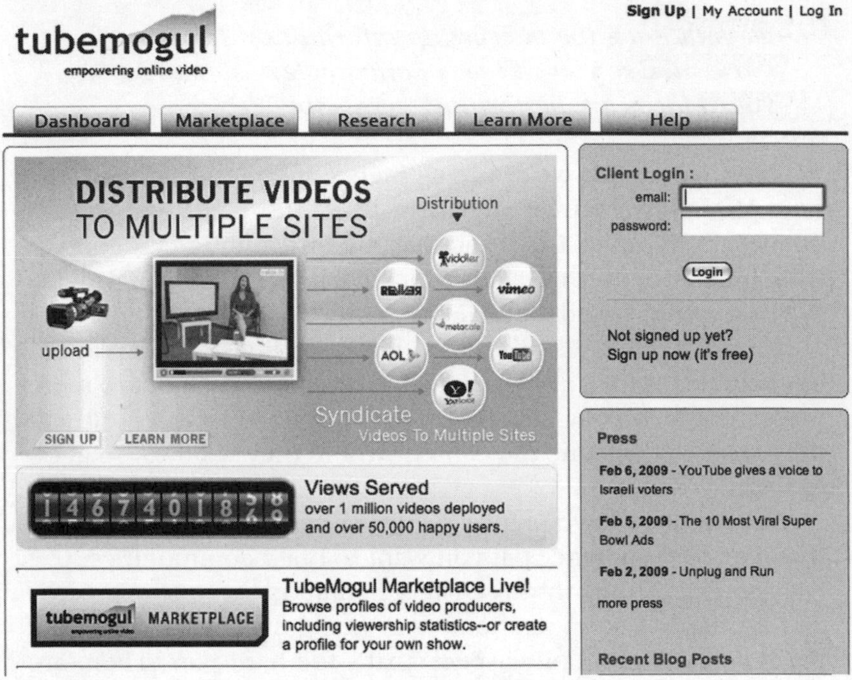

Figure 6.23   TubeMogul Welcome Screen

Step 2: From the TubeMogul Dashboard (see Figure 6.24), click Upload a Video.

Enter a file name by selecting it.

Step 3: While it uploads (see Figure 6.25), you can enter in your video information (see Figure 6.26).

Step 4: Once the video is uploaded to TubeMogul, you can select the sites you want it distributed to (see Figure 6.27).

Sites you can select from include YouTube, Yahoo!, MySpace, Metacafe, Revver, DailyMotion, Blip, Veoh, Crackle, Viddler, Vimeo, or Howcast. New sites are always being added, so check to see if a site you want to upload to is included in the list.

You can change your upload options and select or deselect sites you want to upload to.

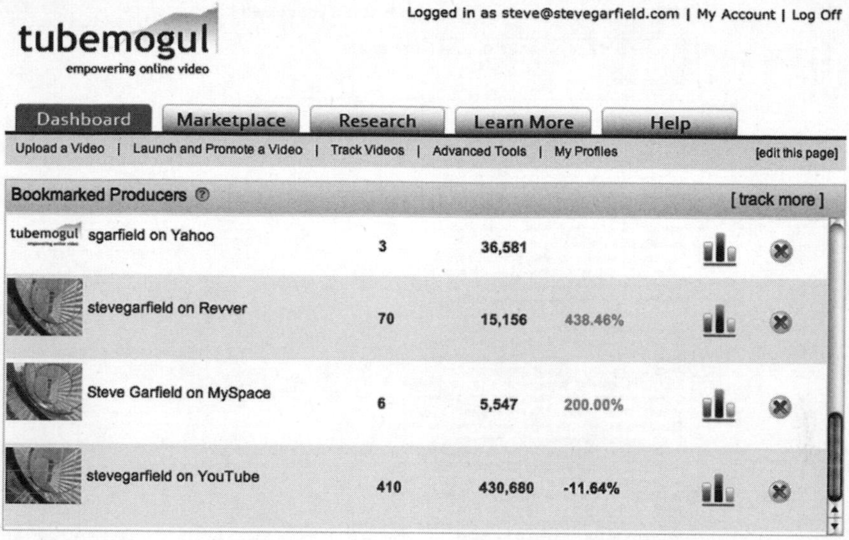

Figure 6.24   TubeMogul Dashboard

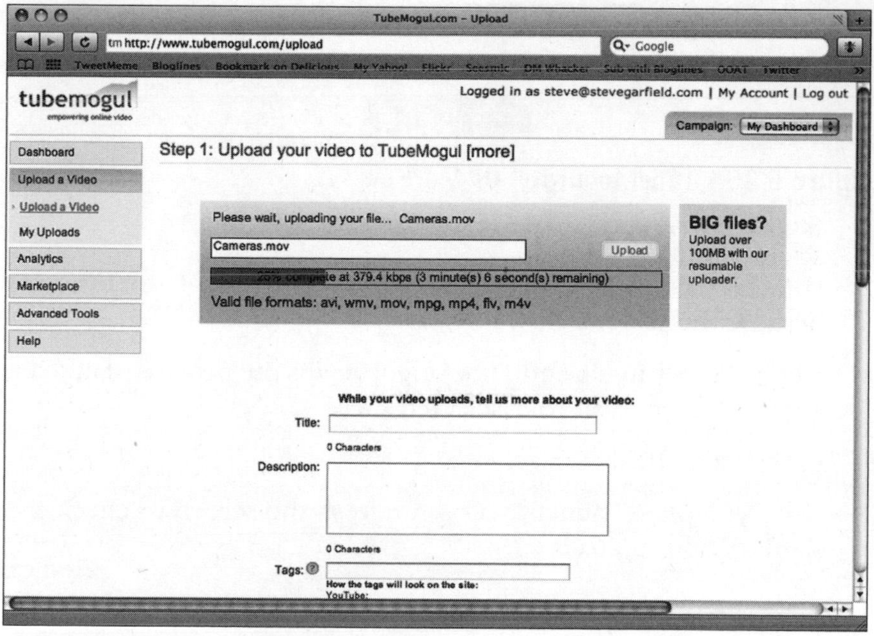

Figure 6.25   TubeMogul Upload Page

While your video uploads, tell us more about your video:

Title: |Obama HOPE poster artist Shepard Fairey arrested i|

58 characters

Description:
```
http://bit.ly/ONc3

I'd like more information.
```

227 characters

Tags: ⓘ |arrested, fairey, obey, giant, ica, boston|

How the tags will look on the site:
Youtube: arrested fairey obey giant ica boston
Yahoo: arrested, fairey, obey, giant, ica, boston
MySpace: arrested fairey obey giant ica boston
MetaCafe: arrested fairey obey giant ica boston
Revver: arrested fairey obey giant ica boston
Break: arrested, fairey, obey, giant, ica, boston,
DailyMotion: arrested fairey obey giant ica boston
Blip.tv: arrested, fairey, obey, giant, ica, boston
Veoh: arrested, fairey, obey, giant, ica,
BrightCove: arrested, fairey, obey, giant, ica, boston
Crackle: arrested, fairey, obey, giant, ica, boston
eBaum's World: arrested fairey obey giant ica boston
Stupid Videos: arrested, fairey, obey, giant, ica, boston
Sclipo: arrested fairey obey giant ica boston
Viddler: arrested fairey obey giant ica boston
Howcast: arrested fairey obey giant ica boston
5min: arrested, fairey, obey, giant, ica, boston
Vimeo: arrested, fairey, obey, giant, ica, boston
Graspr: arrested fairey obey giant ica boston
Webcastr: arrested, fairey, obey, giant, ica, boston
i2TV: arrested fairey obey giant ica boston
Imeem: tags not supported

Category: [News & Blogs ⬦]   See how these categories map

Terms and Conditions: By clicking "Upload," you agree that this video does not violate the Terms of Use of any of the video sites you plan to upload to and that you own all copyrights in this video or have express permission from all copyright owners to upload it. You also agree to TubeMogul's Terms of Service.

Figure 6.26   TubeMogul Tell Us More

For this video I'm going to select all sites except for Howcast because this is not a How-to video.

Step 5: Press Launch and TubeMogul begins the process of uploading your video to all your selected sites.

In this case, 10 sites.

Once you press Launch, you can refresh the screen to check the status of your uploads.

TIP: Navigate directly to each site to have more control over your video's settings.

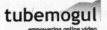

tubemogul
empowering online video

Logged in as steve@stevegarfield.com | My Account | Log Off

| Dashboard | Marketplace | Research | Learn More | Help |

Upload a Video | Launch and Promote a Video | Track Videos | Advanced Tools | My Profiles

Enter Your Credentials and Launch!

sites	login credentials (username or email / password)			
☑ YouTube	stevegarfield	•••••••	[X]	[more options]
☑ Yahoo!	sgarfield@yahoo.com	•••••••	[X]	[more options]
☑ MySpace	myspace@stevegarfield.co	•••••••	[X]	[more options]
☑ Metacafe	steve@stevegarfield.com	•••••••	[X]	[more options]
☐ Revver	Revver launch is temporarily down due to site issues.			[more options]
	stevegarfield	•••••••	[X]	
☑ Dailymotion	stevegarfield	•••••••	[X]	[more options]
☑ Blip	stevegarfield	•••••••	[X]	[more options]
☑ Veoh	stevegarfield	•••••••	[X]	[more options]
☑ Crackle	steve@stevegarfield.com	•••••••	[X]	[more options]
☑ Viddler	stevegarfield	•••••••	[X]	[more options]
☑ Vimeo	Using Vimeo authentication token.		[X]	[more options]
	••••••••••••••••••••			
☑ Howcast	stevegarfield	•••••••	[X]	[more options]

More sites ▶

Credentials saved ▶

(LAUNCH!)

[Change Thumb]

Obama HOPE poster artist Shepard Fairey arrested in Boston

The Boston Globe is reporting that artist Shepard Fairey was arrested last night on his way to DJ an event at the ICA art museum. No details on the arrest warrants were given. http://bit.ly/ONc3 I'd like more information.

Filename:
ShepardFaireyLarge.m4v [info]
Tags: arrested fairey obey giant ica boston
Category: News & Blogs
Added on: 02/07/2009

✎ Edit Info

⟳ Refresh Upload Status

FAQ

What happens after I push Launch?

Figure 6.27 TubeMogul Site Selection Page

For example, go to blip.tv to change copyright information from No License (see Figure 6.28) to Creative Commons (see Figure 6.29).

How Do Sites Handle 16:9 Video?

This is an interesting exercise to see how each site handles a 16:9 formatted video.

Primary File	Stevegarfield-ObamaHOPEPosterArtistSheparc	(Change..) Add additional format
Thumbnail	Stevegarfield-ObamaHOPEPosterArtistSheparc	(Change ...)
License	No license (All rights reserved)	▾

Figure 6.28 Blip.tv—No License

Primary File	Stevegarfield–ObamaHOPEPosterArtistShepard	(Change..) Add additional format
Thumbnail	Stevegarfield–ObamaHOPEPosterArtistShepard	(Change ...)
License	Creative Commons Attribution–NonCommercial–ShareAlike 3.0 ⬦	

Figure 6.29   Blip.tv—Creative Commons

Let's take a look.

YouTube

Figure 6.30 shows what the video looks like on YouTube. You can also click Watch in High Quality.

MySpace

Figure 6.31 shows what the video looks like on MySpace.

Metacafe

Here's what the video looks like on Metacafe (see Figure 6.32). Letterbox maintains aspect ratio.

Switch off annotations editor   watch in high quality

Figure 6.30   YouTube Video

Figure 6.31   MySpace Video

Figure 6.32   MetaCafe Video

Figure 6.33   DailyMotion Video

DailyMotion

Here's what the video looks like on DailyMotion (see Figure 6.33).

Blip

Here's what the video looks like on blip.tv (see Figure 6.34):
   Aspect ratio is maintained.

TIP: With blip.tv you can go in and upload a custom thumbnail image (see Figure 6.35).

TIP: You can set up blip.tv to automatically cross-post to any number of blogs upon completion of the Flash conversion.

TIP: You can set up blip to play the source .m4v high-quality file from the embedded flash player on your blog if the viewer has the most current flash player installed. http://www.blip.tv/file/1748203.

Obama HOPE poster artist Shepard Fairey arrested in Boston

Figure 6.34   blip.tv Video

Internet-Based Video Networks

Another alternative to hosting your video on a site like blip.tv and distributing it via TubeMogul and iTunes, is to join an established Internet-based video network. These networks will handle all the distribution for you.

Obama HOPE poster artist Shepard Fairey arrested in Boston

Figure 6.35   Video on blip.tv with Custom Thumbnail Image

Next New Networks has shows like: Channel Frederator—Cartoons, Threadbanger—Fashion and Beauty, and Fast Lane Daily—Auto News.

These are the types of shows you might want to produce and have Next New Networks distribute for you.

Other Internet-based video networks include Revison3 and Wizzard Media.

Going Viral

Before everyone was concerned about going viral, video bloggers were just interested in having friends share stories. That might be the key to having video go viral today—telling a good story.

The site eguiders[32] recently launched to help people find good video online. That's a good way to get seen and get featured on a site that features online video.

Interview: Kevin Nalts

Tools: Canon HV20

Why You Should Know Kevin Nalts

Kevin Nalts[33] is a career marketer and prolific online-video creator. He's learned how to get his videos seen on YouTube, one with more than 6 million views.

> *Steve Garfield: You've got over 60 million views on YouTube for your videos. How did that happen?*
>
> *Kevin Nalts: About 80 percent of my views are from my most 10 popular videos, which presumably tapped into a common denominator of humor. But what separates the YouTube "stars" from the "one-hit wonders" is a large subscriber base, and regular videos that jump to the "most popular videos of the day" on YouTube. That takes time to build, and requires determination and thick skin. In my free eBook (How to Become Popular on YouTube Without Any Talent), I*

---

[32] http://www.eguiders.com/
[33] http://naltsconsulting.com/

urge people to be patient but persistent, and start by participating actively in the YouTube community—do collaborations with popular YouTubers and actively watch, comment, and reply to viewers. That took me about nine months to understand and achieve.

SG: You involve your family in making many of your videos. How has that affected your relationship with them?

KN: There are times where my wife and kids want me to put the camera away, or surface from my editing cave. But for the most part my kids are used to seeing their lives online, and it's a fun activity we share. Often they come up with the ideas, and get excited about the attention. I suppose as a parent I'm overcompensating for the fact that I don't have videos to remind me of happy childhood moments, and I want them to always be one click away from reliving a fun memory. Now that online video is a source of revenue, my wife is far more patient with what was once a hobby/obsession. And my kids are excited to earn a few dollars for appearing in a video, even though they are far less interested in watching them than their friends.

SG: Your YouTube video, "Farting in Public (Farting in Library) by Nalts "[34]* has gotten over 6 million views. It's funny that you are associated with farting, yet you aren't the one farting in the video. Is there a market for farting in public videos? How does Spencer, the teenager in the video, feel about being in a YouTube with that many views?*

KN: I'm proud to be one of Google's top search results for the word "fart" thanks to my "Farting in Public" video where a teenager uses a fart machine to solicit funny reactions in a public library. Farts sell, but what makes this video interesting is the deadpan humor of Spencer contrasted against the candid reaction of strangers who want to spare him embarrassment.

(continued)

---

[34]http://www.youtube.com/watch?v=O3ejlkzDCuc

My nephew told me one Friday that his friend Spencer was a fan and wanted to be in a video. The very next day we met for the first time, and minutes later were shooting that video. Spencer is a confident teenager, and is almost indifferent about his local fame. My viewers beg to see him in new pranks, and to get him back on camera I usually have to stalk him and bribe him (gift cards work well).

SG: What equipment would you suggest to someone getting started? People can get started using a laptop with an inbuilt webcam, right? Is that a good idea?

KN: You don't need anything fancy. I usually tell people to stay under $500, and concentrate more on good audio and lighting.

Image quality does not currently correlate with views. I'm sure that as professional content moves online, the bar will rise.

SG: Why are you using YouTube to host your videos? Are there drawbacks to using YouTube?

KN: I spent almost a year trying to generate an audience across other video-sharing sites, but YouTube is where 95 percent of my videos are seen. Occasionally I'll be featured on Yahoo! or Yahoo! video, but none of the dozen sites on which I post have a recurring audience. The only downside of YouTube is that I'm dependent on it to keep a recurring audience, and if it goes "pro" that could soften my growing audience.

SG: You are a member of the YouTube Partner program. That means you get paid based on views right? Would you suggest that people apply to the YouTube Partner Program?

KN: There's a myth that people can make a fortune via YouTube's Partner program, but most of the partners are making nominal income. Unless you're going to produce regular content and gain a large audience, it's not worthwhile to you or YouTube. When people submit and are rejected, I tell them to do two things: remove copyright material, and continue creating videos and working to popularize them. Then their chance of being accepted (and making income) increase.

SG: Have you figured out the best method for producing web video? What camera do you use, computer, and editing software? What settings do you use to get the best quality on YouTube?

KN: I shoot with a semi-pro (Canon HV20) and I'm in the dark ages on editing. I use iMovie version 6 because I have a low tolerance to use the fancier tools I've purchased. The single biggest factor in getting a quality image on YouTube is by exporting the video per the correct specifications and sending the largest file size possible. I regret that many of my earlier videos were compressed to 10 MB and now I try to submit videos no smaller than 500 MB.

SG: What makes a successful video?

KN: There are some basic ingredients for a popular video, and the most important tricks are to keep it brief, shock the viewer, ensure the first 15 seconds captivate the viewer, and end with a surprise (that last impression is when a viewer decides whether to share the video with friends). Thumbnails (the image that represents the video) are vital, and tagging with key terms also helps. Topicality is also very important—my parody of the Mac Air did well because I posted it within an hour of the announcement. And my Superbowl ad video was seen several million times because I posted a review of the ads just as the game began.

SG: What advice would you give to a business getting started in online video.

KN: My goal is to make a career showing large brands how to better participate in online video, and most are wasting money trying to produce "viral videos" or buy online video ads alone. I encourage businesses and marketers to partner with already popular creators, which is a proven recipe for success. I shudder when I see brands create large web sites packed with

(continued)

videos, instead of distributing their content via already popular web sites and channels. Fish where the fish are. What brands fail to realize is that there are hungry amateurs with larger audiences than many cable television shows, and that's a smart way to engage.

SG: Any other thoughts . . .

KN: Your reader might be interested in my free eBook, How to Become Popular on YouTube (Without Any Talent).[35]

SG: What is the secret to online video?

KN: The secret sauce of online video is constantly changing, but the most important element is to be true to your own style. It's easy to let the audience feedback take you to a place where you aren't having fun and are making videos for others instead of yourself. The biggest challenge is to balance the needs of the audience with what you find personally satisfying. New "stars" are constantly emerging, and they're not always what you'd expect. It's exciting to find amateurs with great talent that would otherwise have no audience beyond their friends and neighbors. Each new media—radio, television, film, and now online video—creates a new group of stars that translate to that medium. Many of the "most subscribed" YouTube stars are friends, collaborate, and promote each other to their audiences. We also speak often to share new learnings about how to make our videos better, and market ourselves effectively. It's a vibrant community, and most of the "stars" share their secrets willingly with others.

Now the big video sites have curators that decide which videos to highlight on their front pages. This is an area that you might want to focus on figuring out, how to get featured on the front page of a video-sharing site.

On YouTube, becoming part of their partner program might help.

---

[35]http://willvideoforfood.com/2008/01/04/how-to-become-popular-on-youtube-without-any-talent-active-version/

GET SEEN: What separates the YouTube "stars" from the "one-hit wonders" is a large subscriber base.

GET SEEN: Editing and proper compression is more important than camera quality.

GET SEEN: Get highlighted in the front page of a video-sharing site.

Viral Is the Reward, Not the Tactic: Corey Kronengold on Online Video Advertising

Corey Kronengold is the Senior Director of Corporate Communications & Marketing for Tremor Media,[36] a leading online video advertising network and publisher technology provider.

Steve Garfield: You've said "Viral is the reward, not the tactic." What do you mean by that?

Corey Kronengold: When someone comes to me and says, "I want to create a video to go viral," I cringe. Videos going viral is the result of creating compelling, funny, engaging content that resonates with your target audience and makes them so excited that they want to share it with their social network.

I'd compare it to the music industry, where I used to work. It would be like any band sitting down and saying, "We want to write an album that goes double platinum." Of course they do. And if you make a good album, and your fans love your songs and want to bring their friends to your concert, it will. The success metrics shouldn't be confused with the objective of the project. How many people view a viral video is a measure of how much you resonated with your target audience.

(continued)

---

[36]http://www.tremormedia.com/

> *That's not to say that there isn't an art and science to viral videos. But it's definitely more art than science at this point.*

Building Community

One of the many reasons people choose to put video on the Web is to help them build community. Videos on YouTube and links to videos in e-mail, help tell a story. Personal videos can engage and can promote participation.

Chris Brogan and Julien Smith talk about the value of commenting in their book, Trust Agents:[37]

> *Due to the rarity of comments, those who comment are remarkable and are noticed. A first-time commenter is usually recognized as new, whereas a regular is often recognized for his or her regular participation in guest posts[38] or hat tips.[39] Because of this, being a regular commenter transforms you from an invisible presence into a real community member.*

If your goal is to increase the number of people in your online community, using video could be a great way to make it happen.

The Obama campaign was brilliant in its use of video.

LESSONS FROM THE OBAMA CAMPAIGN

In the 2008 United States presidential campaign, the Charles Meets Barack[40] video on YouTube was the most popular of the campaign and it was recorded on a Flip video camera.

It's not all about Twitter, Facebook, or MySpace, it's about getting people to connect with each other to do something.

---

[37] http://www.trustagent.com/

[38] A blog post by someone other than the blog owner is a guest post.

[39] A hat tip is when the blog author mentions you in a blog post. Preferably this includes a link to you.

[40] http://www.youtube.com/watch?v=TW-6DpC-mj8

Interview: Thomas Gensemer—Blue State Digital

WHY YOU SHOULD KNOW THOMAS GENSEMER

Thirteen-and-a-half million people were on the e-mail list of the Obama campaign.

Some videos were recorded on laptop webcams and then sent out to millions within minutes.

You have to build and sustain relationships; it's more than just video.

We had the chance to interview Thomas Gensemer, Managing Partner of Blue State Digital[41] to get his thoughts on how video played a role in the Obama campaign for President in 2008.

Steve Garfield: Tell me about how the Obama campaign used recorded video.

Thomas Gensemer: We had a new media team in Chicago, which ended up being 100 people by Election Day. There was a group of editors, very talented, people from documentaries, CNN, etc. There was a flood of content inbound, from either grassroots activists . . . from volunteers in state offices, or from people who would follow the candidate or surrogates around. How do you package that to make a compelling story . . . that really became the fodder for the best fundraising days, the best volunteer days. Some of the stuff was seen at the convention, some of the stuff was seen on election night. It really highlighted the story of the campaign, as told through—not from—the candidate, not really from the official videographer of the campaign but from a collection of resources on the ground by way of millions of volunteers. That was really part of the story of the campaign more than anything else, video was what separated this campaign from one, two, and four years ago.

SG: The other way you used video was to live stream events. With things like Ustream and streaming live

(continued)

---

[41] http://bluestatedigital.com

and twitter . . . to notify anyone who was interested, that was revolutionary.

TG: It comes down to transparency. Few people understand the significance of the Jefferson Jackson Dinner that happened in Iowa, how that is such a big deal, but if you are there, backstage, with the candidate, and you go out on stage and you feel it, it suddenly opens the door to a campaign.

The whole logic of the campaign was to sell a piece of your involvement, your donation means you own a piece of the campaign, how do we flood you with so much content . . . that you are a part of it. Not everyone wants to watch a streaming video, the numbers are relatively low, the edited video tends to get absorbed far more. But for those who are interested, they should have a seat at the table. They should be invited to the Jefferson Jackson Dinner, they should be invited to the State dinner, they should be invited to the State of the Union. So those tactics are simply meant to lower the barrier to entry, for what has been for a long time a closed community of people inside the beltway, inside the campaign. We've talked a lot about how we lowered the barrier to entry while raising the level of expectation for what it is to be a member of a campaign, a supporter of a campaign. And the streaming video is just another piece of that recipe.

The Story of the Campaign

Some 11,000 videos were produced over the course of 22 months, fewer than 10 percent of them probably actually featured the candidate, fewer than 2 percent actually took time from the candidate.

The story of it was about people like you going to events with your video camera, or someone going with a clipboard to sign people up—that became the excitement around this campaign. It ended up materializing a lot of support for the candidate, it inverted the political model . . . the person on the ground, the person hosting the house, the person giving an hour of volunteerism, party meant just as much as the surrogate on the podium.

That was intentional. Little did we know it would be so successful, but it started with the fact that we elected a political organizer 20 years ago. Those individual stories, those knocks at the door are what he knew was going to build this. It wasn't about technology. It was about a candidate and an inner circle who understood that one neighbor knocking on the next was more important than flooding the airwaves, and putting things in the mail, that was the essence of the campaign. We had a great pleasure to be part of it. It's not a technology story, it's an organizing story.

GET SEEN: People going to events with video cameras became the excitement around this campaign.

Open for Questions

President Barack Obama had an online town hall (see Figure 6.36) on March 26, 2009. The first live-streamed town hall from a president who answered questions submitted to WhiteHouse.gov[42] by text and video (see Figure 6.37).

Interacting with Your Audience

Interview: Amanda Congdon

WHY YOU SHOULD KNOW AMANDA CONGDON

Amanda Congdon created and co-created many different web video projects including AC on ABC, "Amanda Across America,"

(continued)

---

[42] http://www.WhiteHouse.gov

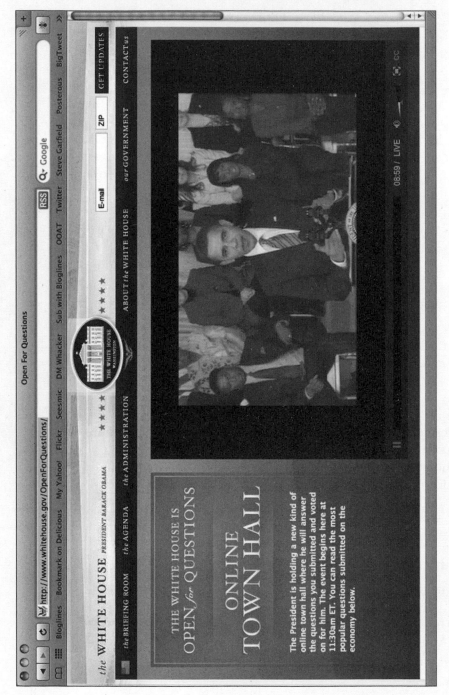

Figure 6.36   White House Online Town Hall

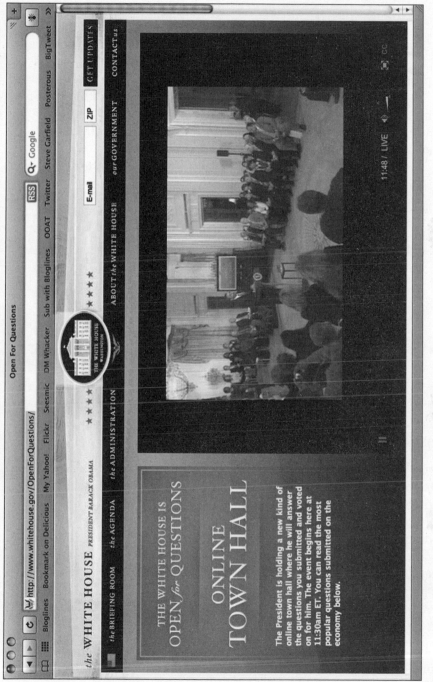

Figure 6.37   White House Online Town Hall

"Rocketboom," and "Starring Amanda Congdon." She now hosts "Sometimesdaily," an interactive variety show with new videos posted to the Web every weekday. As of April 2009, "Sometimesdaily" can also be seen four days each week on FLO TV—live mobile TV. Congdon also produces a *live* show every Thursday at noon PT/3PM ET on her 35-minute show, "The Controverse," at Sometimesdaily.com.

Congdon has three main ways they interact with the "Sometimesdaily" viewers:

1. They talk back and forth with them during the weekly live show.

2. When Congdon does "Amanda-on-the-Street" episodes they ask their friends on Twitter and Facebook the same questions they ask people on the street. They combine voices from the Internet with real-life voices.

3. Congdon responds to viewer comments and questions on Facebook, Twitter, and Sometimesdaily.com. Viewers share their ideas and links as well as give us feedback about the show.

Charging for Content

If you have content that you want to charge for, you'll need a hosting solution that supports all the back-end processing that's necessary to handle this kind of transaction.

One site to consider is MyContent.com. There, you can sell your content at any price between $0.69 and $299. You can sell each piece of content individually, as a package, as a monthly subscription, or as a rental. They split the sales 65/35 percent. If you set up a site there, let me know. Another option is ooyala at www.ooyala.com.

Choices

I've covered a lot of choices in this chapter. We've gone from simple four-step video uploads, to more feature-rich choices. The good news is that you can start with the method that's most comfortable to you.

I'm interested in seeing your videos online. Join me over in the *Get Seen* community at stevegarfield.com and share your progress.

7

Broadcasting Live

A Stream of Information

In 2004, when I started my video blog, it was the easiest way to share new videos.

When media enclosure support was added to RSS, people could subscribe to videos and have them automatically delivered to the desktop. That was video podcasting. I experimented with video podcasting in November of 2004.[1]

Now there are numerous ways to stream live video to the Web. In 2004, we weren't even thinking about live, we were just trying to figure out the best way to deliver recorded video.

A quick look at my web page shows two embedded players from Livestream and Qik. Whenever I stream live, you can watch the stream on one of those players. The Livestream player shows video I'm broadcasting from a webcam, and the Qik player shows video I'm streaming from a cell phone. If I'm not live, the embedded players show recent broadcasts.

Let's take a quick look back at my early thoughts on live streaming, then get into the details of how to broadcast live video with Livestream, Qik, and other solutions.

On Monday, August 7, 2006, Dan Gillmor, director of the Center for Citizen Media, and his cocoordinators brought about 100 people together, at the Berkman Center for Internet and Society at Harvard Law School, to discuss citizen journalism. The purpose was "to brainstorm

---

[1] http://stevegarfield.blogs.com/videopodcast/2004/11/videopodcast_20.html

some key aspects of citizen journalism, including principles, techniques, tools, business models and more."[2]

I spoke about using multimedia tools for better citizen journalism.

At that time, there weren't any easy-to-use solutions for live streaming. People were talking about using custom QuickTime Broadcaster[3] solutions. This meant installing software on a server, which wasn't exactly broadcasting for the rest of us.

In my presentation I said, "A lot of what we do is record something and then we have to bring it onto our computer and upload or edit it . . . if there was a way to hook into Wi-Fi where you are and broadcast, it's something I would do or would like to see . . . I think there needs to be a live streaming solution."

At that time, people were looking for tools to allow remote people to participate in conferences. We wanted a simple video-streaming solution with integrated chat that would allow a conversation.

On March 6, 2007, I experimented with live broadcasting from a cell phone with ComVu PocketCaster software. I was able to stream live to a web page;[4] it was exciting.

Fast-forward to today and there are multiple solutions out there for live streaming. Keep in mind that even though you might have a small audience when you initially broadcast your show, the archived version lives on and will probably get more views than your live broadcast.

GET SEEN: The revolution of recording video is the ability to share from the device you record with.

Live from a Cell Phone—Qik: Stories

Here are a few stories where I used Qik to broadcast live from a Nokia N95 from the campaign trail of the 2008 Presidential Election.

BEATING CNN TO A STORY WITH LIVE VIDEO FROM A CELL PHONE

As I was walking down the sidewalk in Manchester, New Hampshire, I saw a crowd of people hurrying down the sidewalk. I asked people

---

[2]http://wikimania2006.wikimedia.org/wiki/Citizen_Journalism
[3]http://www.apple.com/quicktime/broadcaster/
[4]http://stevegarfield.blogs.com/videoblog/2007/03/broadcasting_li.html

Figure 7.1   Duncan Hunter on Streaming Video

around me what was going on. The response I got was that Congressman Duncan Hunter was going on CNN to make a major announcement. I asked if I could do a live interview with him about it. An aide told me to walk back down the sidewalk and find another staff member to ask. I replied, "No. I can interview him *right now* with this cell phone!" The aide said to go right ahead, so I ran up to him and started streaming live video from the cell phone (see Figure 7.1).

You can see an archived version of the live-streamed video.[5]

As soon as I streamed the interview, people started blogging about it. They were talking about how I beat CNN to the story by being in the right place, at the right time, with the ability to stream live. Jose Castillo said, "Watch out, news world, here comes instant media."

At the time I was using a Nokia N95 that did not support 3G, and I had the Qik software set to Better Performance and Lower Quality.

The cell service was not great up in New Hampshire so I adjusted the streaming settings to make sure that the stream worked, sacrificing video quality for stronger streaming performance.

It's a good idea to set the Qik software settings to get the most reliable stream. That way your broadcast won't get interrupted by a dropped signal.

---

[5]http://bit.ly/qik_duncanhunter

What's interesting to note is that the other news crew wanted an interview, but were told that they'd have to schedule another time.

When I do a live stream, a notification is sent right out to my Twitter followers, so they can watch the live stream as it is broadcast from the cell phone. You set this up on the Qik site, in the networks settings, by authorizing Twitter and setting up a default message.

Citizen media will help cover stories that mainstream media will not.

With new technology that allows people to stream live video from cell phones to the Web, you'll start to see more reports from the street.

BROADCASTING LIVE FROM A CELL PHONE TO LIVESTREAM VIA QIK

A week before Super Tuesday 2008 I thought about the campaign coverage I watched on the UpTake,[6] a citizen journalism site, where they would regularly switch between remote reporters in different cities within one broadcast. The UpTake was using Livestream technology, which allows one video stream to be able to be switched between multiple live cameras, even if they are remote. After broadcasting live from New Hampshire and other places, I wondered, "If Livestream could switch between live cameras in multiple locations, and I was streaming live with a cell phone, why couldn't Livestream switch to a live broadcast of me?"

So I contacted Max Haot at Livestream and Bhaskar Roy at Qik to see if they'd be interested in making their services work together. They said yes!

We had a week until Super Tuesday to make it work. The technical teams joined forces and made it happen.

Livestream and Qik (see Figure 7.2) were working together for the first time. From my N95 in Boston, I transmitted from a bar near Fenway Park and interviewed fellow bloggers.

I streamed live over the AT&T 3G network. I communicated with a remote UpTake producer with my iPhone. They cued up my live cell phone feed on Livestream, then switched to me, and I broadcast live from the street. My stream was sent out over the UpTake's Livestream channel both on the Livestream site and embedded on the UpTake site.

---

[6]http://theuptake.org

Figure 7.2   Live Stream on Qik

I made a 23-minute, 41-second video of my *live* broadcast from Boston Beer Works on Primary night 2/5/08.[7]

Live Streaming Cell Phone Tips

Wi-Fi: Use Wi-Fi when available. Gives the smoothest stream.

Battery: Carry extra batteries, or an IOGEAR battery pack. Continuous live streaming drains the battery in about an hour.

Sound: Add an external microphone. On the N95, add a powered mic to the Yellow A/V cable. It's not meant for this, but works.

Interview: If you are using the camera's in-built mic, be aware of its location and speak directly into it.

Tripod or Monopod: Use a tripod or monopod to get a steady shot. If you don't have that available, lean against something.

Interrupted Stream: Make sure that your streaming provider can recover an interrupted live stream. Do they record to disk

---

[7]http://offonatangent.blogspot.com/2008/02/reporting-for-uptake-massachusetts.html

while streaming? Check with your streaming software to see what happens if your stream is interrupted.

Tips for Producing Compelling Short-Form Video

I train many people on the use of Qik.com, which allows you to capture, share, and post live video from a cell phone. I teach people that you don't need to be an expert to produce video for the Web. Authentic and real moments captured and shared produces compelling video.

Live streaming allows you to produce video without having to learn software like Final Cut Pro, or editing procedures like log and capture, editing, exporting, and uploading.

This frees you to capture and share moments.

Stream your story, then move on to the next one.

Which Live Streaming Service to Use?

When you are deciding which live streaming service you want to use, it will help to think about how many source live streams you want to have and if you want to include roll-ins of prerecorded material.

The Barack Obama campaign made use of Ustream for live streaming. That's a good example of using a straightforward platform to stream a live event.

If you are interested in streaming from multiple locations and including prerecorded videos, Livestream is a good choice.

Livestream also supplies a PC-based streaming solution, Pro-Caster,[8] which only requires clicking one button to stream live. Using that program is as easy as Ustream. ProCaster streams and encodes your broadcasts in the absolute highest quality possible, with automatic frame rate adjustment based on your hardware and quality/connection settings.

Other solutions are Wirecast and BoinxTV.

USING THE AUDIENCE AS DIRECTOR AT OBAMA RALLY

On September 4, 2008, I attended a rally for Barack Obama in Boston.[9] I streamed multiple videos from the site (see Figure 7.3).

---

[8]http://www.livestream.com/procaster
[9]http://offonatangent.blogspot.com/2008/02/obama-rally-boston-9408.html

Figure 7.3   Archived Videos at Qik.com

As a citizen reporter for the UpTake,[10] I got a press pass. On arrival at the convention center, there was a huge line, really really long, maybe one-half a mile. I found the press entrance and waited in line. There were many types of people in line: big media, college students, and me. I overheard some mainstream media reporters complaining about all the kids that Obama let into these rallies as press. The Obama campaign was smart to include citizen journalists and students as press. It got them a lot of extra coverage.

I entered the packed convention hall (see Figure 7.4). There was Wi-Fi available so I set up Qik on the Nokia N95 to use Wi-Fi.

The Nokia N95 can stream over Qik using the Edge network, the 3G network, or Wi-Fi.

Streaming over Wi-Fi provides the best quality.

CONVENTION CENTER

When streaming with Qik, viewers can text chat from the Web to the cell phone.

This is a groundbreaking development. Viewers can interact directly with the producer of the video. On the camera!

These text comments, entered on the Qik web site, or the page where the stream is embedded, are displayed on the cell phone as it's broadcasting live.

---

[10] http://theuptake.org

Figure 7.4   Obama Rally in Boston

I received comments from viewers like, "Wow, this is exciting, I've never been to a political rally before." By streaming live, I was able to bring viewers into the rally, allowing them to experience it from my point of view.

As they sent text messages to my streaming cell phone, they were also directing my coverage. C-Span was also broadcasting the rally. My viewers wanted me to find the C-Span camera. So they guided me as I walked, giving me directions along the way. "Find the guy with the red hat in the crowd."

I finally found him.

I pointed the camera at him and a text message come across my screen, "You found the red hat guy!" Next they wanted me to find the C-Span camera. I turned around and saw the camera. I asked the camera operator for a quick live interview and he said, "Hi." Then I held my camera up to take a similar live shot of what the C-Span camera was getting. I did that to show that with my little Nokia N95 I could approximate the live coverage similar to that of a cable network with lots of expensive equipment.

Then I saw a text message on the screen, "I just saw your Nokia N95 on C-Span."

I had held the camera up so high that it was visible on the C-Span live broadcast.

It was a great experience.

Figure 7.5   Comcast and TiVo

GET SEEN: To see if your cell phone is supported by Qik, check the supported phones page on the Qik web site.[11]

GET SEEN: I broadcast live via Qik over Wi-Fi with chat between remote viewers and my cell phone.

COMCAST—A CUSTOMER SUCCESS STORY USING TWITTER AND QIK

I live streamed a Comcast TiVo problem to Comcast technicians using Qik and my cell phone.

I recently used video to assist in solving a problem I was having with my cable service. I was trying to record *Terminator: The Sarah Connor Chronicles* (never should have been canceled), but I could not record any HD Fox or HD WLVI programs. There also wasn't any detailed program data in the online guide for those two channels.

A customer service rep had been relaying instructions to me from the Comcast/TiVo support people. I was frustrated because the suggestions did not match my problem and something was getting lost in translation. After being unhappy with the support I was receiving, I contacted Frank Eliason, Comcast Director of Digital Care, @comcastcares on Twitter. Frank arranged a conference call with Comcast *and* TiVo (see Figure 7.5) to solve my problem.

---

[11]http://qik.com/info/supported_phones

While on the phone call, I offered to stream my TV's TiVo display live, so they could directly see the issue. I streamed the problem over Qik,[12] using a cell phone while talking with them on the landline-based phone.

The call and live video helped solidify the issue so that they could go back and solve it.

Being able to send Comcast a visual image of the problem was much faster and more efficient than trying to explain verbally what I was seeing.

Frank at Comcast deserves a lot of praise for his handling of this. He tweeted about it (see Figures 7.6 and 7.7):

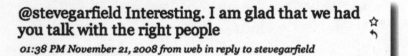

@stevegarfield Interesting. I am glad that we had you talk with the right people

01:38 PM November 21, 2008 from web in reply to stevegarfield

comcastcares
Frank Eliason

Figure 7.6   Frank Eliason on Twitter[13]

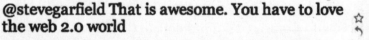

@stevegarfield That is awesome. You have to love the web 2.0 world

01:49 PM November 21, 2008 from web in reply to stevegarfield

comcastcares
Frank Eliason

Figure 7.7   Web 2.0 Works[14]

They were able to resolve my problem by refreshing my box with new guide data. They even called back to make sure everything was still working.

---

[12] http://qik.com/stevegarfield#v=597823
[13] http://twitter.com/comcastcares/statuses/101695341
[14] http://twitter.com/comcastcares/statuses/1016971017

TIP: Live video streaming is a great way for remote support staff to see problems first hand.

Thanks Twitter, Qik, Comcast, and Frank!

I Got on the BBC by Streaming Live with My Cell Phone on Qik

Broadcast networks can engage viewers who want to contribute their stories. The BBC has an initiative called "Have Your Say," which solicits people to send in their stories.

During the 2008 U.S. Presidential election, the BBC wanted to hear from U.S. citizens. The BBC monitored Qik and selected videos to highlight on their web site and on TV.

The BBC wasn't looking for high-quality broadcasts, just real stories about how people thought about what was happening in the campaign.

I used Qik to stream some live videos during the presidential debates. The BBC liked them and featured them on their web site.[15]

TIP: It's the authentic storytelling that's important and not always the quality of the video.

Camera Operation

Using a cell phone as a camera is similar to using a small digital still camera as a video camera.

You'll be streaming live as soon as you press the Stream menu item on your phone.

Prior to starting your live stream, point your camera at whatever you want to have as a thumbnail image on the archive version of your video.

Note where the microphone is located on our phone. If it's at the front of the phone near the camera lens, you'll get better audio quality than if it's on the side.

---

[15] http://offonatangent.blogspot.com/2008/10/bbc-qik-videos-from-us-debate.html

If the microphone is on the side of the camera, orient yourself so that the person talking speaks into the microphone.

You might want to inform the person in your video about this positioning prior to shooting so they'll be prepared.

Hold the camera steady by resting it against something.

If the person in the video is explaining something, you can get good sound by placing the microphone near their mouth, and aiming the camera lens at whatever they are talking about.

Qik: How To

Steps to get started with Qik from your cell phone.

- Sign up at Qik.com or navigate to d.Qik.com from your cell phone.

- Download the software to your mobile phone.

- Open the Qik application.

SETTING UP QIK ON THE PHONE

Note: These are settings on the Nokia N95. These steps would be different if you are not on a Nokia phone.

My default settings are in bold.

Once you have the Qik application running on your phone, the software connects to the default network. In my case, I'm on AT&T so it connects to Medianet. The default network will vary depending on your provider.

Note: Make sure that you have a data plan that can support streaming live video. Plans often change, so check with your service provider so you don't get surprised by a huge bill after you start streaming live video.

Menu Options

After pressing Menu Options you see the following:

Hide Qik: This moves Qik into the background so you don't start streaming by mistake by hitting the stream button.

Mute: If you press the Mute menu option no one will be able to hear you. I've done this in the past and was told quickly that there was no sound. That's the benefit, though, of instant feedback from a live audience.

Stream Info: Under the Stream Info menu you can set the video's Title and Description. That will override whatever you have set as the default on the Qik site.

Public/Private Privacy: The privacy setting, press 0 for private or press 5 for public, allows you to restrict viewing of your live stream. If privacy is set to private you can see your video stream and archived video from your profile page.

Settings: The Settings menu is the most jam-packed. Let's look at each setting.

Camera: Back, Front

Optimize for: Max Quality, Min Delay

Quality: Low, Normal, High

Audio Start Mode: Enabled, Muted

Access Point: MediaNet

Reactivate Device: No

Stay in Background: No

Economy Mode: Max Performance, Max Battery

Update Qik

Help

About

Exit

TIP: If viewers complain about poor performance or if you notice long delays, switch your settings. Try Min Delay.

The best way to stream video from your cell phone is to use Wi-Fi. You can go into the Options menu from Qik, select Change Connection, and choose Search for WLAN as your access point. The phone acts as a Wi-Fi detector and will find a nearby local Wi-Fi network.

Once the phone detects one or more local Wi-Fi networks, it presents a list for you to choose from. Select one, and if it requires an access key, a dialog box will pop up asking you to key in a password.

SETTING UP QIK ON THE SITE

You can also manage your settings at Qik.com.

When you start streaming with your cell phone, your live stream goes right to the front page of Qik.com. It also goes to your own personal page. Mine is at qik.com/stevegarfield.[16]

You can also grab the embed code and paste it on a web page. The next time you stream live, the video will be broadcast live to the Qik.com home page, your personal page at Qik.com, and any page where you've pasted your embed code (see Figure 7.8).

That's powerful.

In addition, you can also send your video to any or all of Qik's partners (see Figure 7.9).

From the Edit Profile menu, select Edit Networks.

Streaming partners for Qik include:

Twitter: Qik will send an update out to Twitter when you stream a new video.

Livestream: Qik will stream live to Livestream when you stream live with Qik.

12seconds.tv: Qik will stream the first 12 seconds of your video stream to 12seconds.com.

---

[16] http://qik.com/stevegarfiel

Figure 7.8   Qik Page with Embed Code

Figure 7.9   Qik Partner Networks

YouTube: Once you are finished streaming, Qik will archive a version of your video on YouTube as long as it's less than 10 minutes.

Blogger: Qik posts your archived video to blogger when you click Share, Networks, Blog This!

Seesmic: Qik videos with titles will be sent to Seesmic.

Tumbler: Qik posts to Tumbler when you stream a new video.

WordPress: You can embed your Live channel on your Wordpress blog, or you can embed an individual video.

Facebook: Qik videos will be posted to your Facebook account.

Each of these partners integrate with Qik in their own way.

GET SEEN: You can connect your Qik account to Facebook. If you don't have a Qik account, you can sign in with your Facebook username and password, then tell Qik your cell phone number.

Otherwise, if you are already signed up with Qik, go to Edit Profile, Networks, Facebook. Then click Edit, and if you have a Facebook account, click Connect.

The next time you stream live with Qik, your videos will be uploaded to Facebook.

Stream Live from Your Mobile Phone with Ustream

CBSNews.com has a channel on Ustream[17] that features breaking news coverage several times every day, presidential press conferences, Congressional hearings, and online-only content and on-air programs such as the *CBS Evening News with Katie Couric*.

Ustream Mobile (see Figure 7.10)[18] is a platform that enables anyone with a camera and an Internet connection to broadcast live

[17] http://www.ustream.tv/channel/cbs-news
[18] http://www.Ustream.com/mobile

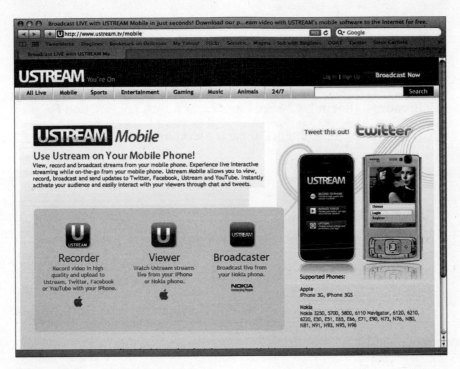

Figure 7.10   Ustream Mobile

interactive video to a global audience. It allows you to stream live from a range of Nokia phones or the Apple iPhone 3G and 3GS.

To get started with Ustream, go to www.ustream.com and select your phone model, country, and enter your cell phone number.

You will receive a text message on your phone with a link in it. Click the link to download and install the Ustream cell phone application.

Once you have installed the Ustream application, you can open it and stream live.

Nokia Instructions:

Open the Ustream program, and select an access point.

MEdiaNet is the AT&T 3G network. If there is available WiFi choose that since the quality will be better.

The program will then connect to the Ustream server.

You have two menu options, Start Broadcast and Options.

Start Broadcast—Starts broadcasting on your Ustream channel. If you've set it up on your account, Ustream can also send out a notification to Twitter that you are streaming live.

If you click options, a menu will pop up with these options:

Broadcast, Record, Change Camera, Settings, Logout, and Help.

Let's look at the contents of each menu item.

Broadcast

Starts broadcasting

Record

Starts recording a video for later use

Change Camera

On the Nokia N95, Change Camera switches the camera between the front and back camera. The "5" key on the keypad also switches between cameras.

Settings

Audio Settings: Audio Enabled or Mute. I leave audio enabled.

Performance: Performance Mode or Max Battery Mode. I use performance mode.

Quality: Auto or Low Quality. I use Auto.

Access Point: Always Ask or Choose from your saved Access Points. I leave it on Always Ask so that if you are near a Wi-Fi network you can choose it instead of defaulting to the 3G network.

Default Channel: Channel you want to start broadcasting on.

Autostart Broadcast: No or Yes. I choose No for this so I can get ready and then choose when to go live.

GPS Data Sending: Whether you want your SPS coordinates sent out.

Auto Twitter: Automatically update Twitter

Twitter Username

Twitter Password

Logout

Log out of Ustream.tv.

Help

Brings up help text.

Once your settings are chosen, you don't have to go back to them each time you broadcast.

Next, choose Start Broadcast and you are streaming live to your Ustream channel and anywhere else you have embedded your Ustream embed code.

The quality of the broadcast stream is good. If you can bring up your Ustream channel on a local computer while streaming from the cell phone, that makes it easier to participate in the text chat. It also allows you to monitor the quality of your broadcast.

Stream Live from a Webcam with Ustream

There are just a few easy steps to get ready to start broadcasting a live video stream using Ustream from a webcam or video camera.

Four Steps

Step 1: Sign in or Sign up for Ustream. The account you are signing up for is free. This means that along with our video, ads will be shown.

Step 2: Click Broadcast Now. A Broadcast console pops up. Click Allow to allow Adobe Flash Player access to your camera and mic. Click Start Broadcast.

Step 3: Optional: Click Start Recording then click Stop Recording. You can start broadcast and selective records segments of your broadcast.

Step 4: Click Stop Broadcast.

I've found that Firefox works better than Safari.

An easy hardware configuration to start with is the iSight camera from an iMac or MacBook Pro and its internal mic. It produces pretty good quality.

You can also use an attached USB mic and USB webcam.

TIP: Use a USB extension cord for the USB camera and microphone to record audio and video live at a distance from the computer.

If you want higher quality, hook up a video camera via Firewire. With a video camera, you could also make use of a mic attached to the camera.

Newer HD video cameras that have SD cards only use the USB port for data transfer and *not* for video streaming. Make sure the video camera you want to use with Ustream has Firewire.

HIGHER QUALITY

Check the Ustream site[19] for more tips on higher quality options. One option is to use a PC to broadcast with Flash Media Encoder.[20]

WATERSHED

See the Watershed site[21] for paid broadcast options like having your own custom watermark on the video, customized player skins, and 16:9 and HD broadcast support. With the paid plan you get 500GB total storage included, $0.30 per GB thereafter.

ANNOUNCING YOUR SHOW TO GET AN AUDIENCE

It's a good idea to pre-announce your show on sites like Twitter, your blog, and by sending out e-mails.

START BROADCASTING

Start broadcasting by clicking the Broadcast Now button.

---

[19] http://www.Ustream.com
[20] http://www.Ustream.com/fme-help
[21] https://watershed.Ustream.com/

START RECORDING

After you start broadcasting live, you can choose to start recording by pressing the Start Recording button. This is important and easy to overlook: If you want to save your recording, you must press the Start Recording button.

Conveniently, the Start Recording button changes into a Stop Recording button, so you don't have to hunt around for it after you start recording.

Some additional features available are adding a text overlay and playing a YouTube video. You can also play an archived Ustream video.

In addition to being archived on the Ustream site, you can also send the video to YouTube.

SEND TO YOUTUBE

The way you do this is go to My Videos, click on the archived video that you want to work with, then click Add to YouTube. Then you'll see YouTube Upload in Progress.

USTREAM SHOW

I recorded a quick show with a Canon GL/2 hooked up via a Firewire card to a MacBook Pro, with an audio-technica AT2020 mic hooked up via USB.[22] Great quality on the recorded broadcast. I sent the recorded show to YouTube and you can check the quality over there.[23]

HIGH-QUALITY CUSTOM BROADCAST

CBS News uses Ustream to stream from the Saturday version of *The Early Show* live on a show called Backstage live.[24] It's a professionally produced broadcast where the anchors make use of the embedded Ustream chat room to talk to viewers. CBS News also uses Telestream Wirecast to display multiple videos in the same Ustream window (see Figure 7.11).

---

[22] http://www.Ustream.com/recorded/1391916

[23] http://www.youtube.com/watch?v=DFCxElZ2a50

[24] http://www.cbsnews.com/htdocs/backstagelive.shtml

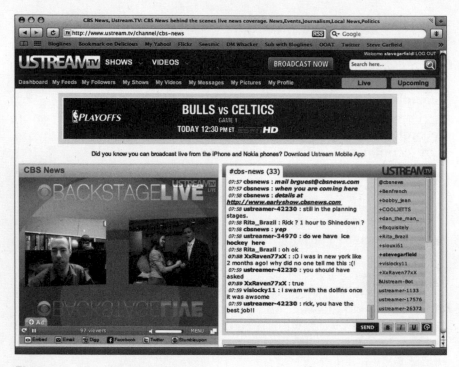

Figure 7.11   BackstageLive

In Boston, HubSpot[25] produces a weekly live show called Hub-Spot.tv.[26]

Note: HubSpot co-founders Brian Halligan and Dharmesh Shah are co-authors of *Inbound Marketing: Get Found Using Google, Blogs, and Social Media,* the first book in the "New Rules of Social Media" series[27] (of which this book is the second).

HubSpot initially used Ustream's white label watershed product, a webcam and USB microphone for their live stream.

---

[25] http://www.hubspot.com/
[26] http://Hubspot.tv
[27] http://davidmeermanscott.com/book_series

Figure 7.12   Karson and Kennedy Live Streaming

They now broadcast on Livestream using a Canon GL/2.

One more local example of live broadcasting is the Karson & Kennedy morning radio show from Mix 104.1 (formerly Mix 98.5)[28] in Boston (see Figure 7.12).

Visit the Facebook Fan Page for *Get Seen* at www.facebook. com/getseen to see an implementation of Ustream Facebook integration.

---

[28] http://www.mix1041.com/

Thoughts on Live Streaming by Brad Hunstable

WHY YOU SHOULD KNOW BRAD HUNSTABLE

Brad Hunstable is a serial entrepreneur and the founder of Ustream.TV.

Brad Hunstable:

Ustream provides a simple, high-quality live broadcasting technology. It allows anyone with a camera, webcam, HD camera, or phone to broadcast live to the Internet. We allow recording of your broadcasts and provide a tremendous amount of interactive tools.

We were lucky to have President Obama throughout his campaign, including his victory speech and inauguration. The Obama team used an HD camera with Ustream streaming in H.264. The key to get this to high quality is a solid high-speed Internet connection.

The inauguration had 3 million people watch online (half a million of whom watched on the iPhone!). His victory speech had 1 million people watch, and during his campaign speeches he had total of 4 million people.

If you broadcast live on Ustream, you can record the live broadcast in the same quality to our servers. This allows you to access it online. You can also record locally to your hard drive and we always recommend to record to tape as well for a backup. If you record to Ustream, we also give you the recorded video for download.

We recommend to have double the upload bandwidth available for whatever bit rate you are looking to stream at. Thus, if you decide to use a 300 kbps stream, ideally you want 600 kbps on the upload.

For hardware, we recommend at least a DV camera connected through Firewire; however, you can use the iSight built into your MacBook as well. We also work with professional production setups as well.

The free Ustream account is for anyone who wants to quickly and easily broadcast live. We are able to provide it free because we serve sponsorships and ads into the feed.

Watershed is a self-serve enterprise product for businesses, online education, and social sites. It has many advance analytics and custom tools that the free account does not have.

It's easy to support co-hosts. When you start a broadcast, you can activate a Cohost feed that will allow your viewers to request to join as a co-host. Then, if they have a camera connection, they can join the Cohost!

It's still the same and will always be the same. The medium may be live, may be recorded, but your audience will only watch if they are enjoying it.

GET SEEN: The secret to online video is to create great content.

You on TV—Cable News Goes Live at CNN.com/LIVE

CNN.com and Facebook joined together to use live streaming and Facebook integration on February 24, 2009, the day of President Barack Obama's first address to Congress. CNN.com's Live host Reggie Aqui hosted four bloggers remotely via Skype.[29]

Figure 7.13 shows what it looked like.

CNN's four-way Skype interview is an example of media opening up the dialog to viewers.

I interviewed some of the participants to get their thoughts on this breakthrough for including the people formerly known as the audience in the major media conversation.

---

[29] http://www.cnn.com/video/#/video/politics/2009/02/24/dcl.what.blogs.say.cnn

Figure 7.13   Pictured from Top Left, Clockwise: Gina Cooper,[30] Eric Erickson,[31] Matt Lewis,[32] Baratunde Thurston[33]

Interview: Baratunde Thurston

Baratunde Thurston is a conscious comic and vigilant pundit who has successfully merged his interests in technology, politics, and comedy. He is Web Editor at TheOnion, blogs at Jack & Jill Politics,[34] the Huffington Post, and his own site baratunde.com.[35]

> *Steve Garfield: How do you feel about CNN's use of readily available technology to bring in voices of bloggers to CNN.com/LIVE?*

[30]http://netrootsnation.com
[31]http://redstate.com
[32]http://news.aol.com/political-machine/
[33]http://jackandjillpolitics.com
[34]http://www.jackandjillpolitics.com/
[35]http://www.baratunde.com

Baratunde Thurton: It's about time.

I'm glad to see legacy media organizations like CNN stop talking about the impact of new technology and start actually using it. There's so much more that can be done, but CNN clearly gets that they have to participate, whether via Facebook live integration, Twitter, Second Life, or sourcing its commentariat from the realm of bloggers piped in via Skype.

SG: What do you see for the future of people formerly known as the audience being able to have a voice on web video broadcasts and TV?

BT: One of the great powers of our emerging networked world is that the burden of intelligence is increasingly distributed across a wide set of people. No single person has to be the smartest. However, the network must be able to deliver that intelligence when needed. We still have a mainstream media model that expects a handful of reporters, producers, and media staff to be experts. We expect them to have the right questions, the right follow-up questions, and the right analysis. All the time.

This is impossible.

Because of our networked world, information spreads much more rapidly through the people formerly known as the audience than it does to the media gatekeepers. Collectively, we know far more than they do. We spot errors more quickly. We find supporting material. We know better experts.

What's happening now is incredibly revolutionary because all that collective wisdom (which has always existed in some form), can now be collected, coordinated, and even be distributed regardless of the wishes of the traditional media model.

The actual way this works is a little more complicated because all these nodes of intelligence still require some tool or glue to coordinate and still don't have the mainstream distribution of our traditional media.

(continued)

That's the power of experiments like the CNN.com/ live efforts. We are moving toward a hybrid model, which marries the brand credibility, formal training, capital resources, widespread distribution, and access of a CNN with the faster collective and corrective intelligence of the people formerly known as the audience.

Interview: Gina Cooper

Gina Cooper[36] is the founder and past CEO of Netroots Nation—the most dynamic and influential political organization to emerge from the early years of the progressive blogosphere.

Steve Garfield: What do you see for the future of people formerly known as the audience being able to have a voice on web video broadcasts and TV?

Gina Cooper: I think what we are seeing right now from CNN.com and similar shows is what is next. The cable channel will only be one of many channels and the prestige of the online shows will be equal to what is shown on TV. Probably as more time goes by because the online content is more readily accessible. No paid subscription required. Here's where I will go off on a philosophical limb—we will also see a lot more diversity and increased tolerance for people with different points of view. People prefer to see themselves as open-minded than dogmatic, I think. The political market is polarized because that is how the choices have been presented. "You're either for us or against us." Don't underestimate the President's ability to set the tone and expectation of political dialogue, and then have that trickle outward into other arenas. What happens next depends on all of us and it depends on leadership. So technologies that support that ethic will be a big part of what is next.

---

[36]http://www.ginacooper.com/

Interview: Matt Lewis

Matt Lewis[37] is a conservative writer and commentator based in Alexandria, Virginia.

Matt is a frequent guest on Fox News, MSNBC, and CNN, as well as various radio shows, including NPR's *Talk of the Nation*, the Hugh Hewitt Show, and the Mike Gallagher Show. He has been quoted by major publications such as, the *Washington Post* and the *New York Times*. He has also authored articles for publications such as *Townhall.com, Politico, Human Events Online*, and *Campaigns & Elections* magazine.

> *Steve Garfield: How do you feel about CNN's use of readily available technology to bring in voices of bloggers to CNN.com/LIVE?*
>
> *Matt Lewis: I think CNN is doing a great job and are on the cutting edge. The quality is superb. And having done a lot of traditional TV hits, I can tell you it is so much more efficient and convenient to do "TV" without leaving your office.*
>
> *SG: What do you see for the future of people formerly known as the audience being able to have a voice on web video broadcasts and TV?*
>
> *ML: I think the Internet will continue to democratize communications. More and more people will have access to getting their views out, but they will also have to compete with more and more alternatives. I also predict that cable news will follow the trend—not just online, but on cable TV, too—and more and more guest "talking heads" will do their interviews from home over the computer.*

A TV Station in Your Computer—Livestream

Livestream, formerly known as Mogulus, allows you to broadcast live and has the ability to incorporate multiple cameras into the broadcast.

---

[37] http://www.mattlewis.org/

There are three ways you can broadcast live with Livestream.

1. Web-based Livestream Studio[38]

2. Web-based Webcaster or Twitcam[39]

3. External sources such as Procaster[40] or a Qik phone[41]

Livestream Studio is the fully featured interface to Livestream that gives you many of the same features you see in a TV station. Webcaster and Twitcam are simpler web interfaces to Livestream, which lets you get started quickly. Procaster is a computer-based application that is similar to Webcaster because it's easy to start streaming.

I used Livestream to broadcast from the Consumer Electronics Show (CES), as shown in Figures 7.14 and 7.15.

Figure 7.14 Broadcasting Live from CES at the TechKu Booth[42]

---

[38] http://www.livestream.com/studio

[39] http://www.livestream.com/webcaster, http://twitcam.com

[40] http://www.livestream.com/procaster/

[41] http://qik.com

[42] http://www.flickr.com/photos/stevegarfield/3181522703/

Figure 7.15   Broadcasting Live from CES at the
Livestream Booth[43]

On February 6, 2009, Mark Gillins wrote a blog post[44] about
watching this live broadcast. Mark says, "Perhaps the most mind-
blowing use of social media I saw at CES was a livecast[45] by social
media celebrity Steve Garfield from the Sands show floor, where he
shot live footage of the show *while following what people were saying in an attached chat room—and responding*! You have no idea
how awesome it felt to know I was a part of the livecast's content,
seeing Steve repeat something out loud that I had mentioned in the
chat room!"

**GET SEEN: What's exciting to viewers, even technical savvy
viewers like Mark, is the feeling they get of being part
of the show, when they are able to interact with the
host.**

---

[43] http://www.flickr.com/photos/stevegarfield/3184563922/
[44] http://blog.ce.org/index.php/2009/02/06/ces-social-media-amazing/#comment-
1384
[45] http://www.Livestream.com/stevegarfield

Livestream How To: Webcaster

SETTING UP LIVESTREAM

The first thing you need to do is visit Livestream.com and set up an account and name your channel.

To get started on the quick web-based version, launch Webcaster.

Three Steps

Step 1: Launch Webcaster[46] and allow access to your camera and microphone.

Step 2: Choose the quality of your broadcast, Low, Medium, or High.

Step 3: Click Go Live.

Livestream How To: Livestream Studio

Using the Livestream Studio requires a few more steps than Webcaster. You get more features, though, by using it. Here's a rundown of the steps.

On this page (see Figure 7.16) you enter information about your channel.

You can also style your channel (see Figure 7.17), including the corner bug, text, and background color.

Here you can add members to your team (see Figure 7.18). This allows them to manage your station or be restricted to being a remote camera only.

Here you can add videos for broadcast on your channel (see Figure 7.19). You can either upload them from your computer, or import them from the Web. Sources for web video you can use are YouTube, by username or Video URL, Video podcast, or video from a web server.

On this page you can see all your camera sources (see Figure 7.20). In this image we are looking at a DV camera as source. I'm using a Canon GL/2 miniDV camera, connected via Firewire to a two-port Firewire card, which is plugged into a MacBook Pro.

Using the Firewire card gives the camera its own bus, kind of like an express bus into the city.

---

[46] http://www.livestream.com/webcaster

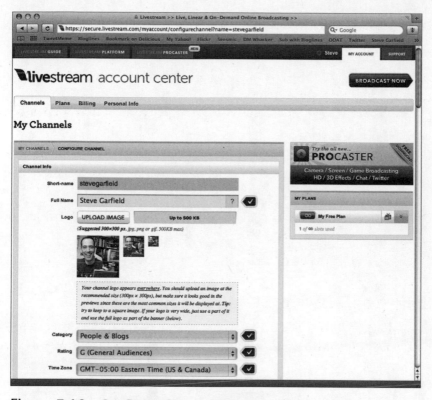

Figure 7.16   Configure Channel Page on Livestream.com

You can also cue videos to be played on your live broadcast. Other configuration options on this page include the ability to set up Overlays, full-screen text, Tickers, Branding (bug or test card).

You can also see and participate in your show's chat room from this page.

If you set up Qik to Auto Go Live to Livestream, when you start streaming with Qik from a cell phone, it can automatically go live on your Livestream channel.

The way you set this up is to go to the Network settings on your Qik account at Qik.com and enter the Channel you want Qik to broadcast to, enter your Livestream username and password, and then choose if you want to check off the Auto Go Live selection. Then save your choices.

If you set it so it doesn't automatically go live, a producer in control of the Livestream studio would decide when to take the cell phone video live.

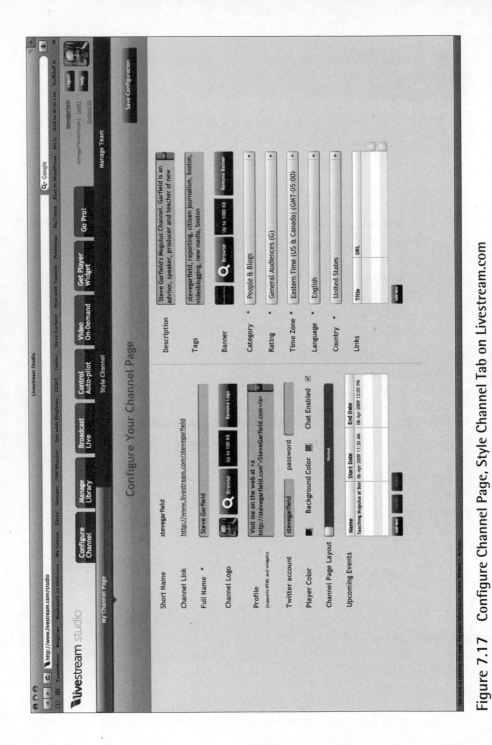

Figure 7.17 Configure Channel Page, Style Channel Tab on Livestream.com

204

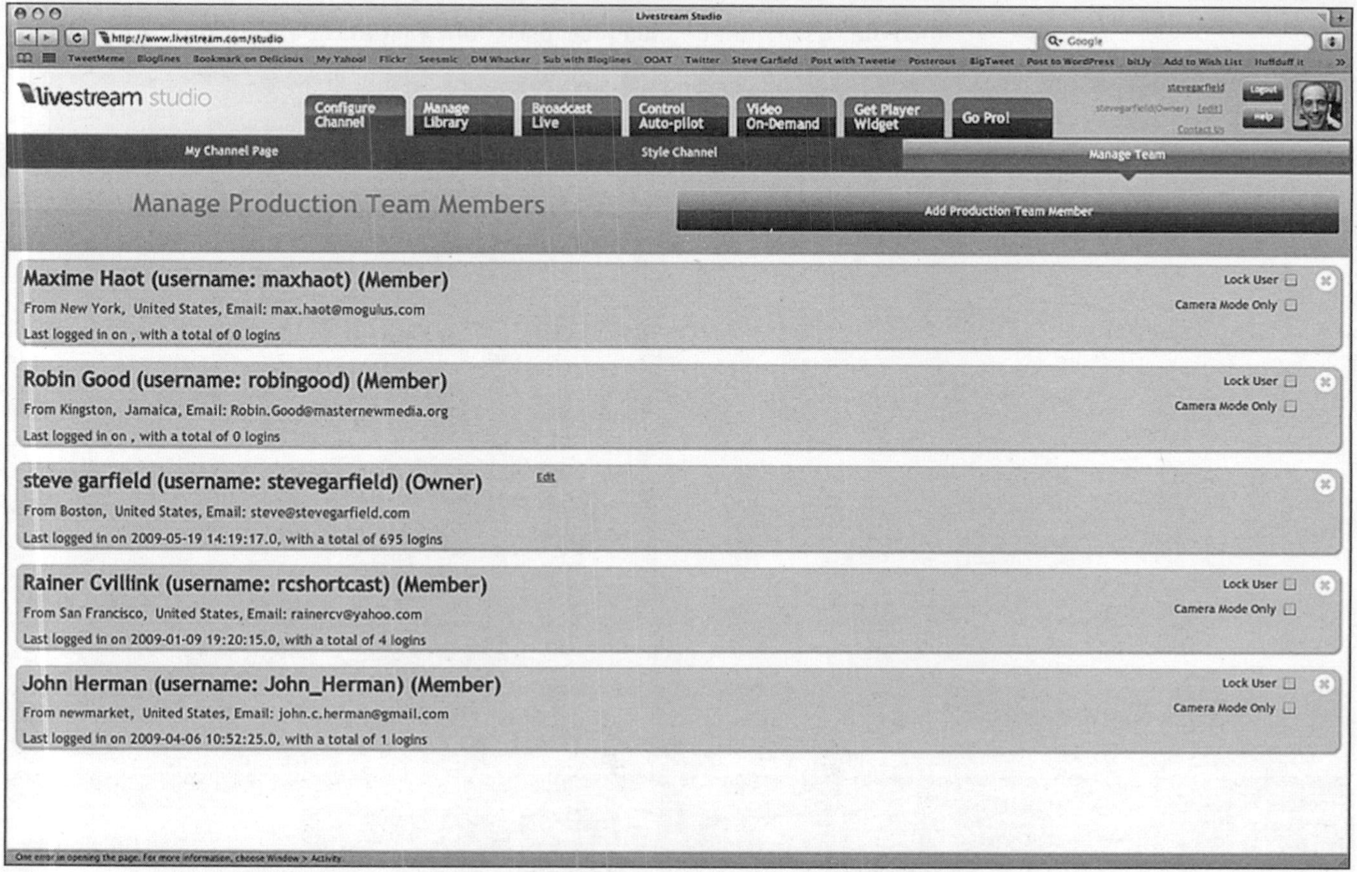

Figure 7.18   Configure Channel Page, Manage Team Tab on Livestream.com

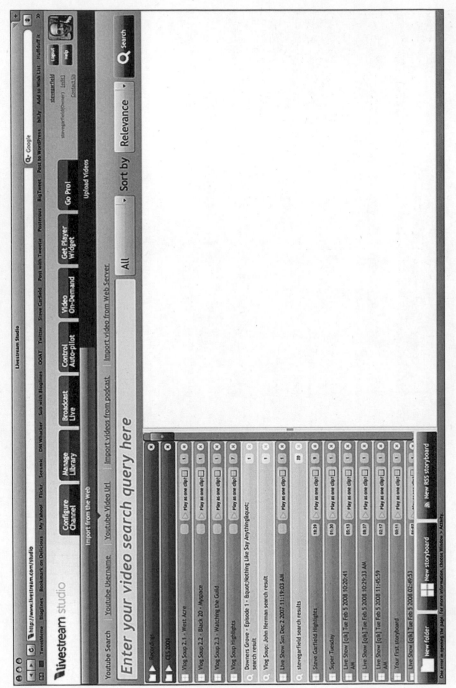

Figure 7.19   Manage Library Page on Livestream.com

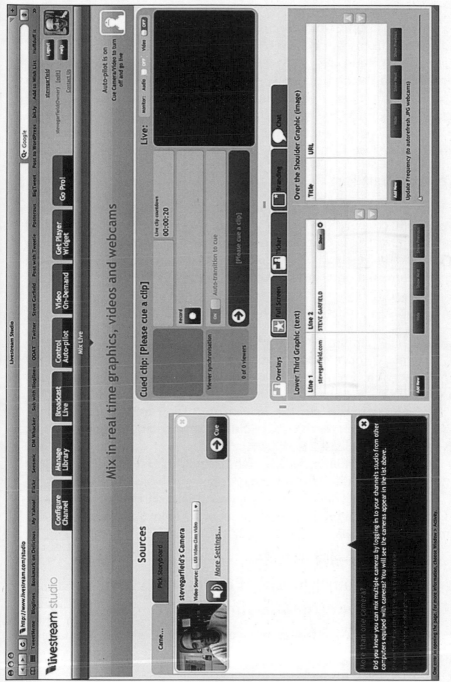

Figure 7.20   Broadcast Live Setup Page on Livestream.com

You can use the Auto-Pilot page (see Figure 7.21) to control which videos play from your channel. From the Video On-Demand page (see Figure 7.22), you can select which shows your viewers can video on-demand. On the Get Player Widget page (see Figure 7.23), you can customize the look of your embedded player and grab the code to use to add your video player to a web page. If you choose to get a premium account, you can do that from the Premium Features and Pricing page (see Figure 7.24).

VERIFYING YOUR FREE CHANNEL

Livestream Free channels are "unverified" and can stream to a maximum of 50 concurrent viewers at a time, and your channel is not listed at www.Livestream.com.

📁 Verified Livestream Free Channels get unlimited concurrent viewers, Livestream.com listing, and promotion eligibility.

UPGRADING TO A PREMIUM CHANNEL

Livestream Premium enables producers to stream at bit rates up to 1700 kbps. You can change the quality on your channel from the My Profile section. Premium channels receive priority transcoding and imported clips are encoded using the best-in-class On2 VP6 codec.

Broadcasters can put the Livestream player full screen and take this into the live mixer to display either a Livestream live feed or a Qik live feed on broadcast TV.

Livestream Premium is fully whitelabel (no Livestream branding) and can be embedded on any page/iframe (flash-based player).

Livestream Premium also supports monetization. Premium customers can plug in their advertising accounts from Scanscout, Adap.tv, and display pre-roll/overlay on their channel.

Estimate Your Monthly Premium Account Costs with the Livestream Estimator

I interviewed Max Haot from Livestream[47] about their Premium accounts.

---

[47]http://www.Livestream.com/estimator

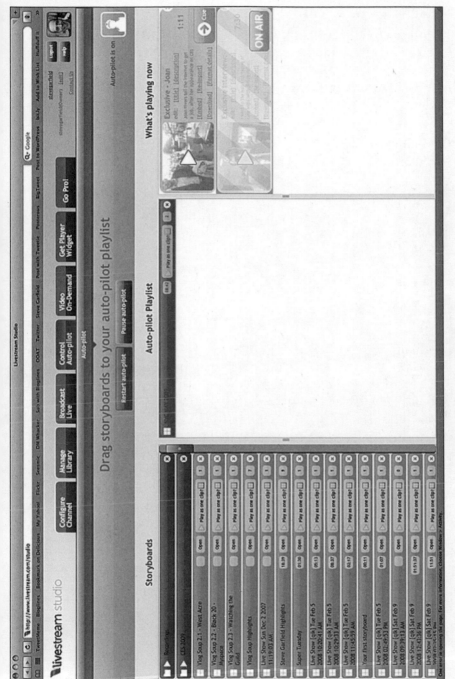

Figure 7.21 Manage Control Auto-Pilot on Livestream.com

Figure 7.22 Manage Video-On-Demand on Livestream.com

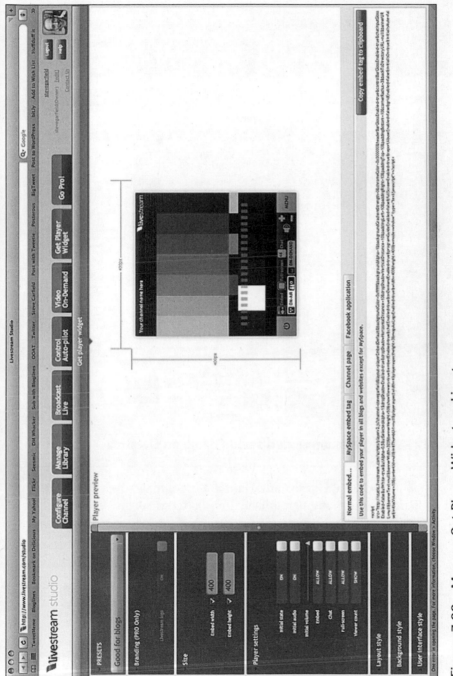

Figure 7.23   Manage Get Player Widget on Livestream.com

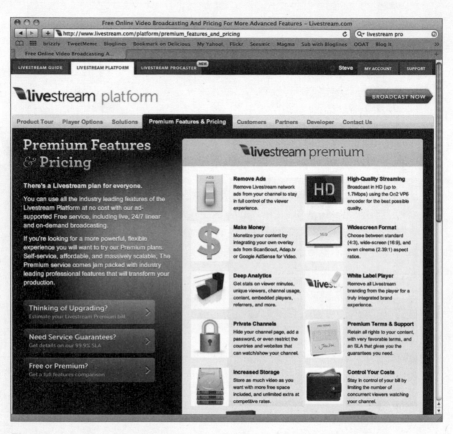

Figure 7.24   Premium Features and Pricing on Livestream.com

Max is CEO at Livestream. Haot is a recognized digital content industry pioneer and is regularly invited to speak and contribute at industry events/forums for the broadcast, broadband, and mobile industries.

Steve Garfield: Which tools make the most sense for TV reporters and how they work? How can TV stations bring the signals into the station or into their web site? Does Livestream have private label channels that can be iframed into a site?

Max Haot: Our Livestream Premium offering is fully whitelabel (no Livestream branding) and can be embedded on any page/iframe (flash-based player).

> *SG: How can TV stations monetize video content on their site?*
>
> *MH: We offer Livestream Premium,[48] which supports monetization. We also allow Premium customers to plug in their advertising accounts from Scanscout,[49] Adap.tv,[50] and display pre-roll/overlay on their channel.*
>
> *SG: Which tools should TV stations be looking at integrating into their news set to bring in the audience or remote reporter live shots?*
>
> *MH: Broadcasters put our player full screen and take this into the live mixer to display either a Livestream live feed or a Qik live feed on broadcast TV.*

Livestream How To: ProCaster

ProCaster is a nice streamlined application that brings one-click live streaming to the Livestream platform.

Livestream describes ProCaster[51] this way:

> *ProCaster is a new free desktop application that will dramatically and automatically boost your broadcasts to the absolute highest quality possible. It's also the simplest broadcasting application available, despite offering some great new features we think you're going to love. If you currently broadcast using the Livestream Studio or Flash Media Encoder you really should check it out. ProCaster is fully integrated with Livestream, including moderated control over your chat, Twitter, and 3D Effects that will turn any live presentation into an instant "Steve Jobs" keynote.*

Wow.

ProCaster (see Figure 7.25) can broadcast your screen, games, and supports chat.

---

[48] http://www.livestream.com/platform/premium_features_and_pricing

[49] http://www.scanscout.com/

[50] http://adap.tv/

[51] http://www.procaster.com/

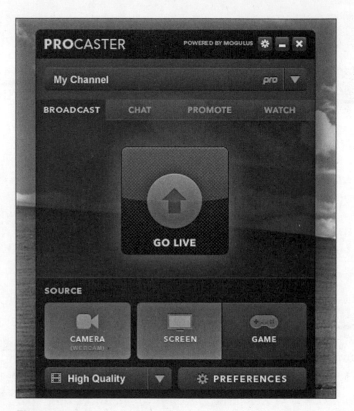

Figure 7.25

Twitter is integrated so you can send out Twitter posts from the system.

I tested this out with a configuration that included a MacBook Pro with a Firewire connected Canon GL/2 and an audio-technica AT2020 USB mic as one camera. The second camera was a Creative Labs VF0380 Live! webcam attached via USB to a Panasonic Tough-book laptop. I ran ProCaster on the Toughbook and it showed up on the Livestream Broadcast Studio on the MacBook Pro.

Then I was able to switch between cameras.

The difference is that with the Livestream Studio you can control camera switching and graphics, and it runs via a web browser off the Livestream web site.

ProCaster allows you to stream video to the Livestream Studio from the desktop application. It's a simple, easy-to-use broadcast application.

Figure 7.26   2–D Animation

The 2-D animation looks like Figure 7.26.

The 3-D animation looks like Figure 7.27.

It's an easy way to do a webcast, showing the presenter and their desktop.

Within the application you can set it to go live automatically. That means that you don't have to have someone running the Livestream Studio to start a live broadcast. You can also set ProCaster to add the recording of your live broadcast automatically to your on-demand library.

Livestream and Ustream with Telestream Wirecast

Wirecast (see Figure 7.28) is another program that allows you to stream live video to the Web. The interface is straightforward and supports switching between multiple cameras.

Figure 7.27   3-D Animation

The Telestream Press Release[52] explains:

Wirecast[53] is a software program for Mac OS X and Windows which allows you to mix multiple cameras and graphics in real time and broadcast to your Livestream or Ustream channel.

This is a fun program to use. Wirecast has a preview mode that allows you to set up your upcoming videos before putting them on air. So, for example, if you are going to switch from a recorded video to a live shot of someone for an interview, you can set up the lower

---

[52] http://www.telestream.net/company/press/2009-03-25.htm
[53] http://www.telestream.net/wire-cast/overview.htm

Figure 7.28   Wirecast Tutorial

third of the screen to display the interviewee's name and information. There are many templates to choose from for this feature. Animation is also built in so that when you make the video go live, the lower third graphic and text can fly in from either side. You can also set it to fly away when you switch to your next shot. Other animation options include Fade In, Spin In, Scale In, and Decelerate In. It doesn't have to be just from the side either, top, bottom, middle. It's flexible.

When you visit the Telestream web site,[54] you can download a demonstration copy of Wirecast that is fully functional. It overlays text and audio on top of your video so you won't be able to use the demonstration copy in a production environment, but you will be able to test out all its features.

---

[54] http://www.telestream.net/

Wirecast's broadcast options include the ability to stream to a QuickTime Streaming server, unicast to a single computer, multicast to a local network, and record to disk.

Recording to disk is a cool option that Wirecast offers. It allows you to produce a show "live to tape." That means that you could have multiple cameras, include photos and videos, switch between them all, and then upload your show without having to do any editing. That could save a lot of work, if you don't mind sharing an unedited show with the public.

To stream live to your Livestream channel from the menu bar, choose Broadcast, then Broadcast Settings.

From the Encoder Presets menu choose one of the Flash Encoder Presets.

For destination, choose Livestream and then enter the channel you want to stream to, username, and password.

Note: For Livestream Free channels you need to ensure that the total encoding bit rate is set no higher than 500 kbps. You can check the bit rate right on the Broadcast settings window. Flash Medium Bandwidth has a rate of 496 k. Flash HD Bandwidth as a bit rate of 1,128 k. That's too high for the Livestream Free channel.

From the Broadcast tab go to Network Broadcast and then Start All to begin encoding.

This is the solution for multiple camera support that many people have been asking for.

Wirecast recognizes your cameras and then displays them so that you can switch between them. In my test I used the in-built iSight camera on my MacBook Pro and a Canon GL/2 connected via a dual port Firewire card.

Note: Livestream also supports multiple cameras, but each camera should have its own computer.

GET SEEN: Livestream Livepack lets you broadcast from a DV camera, connected to a LiveU backpack, over cell phone networks. No longer will you need a local Internet connection.

Multiple People in a Video Chat

Do you want to have a video conference among multiple people?

Here are a few options.

TokBox

Video Twitter. That's what TokBox[55] feels like when you have a group of people in a chat room (see Figure 7.29), hanging out and talking. When I tested it, I was in a group that averaged eight people. I had to step away for a moment, and the conversation kept on going—much like Twitter, where there is no focal point. I found this very interesting.

You don't have to be a user to get into a video chat. One click gets you in.

TokBox[56] lets you make a video call, send a video e-mail, and have a free video conference with no sign ups required.

Here I'm having a video call with Phil Campbell (see Figure 7.30). I'm in Boston and he's in England. If you are signed on to TokBox, it's like saying that you are available for a video chat. Unlike video instant messaging tools like the Mac's iChat, by signing on you are saying you are present and available to chat with others.

TokBox has got a nice interface, and you can invite people who are not even signed up to have a video chat or send them a video e-mail.

Easy.

Stickam

I was encouraged to try out Stickam[57] as an alternative. Stickam does a lot of live shows; check them out.

---

[55] http://www.tokbox.com/

[56] http://www.tokbox.com/#

[57] http://www.stickam.com

Figure 7.29   Screenshot of TokBox Video Conference by Phil Campbell

Figure 7.30   TokBox Video Call with Phil Campbell

ooVoo

OoVoo[58] is a video chat for up to six people at once.

Two-way chats are free. For more than two people there are premium plans that are pay per use or a pay per month plan. Premium video plans are high resolution and allow you to record and save video sessions.

TinyChat

TinyChat[59] lets you make your own video chat room that can hold up to 12 people on video and 100 on text chat. It's free for the basic chat room. A Pro version has added features, including desktop sharing, HQ upgraded video, password options, and the ability to record and save your conferences.

FM.EA-TEL

Fm.ea-tel[60] was the original video chat room the video blogging community used back in 2004. With this chat room, one person talks at a time.

---

[58] http://www.oovoo.com/
[59] http://tinychat.com
[60] http://fm.ea-tel.eu/fm

8

Video Blogging—Why You Might Want a Blog

What Is a Blog?

A blog is a selection of posts, usually in reverse chronological order, which are accessible by a permanent link. The content of a blog post can be text and/or media like audio, images, or video.

ARE TWITTER AND FACEBOOK BLOGS?

Yes. Technically Twitter and Facebook are blogs. They meet the technical criteria of being a blogging system. Facebook, in addition to being a blog, also has many more features. But the key feature of being a system where individual posts can be linked to via a permalink is there.

Oprah's on Facebook!

There was a lot of excitement when Oprah joined Twitter.[1] Her first Twitter post linking to a video was to a video someone on her staff recorded with a Flip mino camera and hosted on Facebook (see Figure 8.1).

Here's her tweet:[2]

"Behind the scenes with my flipcam . . .

http://tiny.cc/T4WYl"

---

[1] http://twitter.com/oprah
[2] http://twitter.com/Oprah/status/1587006527

222

Figure 8.1   Oprah Flip Video on Facebook

That leads to this page on Facebook.[3]

That's a pretty straightforward way to put video on the Web, other than using the in-built Flip "post to YouTube" feature.

Everyone Is on Facebook

If you don't have the resources to build your own site, you can make use of community sites like Facebook to build a community.

---

[3] http://www.facebook.com/video/video.php?v=68650473188

As part of the Facebook infrastructure you can upload and share videos, and your community can, too.

There are a number of ways to share videos on Facebook.

Things to consider.

Video quality

Facebook allows uploading of HD quality video. When embedded on a web page, it also plays in HD quality. This is a unique feature.

With their standard embed code, YouTube plays standard quality video. When embedded elsewhere, you need to go back to YouTube and click the Watch in High Quality link to watch HD quality videos.

Play count

If you want to keep track of the number of views your video receives, then uploading it to Facebook is not a good idea. They do not make public those statistics.

Terms of service

Make sure you read and understand the terms of service of Facebook and any site you upload content to.

YOU'VE GOT YOUTUBE IN MY FACEBOOK

TIP: You can post a video on YouTube and embed it on your Facebook page.

Five Steps

Step 1: Go to Profile.

Step 2: Click in the What's on your mind? box. Then click Link.

Step 3: Enter the YouTube URL.

Step 4: Click Attach.

Step 5: Click Share.

FACEBOOK FAN PAGES ARE OPEN TO THE WORLD

A fan page on Facebook is now a lot more powerful than a regular Facebook page because fan pages are visible to Google.

Katie Couric, anchor of *CBS Evening News with Katie Couric*, has a fan page on Facebook.[4]

In preparation for a report on President Obama's first 100 days, Couric solicited videos from viewers. Facebook is a great platform for that.

When Couric started at *CBS Evening News*, I suggested that she solicit videos from viewers and created a sample site for her called "Say it to Katie." She became aware of it and I got to meet her on the set of the *CBS Evening News*.

She is as nice in person as she seems on TV.

Now back to the Facebook video submission process.

On Couric's post requesting videos, people are allowed to comment, but not submit videos. You need to write on her wall to do that.

Here are the steps to upload a video. These are the same steps as uploading a video to your own Facebook account, but here you click on the person's wall to start:

Five Steps

Step 1: Go to the Wall. Click in the white space writing area of the Write Something . . . box.

Step 2: Click Video.

Step 3: Click Upload a Video from your drive.

Step 4: Click Choose File. The video file size must be less than 1024MB and 20 minutes. Choose the file.

Step 5: Click Share.

Figure 8.2 shows my video explaining how to do this.[5]

Once you record your video, you can play it to see if you like it, then click Share to save it. Unfortunately, you can't choose your thumbnail.

---

[4] http://www.facebook.com/KatieCouric
[5] http://www.facebook.com/video/video.php?v=75018002019&oid=41545764992

Figure 8.2   My Video Submission to Katie Couric

The online recording quality is good. If you want to be better you can always record a video locally on your computer and upload it.

Note: Couric also posted the same request for video on YouTube.[6]

The thing to think about is if you want to have your blog live within another system or live on its own.

A Transport Mechanism

A blog can also be thought of as a transport mechanism for your content. Once you post your video to a blog, because it has a permanent

---

[6] http://www.youtube.com/watch?v=JnDHYDHmJnk

Figure 8.3   Embed Code on a YouTube Page

link, you can then share that link to your content with a large number of third-party systems. The technology to do this is Really Simple Syndication (RSS). RSS is used to distribute your blog content all over the Web. So the process of putting a new video on your blog can be looked at as the first step in delivering your content to people.

For those of you reading this book who have not yet put a video on YouTube, the secret is that it's not hard.

You could post all of your videos to YouTube and send people there to watch them. It's easy to do.

Go to YouTube.com, click Upload, then select Video File or Quick Capture.

That's what Miles Beckett and Greg Goodfried, the producers of LonelyGirl15,[7] did when they first rolled out their groundbreaking video series on YouTube.

Once your video is on YouTube you can link to it or post it on your blog.

To post the video to your blog, you just copy the embed code and paste it into a blog post (see Figure 8.3).

The embed code starts with "<object width . . ."

Done.

Times have changed and the LonelyGirl15 team learned from their first web series that what you really want to do is drive people to your own site.

Now LonelyGirl15 lives at its own domain, www.lg15.com (see Figure 8.4).[8]

---

[7] http://www.youtube.com/profile?user=lonelygirl15
[8] http://www.lg15.com/

Figure 8.4 Lonely Girl15 Web Page

The videos are still on YouTube, but they are also embedded in a blog.

There are many benefits to setting up a blog for your content and videos.

A blog gives you:

- A home on the Web to point people to.

- A place to post links to sites you find interesting.

- Features that are not available for you on video hosting sites like YouTube.

Let's look at some blogging platforms so you can get a sense of what's out there.

Starting Your Blog

HOW TO: CREATE A BLOG WITH POSTEROUS

With Posterous you can start a blog by just sending in an e-mail. It's one of the simplest ways to set up a blog.

Send an e-mail to Posterous at post@posterous.com to get started (see Figure 8.5).

Sachin Agarwal, co-founder of Posterous, describes the video features of Posterous:

> *Posterous is the easiest way to share video online because you simply e-mail the file to Posterous, and we handle the rest. We'll do all the transcoding (convert to flash) and hosting, and we'll create a great player for you. Since you have e-mail access at home, work, and on your mobile device,*

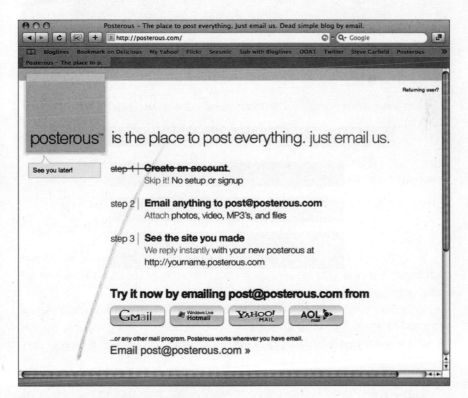

Figure 8.5   Posterous Web Page

Figure 8.6

you can share video quickly and easier no matter where you are.

Sending In a Video

I created a quick video using QuickTime Pro (see Figure 8.6).

Then I attached it to an e-mail and sent it to post@posterous.com (see Figure 8.7).

Posterous takes care of the Flash conversion as Sachin explains earlier, and sends you an e-mail when the video has been transcoded and posted to your blog (see Figure 8.8).

This way you don't need to bother with knowing any compression settings or spend time waiting for a video export to process. So for someone who just wants to quickly post video to a blog, this is a very straightforward way to do it.

Record, Save, E-mail.

Three steps.

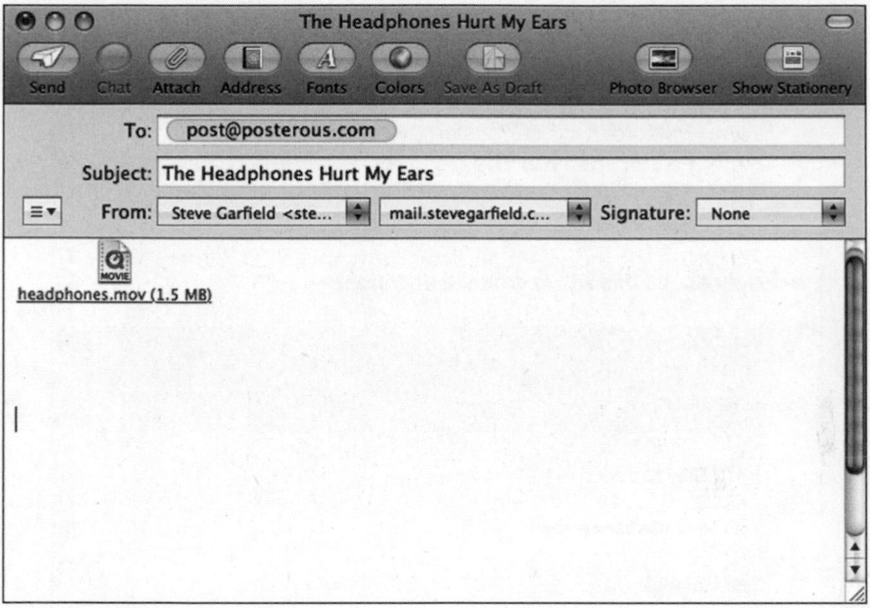

Figure 8.7

Here's the video on my Posterous blog (see Figure 8.9).[9]
The video quality is very good.

Autopost

Once set up, you can have Posterous automatically post elsewhere when you make a post.

I entered my Twitter sign-on information into Posterous, so when I e-mailed the My Video into Posterous, once it was posted to my blog, Posterous automatically made a post to Twitter for me (see Figure 8.10).

Autopost via E-Mail

Posterous also allows you to autopost via e-mail to any sites you register with them.

---

[9] http://stevegarfield.posterous.com/the-headphones-hurt-my-ears

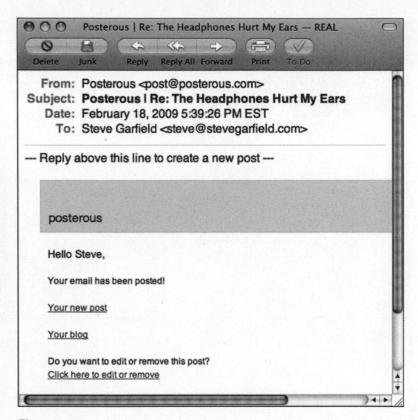

Figure 8.8

Here are some of the sites and the e-mail addresses you can use:

Twitter twitter@posterous.com

Flickr flickr@posterous.com

Facebook facebook@posterous.com

Shopify shopify@posterous.com

Tumblr tumblr@posterous.com

Any other blog blog@posterous.com

Posterous only posterous@posterous.com

Combine them flickr+twitter@posterous.com

That makes it easy if you want to update your sites via e-mail.

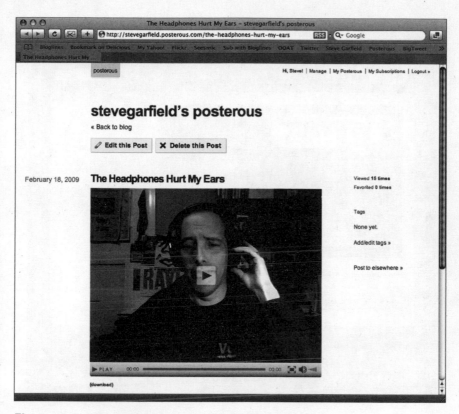

Figure 8.9   The Headphones Hurt My Ears

Figure 8.10   Twitter Post

Figure 8.11   Heather Peterson[10]

How To: Create a Blog with Tumblr

Tumblr is a fun way to blog, easy to set up, and has nice template choices. Hrrrthrrr has a fun tumblr blog (see Figure 8.11).

From the tumblr dashboard, clicking on the Video icon brings you to tumblr's Add a Video page (see Figure 8.12).[11]

Your two options are to Embed a Video or Upload a Video.

Embed a Video

If you've already posted a video somewhere on the Web, or identified a video you want to share on your blog, all you need is the video's URL or embed code.

---

[10] http://hrrrthrrr.tumblr.com
[11] http://www.tumblr.com/new/video

Figure 8.12   Tumblr's Add a Video Page—Embed a Video Tab

For a YouTube video it's easy.

Paste in a YouTube video URL, add a caption (optional) (see Figure 8.13).

Press Create Post.

The post is created. It's so easy (see Figure 8.14).

Upload a Video

The other option is to upload a video from your computer.

Tumblr has teamed up with Vimeo for video uploads.

Click Sign Up or Log In and you'll be able to authorize tumblr to access, edit, upload, and delete your Vimeo videos.

Click Yeah, Let's Do It! to proceed.

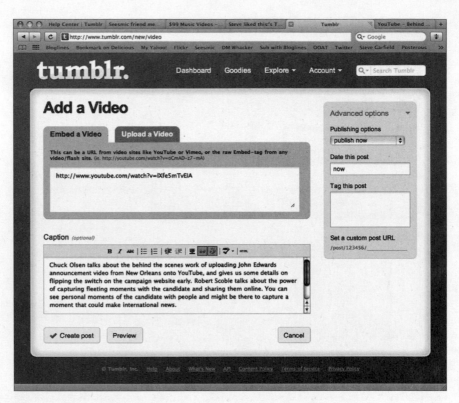

Figure 8.13   Add a Video Page with YouTube URL Entered

Now you can upload a video to Vimeo via tumblr. From the Add a Video page (see Figure 8.15), give it a title, then choose a file and optionally write a caption.

Once you start using tumblr, you'll start to see that it's more than just a regular blog. It's a community of people. Part of the way you can see this is by the reblog feature (see Figure 8.16).

When you are on a post that you like, click Reblog (see Figure 8.19).

This brings up the reblog entry page (see Figure 8.17). Here you can edit what your post will look like. In this example, I want to add, "I like it, too."

Once done modifying your post, click ReBlog Post.

The item you just reblogged is now on your own tumblr blog, ready for being reblogged itself (see Figure 8.18).

Figure 8.14   Tumblr Blog Post with Embedded Video

I "Heart" this Post

Another thing that's easy to use is the Like feature. When you're on someone's tumblr blog, you might like one of their posts and want to indicate that you like it.

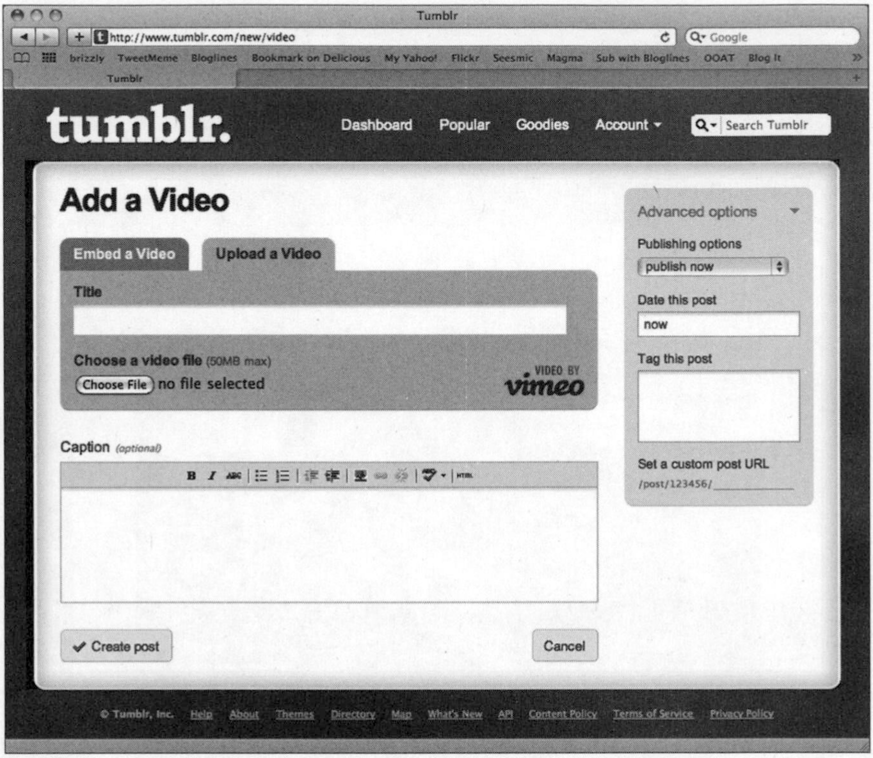

Figure 8.15   Add a Video Page—Upload a Video Tab with Vimeo
Enabled

The way you do that is to click the little heart you'll see near the
blog post. If you don't see a little heart, just go to the posts' permanent
page and there you'll see a heart icon.

Once you indicate that you like it, an entry is posted in that item's
notes.

Figure 8.16

Figure 8.17   ReBlog Audio Post

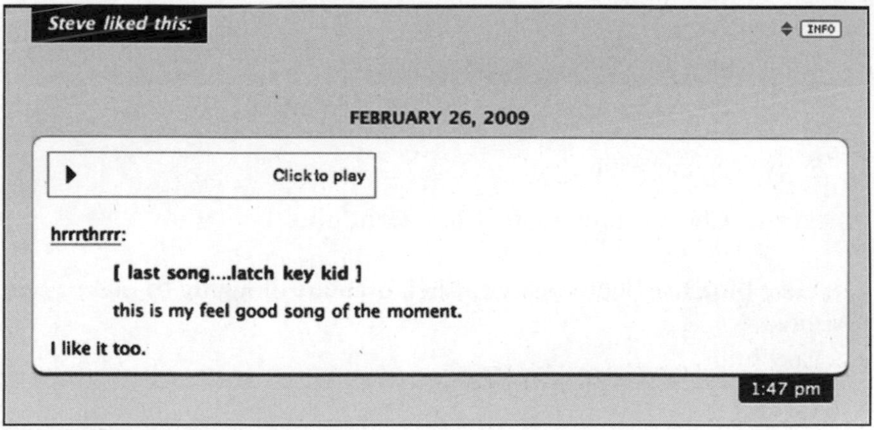

Figure 8.18

Audio Posts and More

Zadi Diaz says, "You can make call-in audio posts on tumblr now.[12] You can now also save drafts and schedule posts. :)"

Gary Vaynerchuk uses tumblr.[13]

Tumble from Your iPhone

The Tumblr Goodies page[14] has neat tools like the iPhone App that allows you to post text, photos, and audio to your tumblr blog from the iPhone.

How To: Create a Blog with Blogger

Creating a blog at blogger.com[15] is one of the easiest ways to get started. Along with being able to post videos on your blog, you can also keep people up-to-date with what you are doing.

I suggest blogger.com for new video bloggers because it lets you embed videos from many different video-hosting sites without having to learn any special codes. It's free and is a good blogging tool to use to distribute your videos out to other sites like iTunes, Twitter, and friendfeed. You can think of it as a video distribution engine.

Want to use another blogging platform? Skip ahead for Wordpress.com, Wordpress.org, and TypePad. They all have different costs and benefits.

Here's how to set up a blog on blogger.

First you need to create an account at blogger.com.

Step 1: Name your blog.

Step 2: Choose a template. Click Continue.

Your blog has been created. Click on Start Blogging to make your first post.

Easy huh?

---

[12] http://www.tumblr.com/goodies
[13] http://garyvaynerchuk.com/
[14] http://www.tumblr.com/goodies
[15] http://blogger.com

Create Your First Blog Post

All you need to do here is type in a title and some content in your first post.

Lots of people use Hello World as their first title. That's a standard procedure for programmers writing their first program. I wrote a Hello World program in BASIC when I learned that programming language, but that's not important right now.

Write your post and click Publish Post.

Adding Video to Your Blog Post—Quick Tip

Adding video to your blog is going to be easy now that you know how to create a post.

Video from Your Computer

To add a video from your computer, from the new post page click the little film strip icon. Then from the 'Add a video to your blog post' dialog box, choose a video and click Upload Video.

Video from YouTube

Here's how you can quickly add a YouTube video to your blog. Let's share the "Where the Hell is Matt?" (2008) video on our blog. Here's a direct link to the video on YouTube.[16]

On YouTube there's a box on the right-hand side of the page that gives information about the video (see Figure 8.19).

Copy the code from the Embed box and paste it into a new blog post.

YouTube embed code:

```
<object width="480" height="295"><param name="movie"
value="http://www.youtube.com/v/zlfKdbWwruY&hl=en&fs=1"
></param><param name="allowFullScreen"
value="true"></param><param name="allowscriptaccess"
value="always"></param><embed
src="http://www.youtube.com/v/zlfKdbWwruY&hl=en&fs=1"
type="application/x-shockwave-flash"
allowscriptaccess="always" allowfullscreen="true"
width="480" height="295"></embed></object>
```

---

[16] http://www.youtube.com/watch?v=zlfKdbWwruY

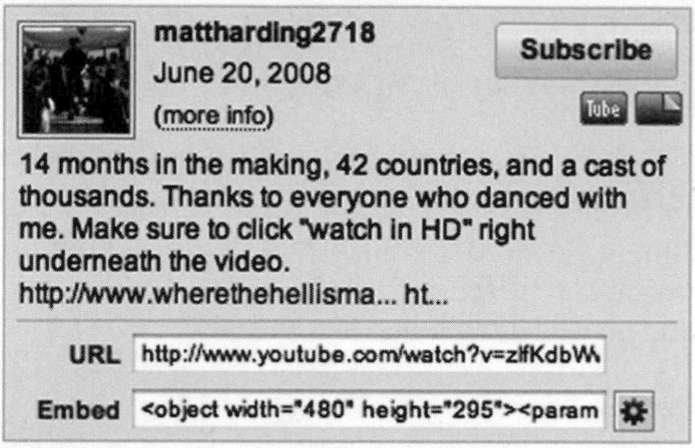

Figure 8.19

Note: The default size is 480 × 295. You can click on the gear icon next to the Embed box to choose other sizes like 425 × 264, 560 × 345, or 640 × 385.

Note: Make sure the Edit HTML tab is selected when you paste in the embed code from YouTube (see Figure 8.20).

Click Publish Post. The video is then posted to your blog (see Figure 8.21).

Adjusting Your Blog Template to Fit Videos

Depending on the template you chose in Step 2, the video might not fit into the width of your blog.

In my example, I used the default minima template. It turns out that the width of the body of the template isn't wide enough to fit the whole width of the YouTube video.

To fix this, you have to edit the HTML of your template, or choose a different template that's wider. The next section talks about choosing a different template, but I want to take a moment to show you how to edit your blogger template because you might need to know how in the future.

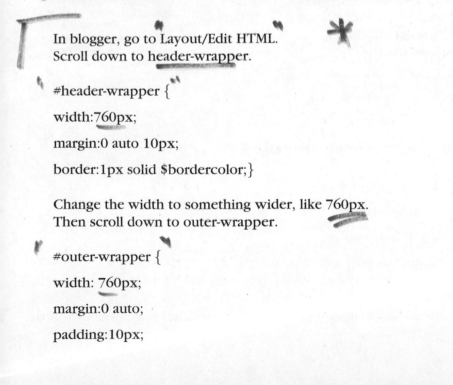

Figure 8.20   YouTube Embed Code Pasted into Edit HTML Page

In blogger, go to Layout/Edit HTML.
Scroll down to header-wrapper.

#header-wrapper {

width:760px;

margin:0 auto 10px;

border:1px solid $bordercolor;}

Change the width to something wider, like 760px.
Then scroll down to outer-wrapper.

#outer-wrapper {

width: 760px;

margin:0 auto;

padding:10px;

GET SEEN: ONLINE VIDEO SECRETS

BLOG FOR THE UPCOMING WILEY BOOK "GET SEEN: ONLINE VIDEO SECRETS" (DECEMBER, 2009)

WEDNESDAY, FEBRUARY 4, 2009

Where the Hell is Matt? (2008)

POSTED BY STEVE GARFIELD AT 4:54 AM   0 COMMENTS

Hello World

This is my first post. Hello.

POSTED BY STEVE GARFIELD AT 4:39 AM   0 COMMENTS

FOLLOWERS (0)

FOLLOW THIS BLOG
BE THE FIRST TO FOLLOW THIS BLOG
0 FOLLOWERS MANAGE

BLOG ARCHIVE

▼ 2009 (2)

 ▼ February (2)

  Where the Hell is Matt? (2008)
  Hello World

ABOUT ME

STEVE GARFIELD

Steve Garfield is an advisor to media and internet companies about online video, a speaker at conferences on mobile video broadcasting, video producer and teacher.

VIEW MY COMPLETE PROFILE

Subscribe to: Posts (Atom)

Figure 8.21   YouTube Video on a Blog

text-align:$startSide;

font: $bodyfont;}

#main-wrapper {

width: 540px;

float: $startSide;

word-wrap: break-word; /* fix for long text breaking sidebar float in IE */

overflow: hidden; /* fix for long non-text content breaking IE sidebar float */}

#sidebar-wrapper {

width: 220px;

float: $endSide;

word-wrap: break-word; /* fix for long text breaking sidebar float in IE */

overflow: hidden; /* fix for long non-text content breaking IE sidebar float */}

Change the outer-wrapper to 760px and the main-wrapper to 540px and the sidebar_wrapper to 220px.

After making the template changes, the video fits on the blog (see Figure 8.22).

More Ways to Post YouTube Videos on Your Blog

Take a look at blogger help, help.blogger.com,[17] for more ways to post YouTube videos on your blog.

CUSTOM TEMPLATES

The default templates aren't the most creative pieces of art ever designed, so you might want to use a custom template. The easiest way to do that is to choose one that's already been designed.

There are a few places I've found where you can find custom templates for your blogger blog:

BTemplates:[18] Free blogger templates for your blog.

Falcon Hive: Zinmag Remedy[19]

---

[17] http://help.blogger.com/bin/answer.py?hl=en&answer=80767

[18] http://btemplates.com/2

[19] http://www.falconhive.com/2008/12/blogger-template-zinmag-remedy.html

Figure 8.22   Video Now Fits on Blog

This is the blogger template I'm going to install:

BTemplates Notepad Chaos (see Figure 8.23).[20]

To get the template, click Download.
A new file is saved to your computer.
In this example the name of the file is Notepad-Chaos.xml
Then in blogger, go to Layout/Edit Html/Upload a template from
a file on your hard drive (see Figure 8.24).
Click Choose File.
Choose the downloaded file. Press Upload, then press Save.

---

[20] http://btemplates.com/2008/09/18/1257/

Figure 8.23   Notepad Chaos

Figure 8.24   Upload a Template

Here's the blog we created with the new template:

newenglandstories.blogspot.com[21]

Note: Choose a new template before adding any widgets. If you have widgets, delete them, then choose a new template. Clearing browser cache might also resolve any blogger errors.

Enhancing Your Blog

Choosing a Theme

You can choose to become a thought leader by focusing your blog on a specific topic and writing about it regularly. Politics, sports, weather . . . You choose. Thanks Chris Brogan.[22]

Standard Domain

When you create a blog with blogger, the easiest way is to let blogger host your blog at blogspot.com. Your blog will have the URL of blogname.blogspot.com.

Many blogs go this easy route. Some people consider blogs that have the blogspot name in their URLs to be second-class or spam blogs, but that is not always the case.

Here are some examples from Google, using the blogspot name in the URL:

News from Google: googlepress.blogspot.com[23]

Google Sites Blog: googlesitesblog.blogspot.com[24]

The Official Google Blog: googleblog.blogspot.com[25]

---

[21] http://newenglandstories.blogspot.com
[22] http://ChrisBrogan.com/
[23] http://googlepress.blogspot.com
[24] http://googlesitesblog.blogspot.com
[25] http://googleblog.blogspot.com

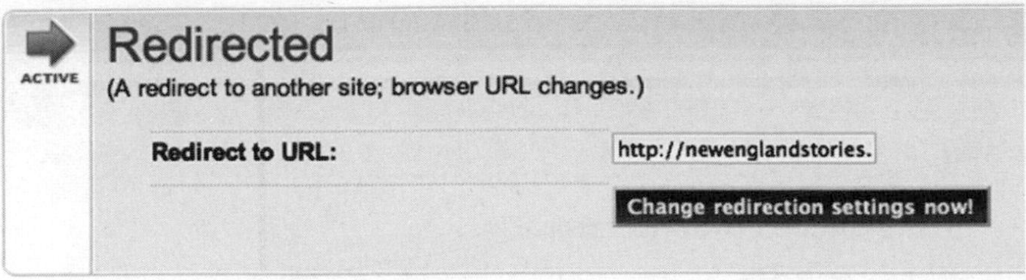

Figure 8.25   Dreamhost Redirect Page

My blog is hosted on blogspot, offonatangent.blogspot.com.[26] I also own the domain name offonatangent.com[27] with redirects to offonatangent.blogspot.com.

Here's how you can redirect or forward domains.

CUSTOM DOMAIN—OWN YOUR OWN: FOWARDING

In this example, when someone keys in nestories.com[28] they will be forwarded to newenglandstories.blogspot.com.

I use Dreamhost[29] to buy domains. This gives you the ability to add lots of hosting options later.

On Dreamhost we used the redirect option to redirect traffic from http://nestories.com to newenglandstories.blogspot.com (see Figure 8.25).

Note: You can also publish your blogspot blog to your own site by FTP but "you will need to Set 'Blog Readers' to 'Anybody' and use a Classic Template."[30] That's not a good idea.

CUSTOM DOMAIN—PURCHASED FROM GOOGLE

In this example your newenglandstories.blogspot.com will be changed to nestories.com.

---

[26] http://offonatangent.blogspot.com
[27] http://offonatangent.com
[28] http://nestories.com
[29] http://Dreamhost.com
[30] http://www.blogger.com/html?blogID=838402916760373941

Figure 8.26   Publishing Settings

On blogger you can go to Settings/Publishing and buy a custom domain for your blog from Google for $10.

You can see that under Settings/Publishing. Click on Custom Domain (see Figure 8.26).

From there you can buy your blog a custom URL (see Figure 8.27).

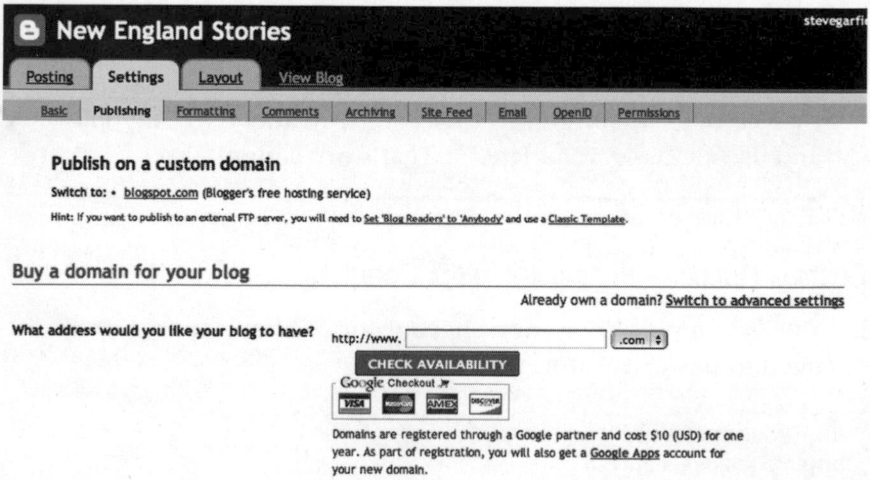

Figure 8.27   Buy a Domain for Your Blog

Domains are registered through a Google partner and cost $10 (USD) for one year. As part of registration, you will also get a **Google Apps**[31] account for your new domain.

Custom Domain—Own Your Own: Creating a CNAME Record

In this example your newenglandstories.blogspot.com will also be changed to nestories.com.

If you already own a domain, click on Switch to Advanced Settings.

From there you can set up your existing domain to point to your blogspot blog. Your blogspot URL will also point to your custom domain.

There are detailed instructions at Blogger Help.[32]

Thoughts On: Creating a Blog with Wordpress.com

Wordpress.com[33] is the free version of the hosted wordpress.org. Wordpress.com is a lot like blogger.com because it's free and easy to use. I use it on some of my sites.

One thing that's nice about Wordpress.com is that in addition to having your main blog page, you can add additional pages on your site. These can be anything, About, Services, Directions. That's a nice feature.

Video

When writing a blog post, you can insert video by clicking the Upload/Insert video icon.

After clicking, you can upload a video from your computer or paste in a URL from somewhere on the Web.

After you paste in the URL, Wordpress formats for display on your blog (see Figure 8.28).

The code looks like this:

The input area is similar to the blogger.com input area. If you are copying and pasting directly into the blog post you need to paste

---

[31] http://www.google.com/a/?hl=en

[32] http://help.blogger.com/bin/answer.py?answer=55373

[33] http://wordpress.com

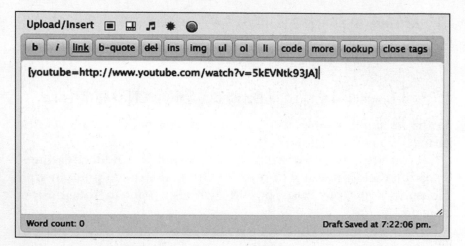

Figure 8.28   Wordpress YouTube Format

in the YouTube URL into the custom WordPress.com embed code [youtube=], like this:

```
[youtube=http://www.youtube.com/watch?v=HfM36BI8ReA&amp;
ap=%2526fmt%3D18]
```

Note: If you paste in the standard YouTube EMBED code, Wordpress.com will convert it to this custom format.

Thoughts On: Creating a Blog with Wordpress.org

Wordpress.org[34] is a popular blog-hosting platform. The wordpress code itself is free, but you need to have a host to run it on. Hosting sites like Dreamhost will let you run Dreamhost on them, but once you install it, you become a system administrator. That means you have to make sure you perform regular backups and keep the wordpress software current by applying regular updates.

If you are technical, wordpress.org-hosted blogging solutions are a feature rich and flexible blogging platform, but you need to learn how to install, maintain, and run it.

---

[34] http://wordpress.org

Figure 8.29   Paul Dateh

You might want to consider getting someone to help you with it, if that's the platform you choose to use for your video blog.

There are some interesting themes that are available to turn the wordpress.org-hosted solution in to a custom video site.

Musician Paul Dateh[35] uses TV elements for his video blog. TV Elements[36] provides a Hulu-style interface (see Figure 8.29).

VIDEOPRESS FOR WORDPRESS.COM.

No Bandwidth worries.

VideoPress[37] is the video upload add-on to WordPress[38] that converts your video into DVD quality, HD quality, iTunes, and Miro. You can embed your videos anywhere. This service includes statistics and costs a monthly fee.

Step 1: From the Add New Post page on WordPress.com, Click the Movie icon beside where it says Upload/Insert.

---

[35] http://pauldateh.com/

[36] http://www.press75.com/demos/tvelements/

[37] http://videopress.com/

[38] http://support.wordpress.com/videos/

Step 2: Click Select Files where it says Choose Files to Upload. After you select the file, it will be uploaded. You'll see a progress bar as the file uploads. Once the video is uploaded, you can add a Title and description.

Step 3. Click Insert into Post.

> **GET SEEN: If a video you've uploaded goes out of sync, where the words don't match the video, try exporting with different settings. Sometimes the encoding process doesn't work well with raw QuickTime files. I know, it's weird.**

Thoughts On: Creating a Blog with TypePad

TypePad[39] is a hosted blogging platform that charges a yearly fee. The benefit of TypePad is that you don't need to install or maintain your own hosted solution.

I've used TypePad since January 1, 2004, when I started my first video blog (see Figure 8.30). Never had a problem with uptime.

You can see my video blog at stevegarfield.com.[40]

TypePad is a clean, paid solution, as an alternative.

Steve Garfield's
Video Blog

Figure 8.30

---

[39] http://typepad.com
[40] http://stevegarfield.com

Thoughts On: Creating a Web Site with iWeb

Apple's iWeb lets you use drag and drop tools to put video on the Web.

You can easily drag a YouTube Widget onto your iWeb page and then paste in a YouTube's video URL.

One feature missing from iWeb is the ability to add custom title tags, meta tags, and alternative image text. These features are used to help search engines find your site. The iWeb SEO Tool allows you to add this information. You can get a free copy at www.ragesw.com.

VIDEO COMMENTS IN BLOGS

There are a number of solutions for adding video comments on a blog.

These include Viddler, Seesmic, and Intense Debate Plug In.[41]

Thoughts on Video Hosting by Dan Rayburn, EVP for StreamingMedia.com

WHY YOU SHOULD KNOW DAN RAYBURN

Dan Rayburn is recognized by many as the voice for the streaming and online video industry.

Steve Garfield: Where do you recommend people host videos and why?

Dan Rayburn: For major media companies and those who need a very customizable platform, services like Brightcove start around $500 a month. There are so many options available on the market so it's important that when it comes to hosting, deciding on the right solution should be based entirely on your business model and your budget.

(continued)

---

[41] http://blog.intensedebate.com/2009/03/05/introducing-intensedebate-plugins-add-the-features-you-want/

For those whose online video business requires things like syndication, advertising, or custom player options, you'll need to use a service like Brightcove, which is enabled for more functionality. In the online video platform world, you do get what you pay for. The more expensive services tend to give customers a lot more custom functionality with their platforms and typically are geared toward those who are trying to make money from online video.

The best way to pick the right solution is to look at what platforms other content owners are using. Find videos on the Web that are similar to yours or in the same industry vertical as you are and see how they are hosting them. Who are they using? Check out their content, see how customized their video player is, see what the video quality looks like and then make your decision. Keep in mind that with most of these platforms, you can usually get a trial account or demo their system for 30 days. Get hands-on with multiple solutions, see what kind of bells and whistles they have and then decide which one is best for you.

Make It Easy for Your Audience to Sit Back and Watch Videos

Embedded show players make it easier for viewers to watch your videos. When you have a single video embedded in a blog, you need to visit another blog post to see another video.

If you use a show player, the viewer can watch one video, and then when that video is over, you can have another video play, or you can have a selection of video to choose from to watch next. Different hosting sites provide different types of show players.

They can live on the video-hosting site or they can be embedded in yours.

YouTube has two kinds of show player, a YouTube Player and a YouTube Playlist.

YouTube Custom Page

Homebuilder Lennar is on Twitter, has Facebook and YouTube pages, but also has a custom page on their web site called Lennar TV,[42] which displays a menu of their YouTube videos that are available for playing right on the Lennar web site. It's a nice-looking implementation.

---

[42] http://www.lennar.com/buy-a-home/podcasts.aspx

Interviews

Interview: Kevin Dando

Why You Should Know Kevin Dando

Kevin Dando is Director, Education and Online Communications at PBS and is working to make PBS videos easy to find on the Web. In our interview, Dando shares tips you can use when posting your video online to help them become easy to find.

Kevin Dando: For a few years now, we've really been syndicating quite a lot of our content out there and we've been really lucky because PBS, also for a long time, has really been thoughtful about getting content out there away from pbs.org. When we first started talking about doing this, we encountered no resistance from anyone who said the only thing we want to do is just drive traffic back to pbs.org. They wanted the content to be out there where people see videos. So, we've been syndicating video to several different video sites including YouTube, Blip, Yahoo!, and Google TV or Google video while it's still around, and we've had great success with it. We're into about 2,000 different clips now. We're putting up about 30 clips a week.

Actually, they're both general audience content and kids content. So, we're putting kids content up in YouTube, too. Ironically, our kids clips are the ones that are most viewed. So, we have a couple hundred clips from PBS Kids and PBS Kids Go shows and they get thousands, hundred of thousands of views actually, and we get great comments. Of course, I have comment moderation turned on in YouTube. Well, we actually have a really good community of people who are watching our clips and really use it quite

259

well and they're actually doing both clips and full length shows, too.

One of the things that we've done—and we've been really deliberate about it—is thinking about metadata, how descriptions are written, how titles are written because especially looking at YouTube, which, of course, when it comes down, that's where the great majority of our views are seen is around YouTube. You can actually look within YouTube in the insides area, the metrics, and see how people are discovering the actual videos. So, you could see the path that people take to actually find something. You use that information in future clips. So, we see that people are seeing our clips in, for instance, the related clips area. When they're watching one clip and they'll see down below related clips and if you write the description in a certain way, the titles, it helps make it be placed down in those related clips areas. That drives a lot of traffic. So, we have a certain naming structure that we have for our files, not the files, the actual names and the video themselves, the descriptions. We're also really deliberate about the URL, the long URL clickable. It will be the very first thing that you see within the description so that people, they don't have to click on "more info" to get the URL, they're seeing it right there. It's really, really important. Just those kinds of things and we give this information to all our producers, to all our stations, and it's had an effect. The traffic from YouTube to pbs.org has gone up 200 percent last year.

The naming structure that we use is series, episode, and then PBS and we recommend that. YouTube has a different opinion about it. YouTube has told us that they think it's more compelling that if the video has animals in it, to talk about the animals or to talk about the actual title itself, but we found it's more searchable if you do that kind of naming structure, but it's up to the individual user, but that's kind of what we've recommend to our stations.

Steve Garfield: I've noticed on series when you look at a page full of videos you'll see only the series name and you can't really see because it only shows a certain length of the title.

> **GET SEEN: Do not make your title longer than 60 characters.**

KD: In YouTube, 60 characters of the title will show up. So, we tell our producers do not make your title longer than 60 characters because it will always show up in the video itself. If the video is embedded elsewhere, YouTube has new functionality that actually shows the title at the top in white. So, we're telling producers, 60 characters, no more, and if the title of the series is "The News Hour with Jim Lehrer," we truncate that down so we can make sure that the whole thing is within 60 characters.

SG: That's great. So, if people want to start and find PBS on the Web, where do you direct them to?

KD: They go to, well, on YouTube it's youtube.com/pbs,[1] but we also have accounts, as I said, on Blip.tv,[2] on Yahoo,[3] and we're going to be doing several other including video here soon.

Watch the interview online.[4]

Interview: Felicia Day

Hosting: YouTube, blip.tv

WHY YOU SHOULD KNOW FELICIA DAY

Felicia Day is most widely known for her work in web video, and co-starred in Joss Whedon's Emmy® Award winning Internet musical "Dr. Horrible's Sing-a-long Blog," voted the Best TV of 2008 by *Time* magazine, *Entertainment Weekly,* and *People* magazine, just to name a few. She also can be seen in the web series "The Guild," which she created, writes, and stars in. We talked about video distribution.

---

[1] http://youtube.com/pbs
[2] http://pbs.blip.tv
[3] http://video.yahoo.com/people/2762492
[4] http://blip.tv/file/1943953/

Steve Garfield: So, for people who are thinking about doing a web series, what advice would you give them?

Felicia Day: I would say that if you make your content not aiming toward TV like pleasing everybody, but rather kind of right toward a niche audience, it's going to be a lot easier for you to get the show off the ground. My show is about online gamers and I think that the success of my show is very tied to the viral aspect to a really devoted fan base who doesn't feel like media is talking to them.

SG: So, what would your suggestion be for people— where would they put their show up?

FD: I would say that people probably—YouTube is where all the most traffic goes or you could try to sell it to, you know, depending on what kind of production values you have or what your subject matter is and how you know people, you could contact other sites like blip.tv and see if maybe they'll feature you if you premiered on their show, their site, or even maybe sell it to some people, although that's kind of hard, but it's always good to try that. Then if you trickle down and just wanted to just put it up and see how people respond, YouTube is probably a really good place or any other place it could be embedded. This is important.

SG: So, it can be spread?

FD: So, it can be spread, yeah.

SG: Tell us about your deal.

FD: My deal? Well, for the first year, we uploaded our show to YouTube, season one. It was self-funded at first and then we had PayPal donations, which is very unusual on a first show, but it got us through the whole season. The second season, we held out for quite a while with studios and producers wanting to invest and own the show and I wanted to keep the rights to my show, which is very unusual, especially in the Hollywood model. We started shooting season two on our own from our DVD money, which we used to pay back our crew that we couldn't afford with the donations. Then Microsoft Xbox stepped in and they said, "We want to fund it. We don't want to own it. We love the show how it is and we're going to distribute it to millions more people." So, it's a real situation where we did it on spec kind of, but we just kept going because the strength of the Web is not asking for permissions to tell your stories.

    SG: And where would people go to find you on the Web?

    FD: Watchtheguild.com[5] is our web site. You can see season one and season two in the center player there.

Watch the video or our interview.[6]

Interview: Bre Pettis of brepettis.com

HOSTING: BLIP.TV, VIMEO, AND YOUTUBE

WHY YOU SHOULD KNOW BRE PETTIS

Bre Pettis (see Figure I.1) is a founder of Makerbot, a company that produces robots that make things. Bre is also a founder of NYCResistor, a hacker collective in Brooklyn. Besides being a TV host and video podcast producer, he's created new media for Etsy.com, hosted "Make: Magazine's Weekend Projects" podcast, and has been a schoolteacher, artist, and puppeteer. Bre is passionate about invention, innovation, and all things Do-It-Yourself.

I host my videos on blip.tv, Vimeo, and YouTube. Each of these places have their own audience so just having them there means that people will watch them. I use the blip.tv player on my blog because it's so configurable and I have it set up so that folks can click on the player and subscribe in iTunes. There are lots of places to upload video and I recommend testing them out to see if folks will watch your video at each place.

> **GET SEEN: The secret to online video is following your passion.**

If you have a camera in your hand and you can banish fear, press the red button at the people that interest you, you'll get

---

[5] http://Watchtheguild.com

[6] http://blip.tv/file/1943775/

Figure I.1   Bre Pettis[7]

good videos that will lead you to great videos. Once you've made a bunch of videos, you'll get a sixth sense for moments when you'd wished you'd pressed the red button and you'll remember to get the camera rolling the next time you feel it. It's important to do a lot of work and put out lots of videos. It's the only way you'll get better and it's really helpful to learn about what works on the Internet.

So get started! Shoot anything you can get your hands on and do your best to make it interesting and share them with the Internet and get feedback and keep going. The only way you'll fail is if you stop producing work. I personally

---

[7]http://BrePettis.com

love to shoot videos that document my projects and focus on people who make things and I invite you to come check them out at brepettis.com.

Interview: Brett Gaylor

WHY YOU SHOULD KNOW BRETT GAYLOR

Brett Gaylor made a movie about remixing that allows the audience to remix the movie.

I first became aware of Brett though video blogging.[8] I had a chance to sit down with him at South By Southwest (SXSW) 2009 to talk about his film and video remixing.

Brett Gaylor: I directed a film called RiP: A Remix Manifesto. *It's a film I made over the course of about six years actually and the kind of the thing that I tried to do all the way through the production of the film was to try and involve the audience in the creation of the actual film. I mean the film is about remix culture, right? It's about this kind of tension between participatory media and copyright law because, of course, people are using copyrighted images to express their culture and this whole war that's been going on over the last 10 years is sort of directly affecting that and I felt it's not getting us anywhere. So, it's a pretty strong viewpoint film,* A Remix Manifesto. *It's not a remix chat. Right from the beginning, I had a web site called opensourcecinema.org[9] and as I was shooting, I would put my rushes and sort of works in progress on this site under a CC license. So, what that allowed me to do is to let the audience know that they can participate in the film. They can use my footage however they want, but I want them to submit it back to the site as well so that I can include it in the final film. So, then I would start to edit these into the film during the editing process and sort of do like a call and response with the audience. So, at some points in the film they kind of take over and it's their part of the film and then I'm back, you know? That's*

---

[8] http://www.etherworks.ca/archives/all_videoblogs/
[9] http://opensourcecinema.org

how I decided to do it, sort of a structured open source sort of experiment.

SG: Okay. So, how do people see the footage, grab it, and send it back to you? Sometimes footage is kind of big. I mean how do you do that? What software?

BG: That's a good question because right when I started doing this, there was no real option for that. It was just basically peer to peer. They would post something and at some point, I might ask them for a higher resolution or I would just eat the bandwidth and download it, but now what I've done since the film has been released is I'm working with a company called Kaltura to integrate onto Open Source Cinema web-based editing. So, it can actually take place on the Web using your browser. You don't have to have Final Cut Pro or iMovie or whatever the PC folks use. You don't have to have that stuff. You can just do it right on the browser. So, that takes care of that kind of part of the question.

SG: Oh, that's cool.

BG: What's cool about Kaltura is that they keep a reference to your high-resolution one and what happens online is almost like an Edit Description List (EDL). So, you can always point back to the original high-resolution version.

SG: So, if people want to find out about this project and the movie, what URL, where would you send them?

BG: Opensourcecinema.org.

SG: Okay, great. Thank you.

BG: Thanks, Steve.

Interview: Chris Pirillo, YouTube Video: We're Gonna Do It Live

TOOLS: STREAM LIVE TO USTREAM

TOOLS: CANON HV 30DV CAMERA

HOSTING: USTREAM, YOUTUBE, BLIP.TV

I love streaming live video to the Web, because once you hit the stop button, you're done and you can move on to something else.

When I stream live video, I like to do it in smaller segments. I think of it like storytelling and make sure my videos have a beginning, middle, and end. I'll start with announcing who I am: "This is Steve Garfield from SteveGarfield.com." Then I'll introduce my video saying where we are, move on to the content of the video, then close. I'll plan out the structure in my mind before going live.

This is what Chris Pirillo does, too. He uses Ustream to stream live, then saves the video to YouTube. No editing. He does have his assistant do a lot of back-end work on the distribution side, too.

Chris has figured out how to get millions of views on YouTube and streamline putting video on the Web quickly by using live streaming. He's got a live stream running 24/7!

His current process involves streaming live video and recording segments of his live stream that are then posted to YouTube. It's a great method for creating a lot of content and posting it quickly.

I interviewed Chris on the topics of streaming live with Ustream and archiving his videos on YouTube.

Chris responded to my interview questions in writing and with a YouTube video.[10]

Chris Pirillo: I've been doing this live video thing for just about two years now. I wanted to talk about online video today in order to answer a few questions Steve Garfield had for me. He's working on a new book, which should be a great read! When talking with me about the book, Steve says:

Most of the video blogging books out there were written a few years ago, so I'm producing a book with real-world examples of tips and tools that people can pick up and actually do. Interviews with people like you will be both inspiring and practical.

Sounds good to me, so let's get going on those answers!

Steve Garfield: You have a background in TV, hosting the TechTV show Call for Help. *What did you learn from your TV experience that would help others produce video for the Web?*

---

[10] http://www.youtube.com/watch?v=SbtD5lX2XYk

CP: The key word in that sentence is "produce." That's what most videos lack—production quality. My production quality has evolved over time—I'm doing my best! My setup is now such that I feel it works very well. I've even worked as a consultant with others who all now use this same setup.

SG: You stream live using Ustream[11] and then post your videos on YouTube. The quality is very good. What computer, video, and audio equipment do you use and why?

CP: It is true that I stream live to Ustream. I do this because it brings a different dimension to my videos. Instead of just being a talking head, I'd rather have the dynamic interaction of the community. I change hardware up frequently, in order to make things better.

I use a Canon HV 30DV camera broadcasting in standard definition connected by Firewire to a Mac mini, the software is CamTwist,[12] and the service is Ustream.

The microphone is an Audio Technica USB AT 2020 condenser microphone. I tend to change things up to make things better over times. Hardware does improve.

SG: What equipment would you suggest to someone getting started if they want to stream live? People can get started using a laptop with a built-in webcam, right? Is that a good idea?

CP: Absolutely, they can start that way. Don't spend any money if you don't have to. That being said . . . if you want your videos to look professional, then spend money, spend some time on your video! I choose going live to file so I don't have to do any editing. I like the live aspect of what I do. It's a matter of personal preference, and what your ultimate goals are when producing content.

Start with what you've got. Improve incrementally. You can also buy a higher quality camera that can shoot HD, it's really not that expensive.

Create something that looks good: That is the key.

You don't just want to shoot just with your head and your face with something in the background that's distracting. Keep in mind what's going on in front of the camera

---

[11] http://Ustream.com
[12] http://www.allocinit.com/index.php?title=CamTwist

is as important as the video and audio quality. Give people something to look at.

SG: Why are you using YouTube to host your videos? Is it because of the integration with Ustream? Are there drawbacks to using YouTube?

CP: I use a variety of video-hosting services, honestly. I don't only rely on YouTube.

I use blip.tv to host the MP4 files that feed into my podcast. At some point in the future I hope to use YouTube's pay per download service.

That being said, YouTube has this vast audience worldwide. It's pretty much the place where everyone goes to find videos. YouTube is actually the second largest search engine on the Internet. A person would be crazy not to put their videos on YouTube. The number of views that YouTube gives me is astronomical . . . around 80,000 to 100,000 views per day!

SG: You just got over 1 million hits for your airplane safety video![13] How'd that happen?

CP: That was the first YouTube video I ever did. It was just a video of me mocking the safety announcement on a flight. I couldn't help it, it was hilarious at the time. I was making up hand gestures, and being silly. For some reason, people just love this video, and find it to be completely funny. When you put something on the Web it doesn't just fade away—it's there forever! The hope is that your video views will increase over time.

It was funny, but the videos I prefer doing are more informative.

SG: Have you figured out the best method for recording a live stream and posting directly to YouTube? Any secrets you can share on how to best do it?

CP: Everyone is going to have a different style. Me . . . I like doing things live, saving the file, and converting it to a different format. I have to thank my assistant Kat[14] for the help she gives on that end. She downloads and converts all my videos, gets them uploaded to the various sites, and

---

[13] http://www.youtube.com/watch?v=ZDepABf9JOg
[14] http://www.katarmstrong.com/blo

writes up the show notes for my blog.[15] *There's a lot involved, and I'm grateful for her help! That also shows you that producing content regularly is not always a walk in the park. If that's all you're doing, you can likely manage it yourself. But if you have your finger in many other pies as I do, you'll need help. I choose to shoot live to file because I hate editing . . . it takes up too much time!*

When I'm not doing something live, I'll have a video camera with me, and I can shoot on that and upload it later. Even then I tend not to do any kind of editing.

My advice is to go at your own speed, produce something that's going to be worth watching again. I tend to produce evergreen content, content that looks and sounds as good today as it will a year from now.

SG: What makes a successful video?

CP: Success can be measured in many ways. For me, success comes from doing something that I myself am proud of. For others, it's getting information from the video that they were hoping to attain, and learning something new from whatever it was I talked about. So success can be measured in number of views, or one of many other ways.

As far as the big picture, I think success lies largely in the arena of attention gotten, so if you've made it this far in the video and want to type the word "pancake" in the comments of this video on YouTube it would be appreciated because it gives me an idea of how many people have watched this far.

(Author's note: If you comment on Chris's video, tell him Steve Garfield sent you. ;-)*)*

SG: What advice would you give to a business getting started in online video?

CP: Just do it. So many businesses and people get caught up in not doing things, or are afraid of receiving bad comments or reviews. The fact is that your video is not a success unless someone has made a negative comment! You've just got to put your best foot forward, and just try. If it doesn't work, try again. The videos that don't work are usually

---

[15] http://chris.pirillo.com/what-do-you-know-about-online-video/#

sales pitches. It is the product demonstrations and screen casts that will work.

SG: What is the secret to online video?

CP: Do something that is unique and stands out. Be sure that both your subject and your set convey your message. Don't try to be someone else. You have to own what you're doing, and make it yours. You've got to make an investment in time and resources and energy and community. If you've got video on your own site, you might as well put it on YouTube also. There are probably more people that know about YouTube than know about you.

SG: What other comments or advice do you have?

CP: Develop a thick skin. There are idiots everywhere, and you'll have to deal with them when your content is distributed. Keep doing your thing, and don't let jerks bring you down or make you question yourself. That isn't to say you shouldn't take constructive criticism—you should! But take everything else and throw it out the window.

My target market is the people who don't know me. As much as I love my audience, I have to do my best to attract the people who don't yet know me. Pay attention to your community, and remember to go after the rest of the people to get them into your community!

Interview: Jay Dedman, Sharing Moments

TOOLS: SANYO XACTI AND iMOVIE

HOSTING: YOUTUBE, BLIP.TV

One of the most important things I've learned about online video is that sharing moments through video helps you get to know someone. Many people are afraid to take the step of recording themselves on video and sharing that video online, but there's something much more powerful that trumps that fear; it's the sense of community that you can build by connecting online.

The first moment I realized the power of online video to connect people was when I met Jay Dedman.

I started my blog, Steve Garfield's Video Blog, as a technical challenge to figure out how to host video and embed that video in a blog. Along the way I posted explanations of everything I learned.

Midway through the year, Dedman left a comment on my blog that said he had started a Yahoo! Group to discuss videoblogging. I joined.

Jay Dedman and Peter Van Dijck started a group on Yahoo! to talk about videoblogging in May of 2004. At that time there was a handful of videobloggers, so few in fact that we were able to watch all of each other's videos.

We probably didn't realize it at the time, but by watching every video that each of us made, we were getting to know each other on a much deeper level than reading traditional blog posts would allow.

The first time Jay and I met in person was when I invited him over to my house. My wife Carol was wary: "You're having someone that you've never met come into our home?" Yes.

Although I'd never met Jay in person, I felt like I knew him. It was a powerful moment that we both experienced.

How could we feel like we really knew each other, having just met in person?

Jay had been watching my personal videos online, and I'd been watching his. I showed him, and the world, a window into my life.

He shared his thoughts on videoblogging, captured moments, and interviews with people.

Sharing those videos helped us get to know each other.

When you look at Dedman's blog, you'll see that he has supporting text in the blog post. A lot of supporting text. That's one of the parts of the structure of a video blog; it's a blog with video, but that doesn't mean you have to exclude text. Many of today's videosharing sites feature video and de-emphasize text. That's too bad; text does a wonderful job of enhancing the story, especially if the story you are sharing is just a moment.

In January of 2005 we all went together to New York City for a gathering of videobloggers and called it vloggercon. That was the first time most of us had met each other in person, and we had that "I feel like I already know you" experience.

I interviewed Jay Dedman about his experiences with video blogging. You can see his videos at Ryanishungry.com (see Figure I.2).

Steve Garfield: You coined the term "moment showing," a phrase I use a lot when talking about the different types of video you can produce for the Web. What does moment showing mean to you?

Figure I.2   RyanIsHungry Site

Jay Dedman: Have you ever had that moment when you're walking down the street and something you see just smacks you in the face? It's that moment of "this is what life means to me right now." It might not mean anything to anyone else, but that moment means something to you. You know a photo wouldn't be enough to capture it, but a small video camera in your pocket might be able to record the 30 seconds of it. You could actually keep that moment as an archive of your life.

It was in college that I realized that being a filmmaker was not for me. I didn't have the right frame of mind to spend months or years of my life on one project. Instead, I just carried around my video camera, lived my life, and recorded these moments that struck me. I never knew what to do with these random, unrelated snippets of life. Everyone else was busy learning "storytelling," while I was focused on "moment showing."

When I found video blogging, I realized I could edit these video moments together and post them on a blog, which would become like a photo album of moving images. The blog itself would be a documentary told over time. I wouldn't have to become a filmmaker or raise a lot of money; I could do this while going about my regular routine. Life and art would be the same thing.

I love working on longer video stories with my wife. But moment showing allows me to have a reason to record those little things happening around me every day. Maybe my great-grandkids will make sense out of them.

SG: What tools do you use for creating video? What would you suggest someone getting started use?

JD: I like the Sanyo Xacti, which is a pocket camera that is shaped a little like the grip of a gun. It reminds me of a miniature 8mm camera. It records MP4 videos onto an SD card. It's important to me that I have a camera that I can whip out at any moment, and doesn't make people feel uncomfortable in public. This camera can start recording as soon as I open the screen.

I personally edit mainly using iMovie. I don't do a lot of fancy editing. Just snip out the boring parts and arrange clips in an interesting order.

I do love the bigger, expensive HD cameras. The quality is amazing and an important evolution for video creators. I can't wait until they create a 1280i HD camera that fits in my pocket.

SG: Where do you recommend people host videos and why?

JD: YouTube.com is the obvious place to post videos these days because that's where everything is.

I use blip.tv because it offers the most creator-friendly tools. Blip transcodes my videos automatically to multiple formats, allows me to add a Creative Commons license, allows me to design my own flash player, and I can cross-upload to Archive.org for archiving purposes.

SG: What is the secret to online video?

JD: Online video is not necessarily TV. Your video blog is a work in progress. Imagine being on your deathbed and looking at your video blog. Don't look back and regret not posting a video because it "wasn't good enough."

> **GET SEEN:** Record those little moments happening every day. Always carry a video camera with you. Record moments that you might want to share with others. Recording the moments doesn't mean you are going to share them, it just means that you've captured them, and they're not lost. You'll be able to decide if you want to share later, but if you never capture the moment, it will just remain a memory.

Interview: Chuck Olsen—Here Now, The News

TOOLS: CANON 5D MARK II AND THE CANON HG20, SONY ECM-77B LAVALIERE MICROPHONE, AZDEN SGM 1X SHOTGUN MICROPHONE, SENNHEISER MD46 HANDHELD INTERVIEW MIKE, LP-MICRO LIGHT FROM LITEPANELS

HOSTING: VIMEO, BLIP, AND YOUTUBE

One day I awoke to loud explosions in my neighborhood. I looked out the window to see sparks flying and fire in the trees. I called 911, then grabbed my camera and ran outside. What I saw was an electrical box that was on fire. Fire engines arrived and a firefighter approached the electrical box as it was exploding and shooting off sparks.

I captured the scene on video. After posting it online, I sent an e-mail out to the residents of my street. One neighbor thanked me for sending it because she had seen all the fire trucks but hadn't known what was happening because she had to rush to work. Another neighbor e-mailed to say her little boy had watched the video 10 times and loved it.

Those comments made it all worthwhile.

I interviewed Chuck to see the path he's taken to share stories.

WHY YOU SHOULD KNOW CHUCK OLSEN

Chuck Olsen and I met in person at the first gathering of video bloggers in New York City in January 2004. I enjoy following Olsen's videos online because he's funny and enlists his wife to take part in short videos that showed me parts of his life.[16]

It's similar to videos that I've been doing with Carol since January 1, 2005.[17]

People watch Olsen's videos because you get to hear stories that are not covered by mainstream media. It's a fresh perspective by someone with a perspective who isn't afraid to share their views and be entertaining.

Chuck Olsen is a co-founder of the UpTake, a nonprofit organization dedicated to training and distributing the work of video-based citizen journalists. He is also the founder of Minnesota Stories, which has been named one of the best video blogs by the *New York Times*. He is the producer-director of *Blogumentary*, the first documentary film about the rise of political and personal blogs. He is the Minneapolis correspondent for *Rocketboom* and works as a freelance producer, videographer, editor, and educator.

I interviewed Chuck about his site and shared a detailed look at the tools he uses to produce video.

> *Steve Garfield: Tell us about The UpTake. How has this citizen journalism site developed?*
>
> *Chuck Olsen: The UpTake is a video-based citizen journalism nonprofit organization, formed by Jason Barnett, Mike McIntee, Chris Dykstra, and myself. We initially formed The UpTake to cover the 2008 Republican National Convention, but quickly realized the idea was more powerful than any one event. We've now produced over 1,000 videos with the help of dozens of volunteers in 26 states. We even had live coast-to-coast coverage of Super Tuesday, with Steve Garfield reporting via a Nokia N95 from Boston.*

---

[16] http://www.mnstories.com/video/63/Review-Bad-Waitress
[17] http://www.youtube.com/carolandsteveshow

SG: Minnesota Stories is now in its second iteration. What's the site about and how is it going to work as a business?

CO: Good question! Minnesota Stories is a video-sharing community for the state of Minnesota. Surfing around a big site like YouTube, it's easy to get lost in wacky videos and you may not feel a connection. Minnesota Stories is more intimate and focused on things happening where Minnesotans live, work, and play. The site is now on a YouTube-like platform, so anybody can create an account and upload video, or even embed video they've uploaded elsewhere (like YouTube, Vimeo, or Blip). I serve as the editor, finding the most interesting videos to feature. Ideally the site will be ad-supported, which is slowly starting to happen.

SG: What tools do you use for creating video? What would you suggest for someone getting started to use?

CO: My two primary video cameras are the Canon 5D Mark II and the Canon HG20. Both are tapeless high-definition cameras with different strengths and weaknesses.

The Canon 5D MKII is one of the first digital SLR cameras to offer high-definition video capability. It can capture absolutely stunning imagery that far surpasses most video cameras, because you can use high-quality professional 35mm lenses, and the size of the camera's sensor is much bigger than a normal video camera, which means the video is richer and more detailed, and performs well in low light.

The 5D has its downsides, and I wouldn't recommend it to a beginner. First of all, there is very little exposure control. There is an exposure lock button, but beyond that the camera is guessing at the best exposure and doesn't always guess well. There is no continuous auto-focus, which is a challenge in any uncontrolled shooting situation. The 5D also has poor audio support. There is a microphone input mini-jack, but no headphone jack to monitor audio. Lastly, it will stop recording after the file reaches 4GB (about 12 minutes), so it's not a good choice for recording events or long interviews. My 16GB CF card holds around 48 minutes of video. Despite these limitations, this camera is a real "game-changer" because it makes the tools of professional videography more affordable and accessible.

The Canon HG20 is much more friendly and forgiving if you are just starting out. Being a hard drive camera, it can hold up to 22 hours of high definition video. It records in the AVCHD format, which is now comparable in quality to the tape-based HDV format. This camera performs great and costs only one-fourth of the 5D. I often use the HG20 as a second camera with the 5D, because I can monitor audio on the HG20. The only word of warning here is that you may need to convert the files into Quicktime before you can edit. I use Roxio Toast to convert the files, though the latest iMovie and Final Cut versions handle the files natively.

When it comes to audio, I have three microphones that cover all my needs. For a sit-down interview, I use a Sony ECM-77B lavaliere microphone. It's an industry standard and guarantees great interview audio. When I'm out in the field, I use an Azden SGM 1X shotgun microphone most of the time. It can capture an interview well, and is also great for recording live music because it has a "bass reduction" mode. I also carry a Sennheiser MD46 handheld interview mike, which allows you to conduct interviews without picking up much crowd noise. It's great for stand ups or interviews in any kind of loud event situation.

Of course, the only way I can use those professional microphones is with the Beachtek DXA-2S microphone adaptor. This particular model is designed for small cameras (like the Canon HG20) and is an absolutely essential part of my kit.

One of my favorite video toys is the LP-MICRO light from Litepanels. It's an LED light that uses AA batteries and is extremely bright and yet very light and portable. It also has a dimmer and includes various diffusers that slide in front of the LEDs. It slides right onto a standard flash mount, which you'll find on most video cameras including the 5D, but sadly not on the HG20. This light really makes your interview subjects, err, shine.

All my gear fits snugly and safely in the Kata R-103 camera backpack. It's heavily cushioned to protect your expensive gear, and even has a laptop pocket.

SG: Where do you recommend people host videos and why?

CO: Vimeo, Blip, and YouTube are my favorites. Vimeo has the best-looking player of anybody, and were among the first video hosts to support HD, making them the choice of filmmakers and video artists. Blip is among the most full-featured of video hosts, especially if you want to have access to your original Quicktime or MP4 for iTunes podcasts or iPhones. YouTube is YouTube—it's where everyone goes to watch video, and where you should be, too. They're starting to support HD and keep rolling out new features like annotations. Most accounts are limited to 10-minute videos, which might be a problem for some folks.

Facebook and Flickr are also great sites to post video. I usually get more comments uploading a video to Facebook than anywhere else, and their encoding looks great. However, at this time they don't provide metrics. Flickr is limited to shorter videos, but supports HD and has always been a great image-focused community.

SG: What is the secret to online video?

CO: A little chili pepper and a squirt of fresh lime. Oh, you were serious? I'll give you two answers. One secret to online video is, just make lots and lots of video until you're good at it. Then make lots more. Steve Martin says you need to invest 10,000 hours into your passion to master it, and I believe him. The other secret is to be yourself. You're probably not going to get noticed doing the same thing everyone else is doing. Do what you love and be original, and you can never go wrong.

SG: What makes a successful video?

CO: Big view numbers aren't the only measure of success. As I mentioned earlier, one reason I upload to Facebook is that I know my friends will see it there and comment. Getting feedback on your video is what I would consider a great success. Likewise, when I find someone has embedded a video on their blog or otherwise communicated that a video has impacted them—that's success.

GET SEEN: Make lots and lots of video until you're good at it and be yourself.

Interview: Steve Woolf—Epic Fu

Hosting: Blip.tv

TV is so good at creating episodic entertainment, why would you want to try and produce a web series or show that has regular episodes?

A web series keeps your audience coming back for more. The added feature of it's being on the Web allows you to engage your audience and encourage them to enter into a conversation with both you the producer and other viewers. When you provide the tools for communication, you can build a community around your show.

One series I produced videos for was Spices of Life. Cookbook author Nina Simonds was looking for a way to share her message of food, health, and lifestyle. At first, the series was imagined as an audio podcast, but after shooting a pilot episode, Nina decided that the show would work better as video. We keep it loose and unscripted. I challenged myself to shoot the episodes with a cell phone and used a Nokia N95. The shows were edited with Final Cut Pro. I also experimented with using multiple cell phones, extra lighting, and external microphones. We ended up moving to a Canon GL/2 miniDV camera for better quality. It usually took a half-day to shoot, and eight hours to edit. Spices of Life has been sponsored from day one by Legal Sea Foods restaurant.

Steve Woolf and Zadi Diaz produce videos for a community of viewers. I first met Zadi while we were both correspondents from Rocketboom. When they first started their show, it was called Jet Set. Their first intro video featured them creating a rocket pack. I was inspired to re-recreate the creation of the rocket pack and share that with them and their viewers.

Why You Should Know Steve Woolf

Steve Woolf co-created the award-winning Epic Fu[18] web show and is co-founder of Pixelodeon,[19] the annual screening festival in Los Angeles for serious Internet video makers.

> *Steve Woolf: I am co-founder of Epic Fu—a 5- to 7-minute weekly online video show that's been on for two-and-a-half*

---

[18] http://epicfu.com/
[19] http://pixelodeonfest.com/

years. We cover independent artists and people who are using the Web in ways that circumvent traditional thinking. We're coming up on our 150th episode.

Steve Garfield: So, for people who are thinking about doing a show on the Web, what advice would you give them?

SW: The advice I'd give them is to pick something that you're really passionate about so that when the going gets rough, you don't hate what you're doing. Take a look at the resources that you have around you or the people you know, what they are interested in, what can they help you to do and what would benefit them in turn, and see if you can put a team together. It's going to be tough to find people who are reliable unless they truly feel invested, but it takes a little time. You have to be prepared for the long haul because even if you put out a show and it's great and everybody tells you how great you are, it doesn't mean people are going to be watching. So, it takes a while to build an audience. You have to be ready for that.

SG: You mentioned money, so how are you guys making money with an online show?

SW: Well, for the last two years, we've been making money through licensing. So, we license the rights to sell advertising on our show to companies like Next New Networks or Revision3. They give us a flat fee and in turn they have the right to sell advertising on our show. We're also going to have a sponsor of our own—a relationship that the very fine folks at blip.tv helped to set up.

SG: So, if people want to start working with a site like blip.tv, do they have to have a show or produce one? How do they start doing a show on somewhere like Blip?

SW: Well, anybody can put a show on Blip, but if you're looking to make money with Blip, well, you probably want to have some kind of consistent format that your audience can recognize. You want to put it out regularly so you have a schedule and people will know what to expect. You want to encourage people to subscribe and you definitely want to call out to your audience and get them involved with the show. That will give them a sense of involvement and will really connect them with the show. That will make them want to tell people about it. The beauty of web shows compared to television or anything else is that your audience can be involved with the show if you want them to be and you encourage them to be.

SG: So, you put your show on Blip, but you also spread it around the Web at sites like YouTube and let it like go wherever it wants?

SW: Absolutely, yeah. I believe that information should be free and widely disseminated. So, if you put it in one place, you might never reach that audience that's living over on YouTube or Metacafe or that's living on Break or Veoh. I like TubeMogul because you just upload once and TubeMogul will disseminate it to all the major sites. So, I would post on TubeMogul and start there.

SG: And if people want to find you on the Web, where do they go?

SW: They can go to epicfu.com,[20] smashface.com,[21] or stevewoolf.com.[22]

Watch a video of our interview.[23]

> **GET SEEN: Pick something that you're really passionate about.**

Interview: Zadi Diaz—Epic Fu

TOOLS: SONY A1U, MANFROTTO TRIPOD, A FEW LOWEL PRO LIGHTS, FLIP MINOHD

WHY YOU SHOULD KNOW ZADI DIAZ

Zadi Diaz is the host of the award-winning web series Epic Fu and she rocks.

---

[20] http://epicfu.co
[21] http://smashface.com
[22] http://stevewoolf.com
[23] http://blip.tv/file/1944617/

*Steve Garfield: You've worked with two of the leading inde-
pendent web distribution/production companies, Next New
Networks and Revision 3, and now are distributing your
show, Epic Fu yourselves. What was the experience like working with these two video networks? What would you advise
people who are trying to decide if they want to distribute
their videos on their own, or join a network?*

*Zadi Diaz: When we started out, we decided to go with a
network because we felt we needed a partner to concentrate
on advertising and distribution while we focused on making
great content. As an independent producer, wearing many
hats can eventually wear you thin, so we wanted to avoid
burnout.*

*We distributed the show ourselves for our first nine
months. During that time, we grew our audience and pol-
ished our show, and basically created the show out-of-pocket.
We then signed on with Next New Networks for a year. They
paid us a licensing fee for the right to distribute and sell advertising for each episode. This allowed us to recoup our costs
and focus on creating the show. When that contract was up,
we signed on with Revision3, which was a very different experience from Next New Networks. Their distribution model
was different, their core audience was different, their culture was different. It was an amazing learning experience
to work with the two leading web distribution/production
companies.*

*Some advice I would give to new content creators is
to think about who you decide to partner with very carefully.*

*Think about where you want to be a year from now
and whether or not a network can help you get there. Think
about whether or not you want to keep full control of your
content, and what it means if you don't. There are pros and
cons to each scenario and in the end it's a very personal
decision.*

*SG: What tools do you use for creating video? What
would you suggest someone getting started use?*

*ZD: To shoot the show, we use a Sony A1U, a really great
and fluid Manfrotto tripod, a few Lowel Pro lights with color*

gels, a Sennheiser lav mike, and we edit on Final Cut Pro. I always suggest diving in and starting with the pro set of tools if you're looking at this as a business.

If you're just testing things out and just want to tell your story, you can most certainly start out with iMovie and an inexpensive camera. For video blogging I carry around my MinoHD Flip cam.

SG: Where do you recommend people host videos and why?

ZD: If you want your video seen, you never know where you may find your audience. The audience who finds you on YouTube may not respond to your work, but you might find an audience on Vimeo who will. Use TubeMogul to upload your video everywhere. Also keep a raw video file backed up on your computer or server, just in case.

SG: What is the secret to online video?

ZD: If you find yourself searching for something to say, chances are you aren't going to create compelling video. Tell stories about things that you're passionate about, that you're curious about, and you will find people who are also passionate about those things. You can usually tell the difference between someone who enjoys the story he's telling and someone who is telling a story just to have something to say.

SG: What makes a successful video?

ZD: Besides being passionate about what you are talking about, make sure you have good lighting, good sound, and that something is being communicated in an engaging and visual way.

SG: What advice would you give to a business getting started in online video?

ZD: Invest themselves in the online space. Be open to change, be aware that the Web is fertile ground for experimentation. Live on the Web for a while, find networks, use the tools, learn about what the Web is and how it works so you can use it to its current potential.

SG: Any other thoughts . . . ?

ZD: Know that this is an exciting time. The possibilities are endless. All the rules haven't been set, and the ones which have are still open for debate. Rush in and play.

GET SEEN: The people you work with ultimately affect how your show is viewed. Ask questions. Ask other creators who are already part of the network whether they are happy.

Do they feel that their distribution network is helping them get more widely distributed? Are they getting additional advertising opportunities?

GET SEEN: Host videos everywhere.

GET SEEN: The secret to online video is to know what your story is. Really know it.

GET SEEN: Ask yourself why you need video to communicate your message instead of just audio.

GET SEEN: Don't think of this as television. If you do, you're missing the bigger picture and possibilities.

Interview: Adam Elend

Tools: HVX 200 Panasonic HD Cameras and Final Cut Pro

Hosting: Blip.tv, YouTube

I met Adam Elend through his work with Moblogic.tv. Moblogic was one of the best implementations of a web video show that incorporated audience suggestions.

Viewers watched Moblogic because they felt like they were a part of the show. They felt that way because the producers listened and acted on their suggestions.

Today, mainstream media is incorporating social media tools to engage the audience with their productions. Some tools being used are Twitter, Facebook, and online chat.

Why You Should Know Adam Elend

Adam Elend co-founded Bright Red Pixels[24] a digital studio specializing in social entertainment—the intersection of great web video and

---

[24] http://brightredpixels.com/

engaging web tools. Elend produced the hit daily web show WALL-STRIP. At CBS, Elend ran the CBSi Web Originals production studio with partner Jeff Marks. He also produced Moblogic.tv, a news show where the host, Lindsay Campbell, showed her bias in the storytelling.

Steve Garfield: Tell us about your experience producing Moblogic.tv.[25]

Adam Elend: Our goal with Moblogic was to blend the traditional newscast format with some of the elements that make the Internet the number one news source for the YouTube generation: interactivity, authenticity, and opinions supported by facts.

Lindsay's job 100 percent of the time was to be an advocate for the audience. That meant reporting important stories that weren't getting covered and offering a new perspective on the ones that were getting covered. We mixed a lot of man-on-the-street stories with location stories and studio reports. We also did "first person experience" stories, where Lindsay experienced things that the audience couldn't necessarily do themselves, and then reported honestly on what she experienced and how she felt about it. Lindsay called it like she saw it, and we involved the audience in the actual creation of the episodes as well as the sometimes heated discussions that emerged from them.

Moblogic's main purpose was to become the catalyst for conversation, and I think we accomplished that.

SG: A large part of the show was interaction with the audience. How much of a role did the viewers play and is that important for video producers to include as an aspect of their shows?

AE: The audience played a huge part in Moblogic. Viewers uncovered stories for us to talk about (we had an idea jar on the front page for this), when we went on location, we asked the audience what they wanted us to find out before we made the show. We even provided a cell phone number where viewers could call Lindsay directly while we were producing shows. Even more important—Moblogic wasn't simply the show we posted each day. It was an ongoing

---

[25] http://www.youtube.com/user/moblogictv

conversation about the topic. Our team participated transparently in this discussion, and it colored how we viewed a given subject, and informed how we reported about future topics.

SG: You have worked independently as well as with the CBS television network. What was the experience like working with both?

AE: Very different, and very much the same. CBS Interactive really gave us free reign creatively. They were and still are, however, much more focused on the business model and revenue than we were as independents. It's hard to know, however, if that emphasis had more to do with the transition to a bigger organization, or a general shift in the industry. The years 2004–2007 were all about innovation. 2007 and beyond has been all about "how do we turn this into a profitable business?"

Additionally, working with a big TV network means huge access to resources. We've tried to take full advantage of that. At the same time, things move much slower. That took some adjustment.

SG: What tools do you use for creating video? What would you suggest someone getting started use?

AE: We use HVX 200 Panasonic HD cameras and Final Cut Pro. If you have the resources, this is the best approach. If not, you can use HDV cameras—lower quality but still HD. We did most of our lighting with an Arri fresnel kit and a set of Lowell Rifa lights. The Lowells are great because they're cheap and can create soft light, like a more expensive Kino Flo solution.

SG: Where do you recommend people host videos and why?

AE: I'm a big fan of blip.tv. They are custom-designed for web show producers, rather than the User Generated Content (UGC) set. Their customer service is unbelievable, and they make a great product. They also have a wide range of instant syndication options with built-in ad solutions. I also think that YouTube is a great solution. The tools there are great, and you can't dismiss the size of the audience. Now that their video quality has improved, the only real downside is that you end up as the small fish in a big pond.

SG: What is the secret to online video?

AE: Marketing. The days of throwing up a video and hoping it catches on are over. There is much too much video out there.

For a movie, at least half the budget is spent on marketing—sometimes more. You need to allocate money using that ratio.

SG: What makes a successful video?

AE: Fundamentally, the same thing that makes good television or good movies: a great story, well told. You need to ask yourself, though, "why does this have to be on the Web." If your answer is "because I can't get it on TV" then it's not web-authentic enough to draw an audience. The big players are going to be able to spend more money and make higher quality content than you can, if you're competing with TV shows.

SG: What advice would you give to a business getting started in online video?

AE: Learn and understand distribution and marketing. In the TV world, you have other people to do those things. In web video, you have to do it all yourself. You need to be as good at that as you are at making good content.

The way we describe it to talent is: on TV, you perform like you're giving a speech to a room full of people. Web video is more like telling a story to a group of your friends. You're still performing for them, but they all know you, all have a connection to you, and want you to be real. That advice doesn't just apply to on-camera personalities, it should inform your approach to content creation as a whole.

GET SEEN: The dialogue in the comments was as critical to the show as the video was.

GET SEEN: You need to have a marketing plan, and you need to be prepared to spend money for distribution.

GET SEEN: You need to give the audience an experience they can't get anywhere else.

GET SEEN: Give your work voice. Voice is critical on the Web.

Interview: Gavin Purcell, A Talk Show That Listens

When I first heard that Jimmy Fallon was going to start videoblogging, to show us the creation of his new show from behind the scenes, I was excited. Prior to this, you might see some random videos from TV shows, but I'd never seen the host of a show let viewers in to see what goes on to put the show together. Beyond that, Jimmy Fallon was actually reading and responding to viewers. I experienced that first-hand when he answered my comments in his video post I talked about earlier.

In this interview we hear from *Late Night with Jimmy Fallon* co-producer Gavin Purcell, who is working to change the way TV shows interact with the people formerly known as the audience.

Gavin Purcell worked with Jimmy Fallon prior to launching the *Late Night with Jimmy Fallon Show* to connect online with viewers. That put *Late Night with Jimmy Fallon* way ahead of the game even before they went on air. People who were interested in behind-the-scenes videos that gave insight into the development of the show had a great place to visit to learn more.

Videos included seeing the plans for the stage construction and a tour of the NBC cafeteria. People watched and became engaged. Many of these videos weren't produced with high-end video equipment, either; some were shot on Flip cameras.

The immediacy and connection that these videos enabled were immensely valuable.

WHY YOU SHOULD KNOW GAVIN PURCELL

Behind-the-scenes video has always been something I could not get enough of. Behind-the-scenes footage engages the audience. Gavin Purcell has said that he's going to be giving guests Flip cams.[26] The most creative thing that's going on here is that the guest's appearance on the *Late Night with Jimmy Fallon Show* will not be the only content created. This is so amazing and creative.

> Steve Garfield: I met you online, through Twitter.
> Gavin Purcell: Yes, yes.
> SG: The show's web site, it's excellent. I love what you're doing like trying to engage the audience prior to the show.

---

[26] http://www.businessinsider.com/the-jimmy-fallon-shows-tv-business-innovations-2009-2

GP: Yeah, yeah. It's a huge part of our plan. We really love the idea of connecting with viewers ahead of time but also the other part is we're going to do this stuff on the show as well. So I think that's a big part of it, too. We wanted both of those things to be part of the show.

SG: So you have the show that's on at a certain time but this web site that you're building can live on like 24/7 and people can go there, and participate with the show all the time. Are you going to do something new or different than we've seen?

GP: We're going to take the web site and we're going to create a content-driven experience that will be different from the show while still being connected to the show. Essentially, we're going to make a content blog on the show as well as community section of the site driven by people that will work for the site itself like on-the-show staff. So, we're going to be one of the first major shows, maybe even anywhere because even at former networks I've worked at the Internet and the TV shows are managed by different departments. We will have bloggers on our show staff and they'll be integrated into the show itself. So, it's going to be really interesting, the web sites, and I think there are so many possibilities to do stuff on the Web that may not work on TV but there are things on TV that may not work on the Web and there are some things that will work on both. It will give us a chance to explore all sorts of different kinds of content as well because some videos and some kinds of content honestly work better on the Web so we'll do those things on the Web; some things work better on TV, we'll do those things on TV and some things work great together and we'll do those things together. It's going to give us an opportunity to do stuff that people haven't really done before.

SG: So, Jimmy's on Twitter and he just recently got on Twitter.

GP: Yes.

SG: And he got a crock pot for Christmas.

GP: Yes.

SG: And he asked for advice on what his audience cooks with a crock pot. He got like pages and pages of recipes. What did he think of that feedback?

GP: He loved it. He absolutely loved it. He went bonkers for it. In fact, he loves—I mean it's funny to see people. What I always love about when you're on Twitter with famous people, the greatest thing is they all kind of get off with the idea of using it like this, and it's an awesome thing when like you can say and have 7,000 people instantly respond to you, but I think more than that for Jimmy, the cool thing is like it's a direct connection to his fans in a way that he's never felt before. He said to me so many times in the last few weeks he's like totally addicted to it because it gives him a chance to connect in this really cool way and it's kind of like what the Web is also doing, too, is like a lot of people get to know who he is rather than kind of through a guise of like what other might people think he is. It's like directly to him and I think most people who have kind of had that interaction with him whether from watching the web series or from Twitter are really liking the person that they're finding, which is so awesome because that's the guy that I know. He's the most awesome guy in the world. It sounds like sucking up but like he's a super cool guy and I think it's one of those things, an opportunity for somebody like that to kind of get to know even better.

SG: I think that Jimmy being on Twitter and actually really using it and listening to people, people, it's like the first time they've ever had a chance to talk to someone on TV and it's like a pent up desire to be part of something.

GP: I think totally. I think that we're big fans, number one, of what Colbert is doing with all of this stuff. I'm also a big fan of what we used to do at the G4 channel because I think G4 does a really interesting job of getting audiences interacting and things like that. They've got a very specific audience but they do really focus on interaction. I think we are definitely going to find ways to get people to interact with the show. So there will be a lot of fun things.

SG: If people want to follow the show, where do they go?

GP: www.latenightwithjimmyfallon.com.[27] That's the main site of the videos for the show, and I think following Jimmy on Twitter is a great thing, too, which is at

---

[27] http://www.latenightwithjimmyfallon.com

@jimmyfallon and I'm at @gavinpurcell if anyone wants to follow me, too.

Watch a video of the interview.[28]

Interview: Adam Quirk—Wreck and Salvage, But I Don't Want to Be on Video

HOSTING: INTERNET ARCHIVE, YOUTUBE, AND BLIP.TV

TOOLS: LIVESTREAM

TOOLS: CANON HV20

TOOLS: ADOBE PREMIERE, AFTER EFFECTS, AND PHOTOSHOP

HOSTING: BLIP.TV, VIMEO.COM

If you don't want to record your own video, you can still participate in online video.

There's a lot of video out there that's available to remix and reuse. Many video producers allow reuse of their videos. Look for a Creative Commons license attached to people's videos, either in the credits or in the associated text where you find the video.

One place to find video is the Internet Archive's Moving Images Archive. There, you have near-unrestricted access to videos that you can use in your own creations.

The upside is that reusing found video makes it easier to get started without having to invest in camera equipment.

The downside is that you need to be cautious that you don't end up using something you aren't supposed to. My general rule of thumb is that if you aren't sure you can use it, don't.

WHY YOU SHOULD KNOW ADAM QUIRK

Adam Quirk and his team create videos from videos. They are commenting on society, mainly without shooting video.

Adam Quirk has an online video show called "Wreck & Salvage."[29] Adam and his team reuse found footage and interact with the audience

---

[28] http://blip.tv/file/1655012/
[29] http://Wreckandsalvage.com

by producing live broadcasts. Adam proves that you don't need to learn how to use a video camera to create video for the Web.

Steve Garfield: Many people think they have to learn how to shoot video and understand lighting and sound to get started. You concentrate on reuse. Where can people go to find existing video they can use in mashups and remixes?

Adam Quirk: We rely heavily on the Internet Archive, YouTube, and blip.tv. There is such a huge amount of video being pushed onto the Internet every day, it is usually fairly easy to find video on any theme you desire. There are a number of tools that can help you download web video. There is also a trend of video-sharing sites opening up their content for download, which bodes well for the remix artist.

SG: What's Tricorn? How does it make use of the inter-active features of the Web?

AQ: Tricorn is our monthly hour-long live show. We use the broadcasting platform Livestream to stream feeds of our live webcams, and also to cue up prerecorded clips. The general idea is to create a sort of on-the-fly television station for an hour, in which each of us have a folder full of video to choose from. If Valdez runs a clip of Arnold Schwarzenegger, I will then find a clip in my folder that complements that, maybe a female bodybuilder or a video about health and fitness. The entire time, we are interacting with the viewers in the chat room, taking requests, and answering questions.

SG: How do you coordinate the live broadcast between the three of you? Are you talking on the phone at the same time? Is there one producer in control?

AQ: We have an IM chat room open privately where the three of us can discuss things on the fly. We are all three in control of all aspects of the production. When someone has a video playing, either of the other two producers can queue up the next clip, depending on who gets to the button first. Even if one of us queues up a clip, though, another producer can trump that clip with something they feel may fit better into the flow. You really have to trust the people you're working with to do what's best for the broadcast. It's instantaneous collaboration with no leader, a very egalitarian show.

SG: What tools do you use for creating video? What would you suggest someone getting started use?

AQ: I use a Canon HV20 for recording video, a Dell XPS 410 PC with 2.44ghz dual processors, two 19" monitors, three 500GB hard drives (2 internal, 1 external), and an Onkyo receiver with Fisher speakers for audio.

I use Adobe Premiere, After Effects, and Photoshop. I also regularly use a transcoding program called Super that is incredibly useful for transcoding to and from any codec and filetype. I use HDVSplit for capturing HD footage.

For someone just getting started, I'd recommend a Canon camera because of their great color and reliability, and Movie Maker for editing.

SG: Where do you recommend people host videos and why?

AQ: Depending on the content of their videos, I would recommend either blip.tv or Vimeo.com. If they are producing more personal videos that don't have writing or plot, or art video, they should use Vimeo.com because the on-site community there is incredible and supportive. Blip.tv is a better platform for someone wanting to produce a "show" because of all their incredible distribution, advertising, and statistics options.

SG: What is the secret to online video?

AQ: The big secret is that anyone can do it but not everyone should.

Interview: Robb Montgomery, Video in the Newspaper

TOOLS: SONY A1U, RODE NTG-1, SONY WIRELESS LAV KIT

HOSTING: VIMEO, YOUTUBE, EMBEDR.COM

Many radio and television stations and newspapers are adding video to their sites.

They use YouTube, Facebook, and Skype to collect user videos.

If they are only collectors of content, they are only doing 50 percent of the job.

There has to be a conversation.

Media companies should send an e-mail to the submitter before they use submitted content; then the submitter will tell their friends to watch.

Companies should send an e-mail after they use the video, thanking the submitter and including a link to an online archive, so they can promote and share that, too.

Media companies need to embrace the people formerly known as the audience in a two-way conversation.

WHY YOU SHOULD KNOW ROBB MONTGOMERY

Robb Montgomery[30] is a journalist, entrepreneur, and teacher. He uses his unique combination of talent and experience, along with his network of global contacts to create seminars, courses, and business models to better serve the needs of journalists and students working in the networked journalism era.

Steve Garfield: Why are newspapers training their reporters and photographers to become video producers?

Robb Montgomery: They have observed the sea change with the medium that YouTube ushered in and are adjusting their model to take into consideration the fact that web video is now a mainstream activity and affordable form of online journalism

SG: What's been the response from reporters and photographers after they've been trained to produce video?

RM: Newspaper journalists are great students to train how to VJ because you don't have to teach them journalism, the reporting, or the ethics. What is harder is to teach their bosses that the web video styles that work online are not the TV news–style reports they grew up with, but rather a range of video forms that must be served up in context with the story. Once you understand that you are not bound by the limitations and conceits of TV news, then you are open to experimenting with what does work. Raw video can work, live streaming video can work, user-submitted video can work, well-produced original documentaries can work. It's a very rich and creative medium and I have seen newspaper

---

[30] http://www.robbmontgomery.com/

reporters fall in love with producing video reports because they can report more information.

SG: What tools do you use for creating video? What would you suggest someone getting started use?

RM: I like the tiered approach. Issue every staffer a camera or camera phone that can record video in a pinch. The Flip is popular with many, the Nokia N95s are great, and the new Samsung phone that will record in Hi-Def could be a game changer. But those are only for getting video in a pinch. For people who do this regularly you need a camera and a high-definition microphone. A small video camera that allows you to attach professional lav or shotgun microphone to it is the most important criteria.

I love small cameras. As a solo VJ I use Sony A1U and have upgraded the mike to a Rode NTG-1 and added the Sony Wireless Lav kit. It all fits in carry-on luggage with my laptop and that means I can, and do, report from just about anywhere in the world. I have filed film reports from the middle of Egypt's White Desert and from 7,000 feet in the Canadian Rockies.

SG: Where do you recommend people host videos and why?

RM: I like Vimeo.com[31] and cross post clips to YouTube. The Vimeo is for quality and YouTube is for search. I like the new Embedr.com[32] player that allows you to put a play list of your work anywhere on the Web.

SG: What is the secret to online video?

RM: Ask those YouTube billionaires! Seriously, producing video is not new to me. What has changed is the price of admission.

The live streaming video is a component every news outlet should embrace because the Web is great at the "What?"

The What refers to "what is happening now." That's why Twitter is so addictive—the now factor. Imagine linking live streaming video to Twitter. . . . Could be a killer news app.

SG: What makes a successful video?

RM: The key is relevancy and pacing. You have to edit film differently for a web audience. The stuff I see newspaper

---

[31] http://Vimeo.com

[32] http://Embedr.com

VJs winning awards for are for films cut in the template of a PBS or CNN segment. No. Web video must be cut faster and get to the point right away.

SG: What advice would you give to a business getting started in online video?

RM: Seriously I got better at short-film filmmaking by giving myself a daily deadline and no excuses for not posting something each day for a week. It worked. That discipline got me over my fear and made the process of reporting with a video camera second nature.

SG: Anything else?

RM: For journalists the key to online success means knowing and serving your community. Web video lets you provide a great service to a community. Start by being smart enough to decentralize your newsroom and get your reporters out from their desks and out in the field where the stories are. Next, embrace the contributions that other eyes and ears in your community can offer. If you have to blow up your newsroom, it helps to have a plan for how to rebuild it around these ideas.

GET SEEN: It costs almost nothing to create or distribute great, timely content. That's the game changer.

GET SEEN: Just do it. Today. Make mistakes, post, improve, post.

Interview: Jeff Jarvis

Tools: Flip

Tools: YouTube

Why You Should Know Jeff Jarvis

Jeff Jarvis, author of *What Would Google Do?* (HarperCollins 2009), blogs about media and news at Buzzmachine.com.[33] He is associate

---

[33] http://Buzzmachine.com

professor and director of the interactive journalism program at the City University of New York's new Graduate School of Journalism.

Steve Garfield: For journalists and newspapers trying to get in the video space, what do you tell them to do now?

Jeff Jarvis: I tell them to get a bunch of Flips. I was at Davos a year ago and I showed the Flip to Kai Diekmann[34] who's the editor of Bild,[35] which is the largest newspaper in Germany. And he's turned all of Germany into paparazzi because he has them text in photos to a number 1414. They are all out there shooting celebrities and he pays them 500 euros and runs them in the paper. So I said Kai, you should be doing video and I pulled out my old Flip and he practically lunged at it and said I must have that I must have thousands.

And indeed he sent his staffers to buy them. I found out he then went to a camera manufacturer, created a Bild-branded camera, and he sold them to his readers. He sold 21,000 in just one month, which means he now has 21,000 readers out there all taking video, able to send them straight into Bild.

It's kinda brilliant.

I teach my students at CUNY to make video of all forms, audio, blogs, and wikis and everything.

Video can enhance most anything you do. Video can come from the audience, it can come from witnesses, it's just one more element of news.

SG: If people are recording video on a Flip, how would you suggest they share it, what would be the easiest way?

JJ: It's so bloody easy with the Flip, because you put it in and it goes on YouTube. I would say put it on YouTube and then embed it on the blogs and wherever, I think it's that simple.

GET SEEN: I don't want them to operate with the orthodoxy of old TV, stand ups, and B-Roll and all

---

[34] http://en.wikipedia.org/wiki/Kai_Diekmann
[35] http://www.Bild.de

that stuff. I want them to just be able to experiment and make video and use it not necessarily in whole stories but use it as a talking moving picture.

Interview: Scott Kirsner

Scott is from the Boston area and we see each other at many local conferences. One time Scott was moderating a panel for MITX about new media tools, and he called me out from the audience to talk about what I was doing. At that time broadcasting live video from a cell phone was fairly new. I started streaming from my Nokia N95 and displayed it on the big screen in the room. It was an eye-opening presentation for many people there.

WHY YOU SHOULD KNOW SCOTT KIRSNER

Scott writes the weekly "Innovation Economy" column for the *Boston Globe*, which runs on Sundays. He also edits the blog CinemaTech.[36] Kirsner has been a contributing writer for *Fast Company* and *Wired* since 1997, and his writing has appeared in other places, too, including the *New York Times, BusinessWeek*, Salon.com, the *San Jose Mercury News, CIO*, and the *San Francisco Chronicle*.

> *Steve Garfield: What is the secret to online video?*
>
> *Scott Kirsner: I think the big secret is how you get lots of people to watch your video, and pass it along. Unfortunately, there's no one answer. I use the term "remarkability," though, to try to suggest that your video needs to be different from other videos out there.*
>
> *Remarkability can come from being funny, outrageous, extremely topical, or aesthetically captivating. It can come from shooting something that doesn't already exist on the Web (one of my most-viewed videos involved a visit to an R&D lab that few people can get access to). It can also come from being useful—for instance, by sharing some expertise*

---

[36] http://cinematech.blogspot.com/

or some advice that you have that lots of people will find helpful.

SG: What advice would you give to a business getting started in online video?

SK: It's hard to tell in advance what people will respond to. Even if you only distribute your first few videos to a small group of friends and business partners to get their feedback, start making videos before you decide exactly what they will be. You'll learn a lot from the process, and be more open to feedback, than if you try to nail everything down before you start production. I'd also note that production values (and the amount you spend on your videos) aren't nearly as important as great content.

> **GET SEEN: You need to make something that's different enough and engaging enough that it gets people to forward it along to others. That's what builds up big audiences online.**
>
> **GET SEEN: Be spontaneous. Don't create a detailed plan before you start making videos.**

Interview: Scott Monty, Social Media

Social Media allows companies to put on a human face. You could think of it as a big set of eyes and a mouth stuck to a 20-story building, but although funny, that wouldn't accurately depict what's happening.

Scott Monty is someone who understands how tools like Twitter and YouTube allow companies to connect with customers and prospects in a personal way.

Many social tools are used for listening. Customers can record a video and post it to YouTube, and company representatives can find the videos via search, and record and post a response video.

WHY YOU NEED TO KNOW SCOTT MONTY

Scott Monty is the head of social media for Ford Motor Company. Scott has been on the cutting edge of the marketing field for some time, having written the internationally recognized Social Media Marketing Blog at www.scottmonty.com[37] since 2006.

Steve Garfield: How is Ford using video on the Web?

Scott Monty: Well, we've got a number of things. We've had YouTube channels for a long time. We've got Ford Video One as kind of our public relations video channel. Our B-roll footage is there, and there is some other storytelling type of footage there. There's also Ford, which is our advertising channel where we show our commercials and some more long-form—well, medium-form—videos that are highly produced, web sonic in nature. They're part of our Drive One campaign where we talk about quality, safe, smart, and green initiatives. We've actually just started a weekly series called, "DigiKnows."[38] That is basically a live stream event every Tuesday at noon where we bring a subject matter expert from Ford together with the camera. Using Ustream, we interview experts from Ford about a variety of things—whether it be the sync system, our new hybrid program, our new seat cushions that are made out of soybeans, or any number of things. We're archiving those and putting them up on the Ford DigiKnow YouTube channel[39] for people to view later.

SG: Talk more about Ford videos and how they're produced. Do you produce videos especially for the Web? Videos that aren't as produced as TV commercials?

SM: Yeah. My department does that. I'm digital and multimedia communications manager essentially. The job involves social media but I've also got a team of people that are doing web publishing for our press release sites. I've also got a team that does broadcast and online media. So, they do all of the professional grade stuff and we're doing everything in HD now because of standards for professional B-roll, but we also do stuff that we know is only going to be on the Web. My video director, she's phenomenal at this. She really understands that you don't need to set up an elaborate

---

[37] http://www.scottmonty.com
[38] http://www.ustream.tv/channel/ford-weekly-digiknows
[39] http://www.youtube.com/user/FordDigiKnows

shoot with lighting and professional cameras. Sometimes it's something as simple as taking out a Flip cam or just having a cameraman who edits the video in a day. That's the kind of thing we're shooting for because as a communications department, our product is not the automobile, our product is information and we need to turn that out as quickly and as effectively as possible.

SG: What is the secret to online video?

SM: The secret to online video is to keep it short—I would say two to three minutes in length. Keep people's attention for as long as you can and give them something that no one else can give them. We have so many great things that we can bring people into at Ford in terms of an experience that the average person wouldn't be able to produce.

SG: Excellent, and if people want to find out more about Ford, where can they go?

SM: The best place to go at this point, and this is a site that's under development now so it will be changing a lot, it's called the fordstory.com.[40] We've got, again, some highly produced things, some regular stuff that's coming, too. We've got aggregated content from third parties across the Web and then a bunch of our social presences on Flickr, YouTube, Twitter, and other sites like that.

Watch the video.[41]

> **GET SEEN: The secret to online video is to keep it short.**

Interview: Schlomo Rabinowitz, I Subscribe to People

Since I started videoblogging I've been excited by the power of video to connect people. I've met people from all over the world, and many of my good friends are also videobloggers.

---

[40] http://fordstory.com
[41] http://blip.tv/file/1944404/

Part of the allure of web video is that you can be authentic and share your passion through video. That passion comes through and people can respond.

WHY YOU SHOULD KNOW SCHLOMO RABINOWITZ

Schlomo Rabinowitz[42] was an early video blogger who now creates video solely for the Web. Rabinowitz also helps nonprofits figure out how to get their message out to the right people. Rabinowitz drinks a lot of tea and owns a bar in San Francisco called House Of Shields.

> *Steve Garfield: What's the secret of online video?*
> *Schlomo Rabinowitz: To me, the secret of online video is really understanding how to deal with my subject, how do I get what I need from them and make them feel comfortable, so in the end they look fun on camera and I'm getting my information out.*

Watch the full interview video.[43]

GET SEEN: Try using a small camera without extra lights and microphones. It'll put your subject at ease.

Kent Nichols: Remember the Pioneers

Kent Nichols, co-creator, director, and producer of AskANinja,[44] wrote[45] about the early days. Nichols explains the importance of video on the net, prior to videoblogging:

> *Ten years ago at the edge of Web 1.0 there were some brave video pioneers making shows for the net alone in the*

---

[42] http://www.google.com/profiles/schlomo
[43] http://blip.tv/file/1944255/
[44] http://askaninja.com
[45] http://kentnichols.com/2009/03/30/thoughts-on-the-first-streamys/

wilderness with no standards of delivery, business model, or format. Shorts like 405[46] and series like Homestar[47] and Red vs. Blue[48] and many, many others that haven't endured are the giants upon which we all are standing.

Four years ago the second wave of video shows appeared, embracing podcasting and the first iterations of flash video (including YouTube). This was the wave AskANinja, TikiBar,[49] Rocketboom,[50] French Maid TV,[51] and LG15[52] were on.

Shira Lazar: Living in Both Web and TV Worlds

Shira takes advantage of the power of online video in many ways. Sometimes you'll see her broadcasting live via cell phone using a service like Kyte to report from a conference or vacation spot, and other times you might see her on *CBS This Morning*, reporting on great travel sites. Lazar is someone who has been able to easily cross between online and broadcast. What Lazar understands is that it's the immediacy and conversation that's important when she goes live from a venue. People will forgive broadcasts that are less than perfect to see what's going on right now. Broadcasters can take advantage of this knowledge by placing live broadcasts that might be coming in from Skype on a computer, or Kyte on a cell phone on their web sites, or within TV monitors on their sets to show that the video is coming from another source than the standard broadcast, which viewers expect these days to be in high quality.

WHY YOU SHOULD KNOW SHIRA LAZAR

Shira Lazar is successful on TV and the Web. Lazar can be seen on CBSNEWS.com reporting on social trends and tech and pop culture.

---

[46] http://www.405themovie.com
[47] http://www.homestarrunner.com/
[48] http://rvb.roosterteeth.com/
[49] http://www.tikibartv.com/
[50] http://rocketboom.com
[51] http://www.frenchmaidtv.com/
[52] http://www.lg15.com/

Lazar has also appeared on Fox News Channel, CNN, MSNBC, NBC, and Direct TV. You can find her on the web at ShiraLazar.com.

Steve Garfield: What's the secret of online video?

Shira Lazar: There are so many different types of online video. There are ones written like the fictional scripted stuff, there's the nonscripted, and then there's just being yourself, which is more like the live casting.

I think it's about finding the balance between being transparent and being who you are, while also constantly delivering content, being a content provider, because when you just start live casting, that's all people know you for, but I think when you deliver that balance, there's respect in that. People will start caring.

It's not about the number as much as who's actually caring because people can be following you on Twitter, but it doesn't mean they're actually reading or watching your stuff.

Just be authentic, find your voice, and be true to who you are, and be consistent because you can't just throw out a video once every year.

Watch the video of our interview.[53]

> **GET SEEN: Be authentic, find your voice, and be true to who you are.**

Justine Ezarik: Cam Girl to Web Star

When Justine Ezarik, aka iJustine, started live streaming almost every moment of her life on a webcam, people started watching. Every moment.

Justine is cute and did interesting things.

People watched.

They did more than just watch, though, they also had a conversation, with Justine and with each other.

---

[53] http://blip.tv/file/1944469/

At the time it was all so experimental, but what it showed was that people would watch online video, for long periods of time, and interact with those who were sharing their lives.

This knowledge of the engaged audience can transfer to archived video, too. Justine knows that if you produce short entertaining videos about things that you love, that emotion will come through, and a community of viewers will watch and comment on your videos.

TOOLS: MacBook and iMovie

TOOLS: Sanyo Xacti, iSight Camera, Blue Snowflake Microphone

Why You Should Know iJustine

Justine Ezarik became well known for strapping a camera to her head and live streaming on Justin.tv. She produces short, entertaining videos that have garnered her a large online following of almost 100,000 subscribers on YouTube and more than one-half million followers on Twitter. Justine has multiple videos with more than 1 million views.

> *Steve Garfield: You gained a lot of exposure by streaming your life live on Justin.tv. That technology has made it a lot easier for people to create video. How do you feel about the state of live streaming and when do you use it these days?*
>
> *Justine Ezarik: Live streaming has come so far since the first day I put a camera on my head (crazy, I know). Then it was unstable, low quality, and it was so new that not everyone had the capability to do it. Now, just about every person has a cell phone and is constantly live streaming every little mundane task of their day to becoming real-time news sources.*
>
> *SG: Your YouTube iPhone Bill video[54] has now been seen over 1.6 million times.*
>
> *Why do you think that became so popular and what came out of it for you?*
>
> *JE: The crazy part is that's just the views on YouTube! There are a few more million across Yahoo!, Viddler, My-Space, Revver, and Break. The iPhone video was so popular*

---

[54] http://www.youtube.com/watch?v=UdULhkh6yeA

*because not only was the video topical, this was the first spot-
ting of AT&T's billing error and it made for a good mainstream story. For me personally, it gave a lot more validity
to what I do and a much more mainstream appeal.*

*SG: You make funny and entertaining videos. Some-
times, when companies hire you as an actor, a portion of
the creativity is taken away from you. What would you
suggest companies consider when hiring an actor for an
Internet video?*

*JE: When companies hire Internet talent as an actor, you
take away from what makes them unique—their distribution network. The only problem is that brands and companies don't want to pay for that distribution and take for
granted how powerful it is. What we are dealing with now
is an education process from content creator to brand on
putting a dollar amount on those views and still being true
to your audience.*

*SG: Would it be better for companies to give you complete
creative control?*

*JE: I wouldn't say that it's necessary for companies to
give Internet talent complete control, but the talent needs to
also know when a project isn't right for them. I've worked
with a lot of smart people at companies who have great
ideas, but in that same instance, I've also run into the ex-
treme opposite. It's important to know how your audience
will react to a product and have it be something that you
actually love and might normally talk about anyway.*

*SG: What equipment would you suggest to someone get-
ting started?*

*JE: The best equipment to get started being a vlogger
is a MacBook. It comes with an integrated webcam and
iMovie software. It's extremely simple and the quality is
actually quite impressive. After you've mastered that, look
into getting a better microphone. Sometimes audio is even
more important than the video quality.*

*SG: What do you use for editing videos? What's your
procedure and what settings do you use to get the best online
video quality?*

*JE: The equipment that I use varies from video to video.
Currently I'm testing out a wide range of consumer HD video*

cameras and have found that Canon and Sanyo Xacti are the best for audio, video, and ease of use. For a lot of my Ask iJ series,[55] I use my iSight camera, a Blue Snowflake Microphone, shoot the video in iMovie, and export that footage over to Final Cut for all of the audio edits, color correction, and effects. I then upscale that video out to an HD version to upload.

SG: You use a lot of sites to host your video including YouTube, Viddler, and Vimeo. What sets them apart? Where would you suggest people host their videos?

JE: There are so many video sites out there and choosing the one for you is important. Most of the time, what you ideally want is views and unless you have a lot of traffic to your web site, you'd be crazy not to use YouTube. I didn't for a long time and am just now realizing that error.

I put my videos everywhere because you never know when or how someone is going to surf across one of them on a various platform, but with YouTube being the number two search engine, you are much more likely to be discovered there. Now, I'm not saying to completely neglect these other video sites, because a lot of them have extremely amazing communities and features that you won't find anywhere else. Explore them and see what's right for you.

SG: What selection of video and audio equipment do you use and why? Do you decide when to use each type?

JE: Again, when choosing the right video equipment, it's really up to whatever feels right for you. For me personally, it's easiest to use my iSight to shoot my videos because I can edit as I shoot the video and know if I need to retake something. When I'm on the go, having a small compact HD camera like the Sanyo or Canon is ideal to keep in my purse at all times.

SG: What makes a successful video?

JE: As much as some people preach that 30-minute unedited videos for the Internet are successful . . . ask the person who just watched it how many times they skipped forward to get to the end. With a successful video, you want

---

[55] http://www.youtube.com/user/ijustine

to get the most information in the shortest time possible and have the viewer walk away with that information.

SG: What advice would you give to a business getting started in online video?

JE: Don't think too much about the first few. Have a general idea of what you want and jump right into it. The best part about the Internet is we're all kind of learning about what works. You're going to have some failed videos and you'll have some successes. Learn from both as you continue creating your content.

SG: What is the secret to online video?

JE: Create engaging content and love what you're doing.

GET SEEN: Present the most information in the shortest time possible.

GET SEEN: Create engaging content and love what you're doing.

Jeff Pulver: I Am a Person

WHY YOU SHOULD KNOW JEFF PULVER

Jeff Pulver[56] is the Chairman and Founder of pulver.com, and one of the true pioneers of the VoIP industry and a leader in the emerging TV on the Net industry. Leveraging well over a decade of hands-on experience in Internet/IP communications and innovation, Mr. Pulver is a globally renowned thought leader, author, and entrepreneur.

Jeff Pulver: For the past few years, I have done my own videos and I found the most effective ones are the ones where I remember that I am a person.

The best advice I could offer is before you start rolling those cameras to figure out what it is you want to do and then turn the cameras on and see what happens. Allow yourself to be creative.

---

[56] http://jeffpulver.com

What's wonderful about video is that you learn as you go.

The one thing you should always remember is that there's a person behind that camera and there's a person in front of it. If you're using video to connect with people, showing some humanity and allowing your viewer to connect on some level with the person behind the camera or the person in front of the camera is a much more effective strategy than rattling off a pitch like, "Hi, it's Jeff Pulver. Come to jeffpulver.com now!"

People are tired of hearing sales pitches. If I hear a pitch, five seconds into it, I click away. But if something about the person, the setting, or the video resonates with me not as a consumer, but as a person, you have a much better chance to actually be effective.

One thing to also keep in mind is that no matter what all the experts are saying, if you feel comfortable doing what you're doing, you're right.

It means you do it. Don't ask for permission. Just make it happen.

Watch the video of our interview.[57]

> **GET SEEN: Life is about figuring things out, making great mistakes.**
>
> **GET SEEN: Online video is never having to say you're sorry.**

---

[57] http://blip.tv/file/1943875/

Acknowledgments

First a disclosure: Because I am deeply involved in the online video community, I have developed friendships, worked with, and invested in some of the people and companies mentioned in this book.

Thanks to David Meerman Scott for encouraging me to write this book, and to Shannon Vargo and the team from John Wiley & Sons for helping me navigate the world of book publishing.

About the Author

Steve Garfield is one of the Internet's first video bloggers, having launched his own regular video blog on January 1, 2004.

Garfield likes to capture and share fleeting moments and teach others how to do the same. This led to his becoming co-creator of the first vloggercon, and a co-organizer of the first PodCamp held in Boston. He currently runs the Boston Media Makers (http://bostonmediamakers .com).

On February 3, 2005, Garfield posted what is believed to be the first video blog from a United States elected politician, Boston City Councillor John Tobin.

In 2007, Garfield produced Nina Simonds' Spices of Life video blog.

Garfield works with and advises Fortune 500 brands such as AT&T, Kodak, Nokia, and Panasonic, and media outlets including CBS, NBC, NECN, and Turner Broadcasting.

Garfield is a video producer and teacher. Garfield lectures on new media at Boston University, Emerson College, Northeastern University, and Simmons College.

Selected speaking engagements include Inbound Marketing Summit, New England Newspaper Association, Streaming Media East/ West, New Media Expo, PodCamp Boston, Video on the Net—Boston and San Jose, NH Film Festival, Woods Hole Film Festival, and Podcast Academy Boston.

Nationally featured on CNN, Garfield is the Boston correspondent for the pioneering video podcast Rocketboom, and currently provides citizen journalism reports for CNN's iReport, the UpTake, and techPresident.

Garfield also serves as an advisor to many of the Web's early video startups.

Index

315

YOUTUBE

Set up auto share + Twitter
faceb.

BLIP TV

pro account?

Interview all the homeless
on the subway.

BLIP. TV

Youtube   Vimeo

Need   to get   'NY video' ✓
New York video Service ✓

provide "Tweet this" buttons
"email this"